# FLIGHT FACTS
## for
# PRIVATE
# PILOTS

Piper Aztec

# FLIGHT FACTS
## for
# PRIVATE
# PILOTS

*By*

### MERRILL E. TOWER

*Educational Consultant,
Former Coordinator of Aviation Education for Los Angeles
City Schools, and former member of the staff of Northrop
Aeronautical Institute and Convair, Member of
American Association of Engineering Education,
and Institute of the Aerospace Sciences.*

## 1971

*Cover photo reproduced thru courtesy of Cessna Aircraft Co.*

ISBN–O–8168–5803–9

*Aero Publishers, Inc.*

*329 Aviation Road
Fallbrook, California 92028*

Printed and Published in the United States by Aero Publishers, Inc.

# PREFACE

This factual book is a companion to "Federal Air Regulations and Flight Standards For Pilots", also published by Aero Publishers, Inc. It presents basic facts that private and the more advanced pilots should know, and will enrich and review their knowledge, thereby increasing their flying skill and confidence.

No attempt is made to philosophize about various flying techniques. The book does not aim to produce self-learned pilots; because there is no substitute for flight lessons by competent flight instructors.

This book contains information for the private pilot and goes beyond enough to prepare him partially for his next rating. In this day of crowded airways and areas, it is necessary that the private pilot advance as quickly as possible. The crowded conditions and faster aircraft makes advancement a must.

Acknowledgement is hereby given to the following organizations for their courtesies in presenting material for this volume:

Aero Design & Engineering Co.; American Airlines; Bendix Aviation Corporation; Bendix Radio; Cessna Aircraft Company; Continental Motors; Eclipse-Pioneer; Federal Aviation Agency; Flying Magazine; Friez Instrument Division of Bendix Aviation Corp.; Grumman Aircraft Engineering Corp. Killsman Instrument Corporation; Los Angeles City Department of Airports; National Aeronautical Corporation; Piper Aircraft Corp.; Sensenich Corporation; United Air Lines; University of California Airport; Western Air Lines; and Wright Aeronautical Corporation.

The author also expresses his appreciation to the following: Mr. Ernest J. Gentle, Mr. Delbert P. Canning and Mr. Walter Winner of Aero Publishers; To Mr. Paul N. Bell of Bellair (deceased); and to Mr. D. F. Peterson of the F.A.A.

Furthermore, heartfelt thanks is also extended to Mrs. H. C. Tower, Mrs. Carla T. Anderson, Miss Carin A. Anderson and Mr. Ben E. Anderson for their constant source of inspiration and help.

Cessna Skylane

# TABLE OF CONTENTS

## INTRODUCTION

## PART ONE - - THE AIRPLANE

**CHAPTER 1. WHAT HOLDS THE AIRPLANE UP?**
. . . . . . . . . . . . . . . . . . . . . . . . . Page 17

Two theories of flight
Bernoullis theory
Action - reaction theory

Angle of attack

Forces in flight
Thrust
Drag
Gravity

Factors affecting flight
Speed
Angle of attack
Altitude
Temperature
Weight and balance

Stresses
Compression
Shear
Tension
Bending
Torsion

Stability of the airplane
Stability in pitch
Stability in yaw
Stability in roll

**CHAPTER 2. HOW TO CONTROL THE AIRPLANE DURING FLIGHT** . . . . . . . . . . . . . . Page 29

Parts of an airplane

Airplane controls
Control surfaces
Elevators
Rudder
Ailerons
Flaps
Stalls and spins
Making a turn
Lift force during a turn
Losing altitude
Climbing flight
Flight instruments
Airspeed indicator
Altimeter
Compass
Turn and bank
Directional gyro
Gyro horizon
Torque

**CHAPTER 3. THE POWER PLANT AND HOW TO USE IT.** . . . . . . . . . . . . . . . . . . . Page 39

Parts of an engine

The four-stroke cycle engine
Intake stroke
Compression stroke
Power stroke
Exhaust stroke

Cooling the engine

Proper fuel essential

Carburetor icing

Fuel system

Idling procedure

Swinging the prop

Propellers
Parts of a propeller
Types of propellers
Fixed pitch
Adjustable pitch
Variable pitch

Engine warm up

Engine Maintenance

**CHAPTER 4. BEFORE TAKE OFF** . . . Page 48

Radio equipment

Radio Communications
Communications terms
Using an aircraft radio transmitter
Airport and en route communications
procedures
Radio frequencies
Aircraft receiving frequencies
Tuning a radio receiver

Pre flight planning

Pre flight check

Let's get on board the airplane
Before starting the engine
Starting the engine
Before take off

Effect of flight
Effect of speed and motion
Effect of changing speed
Air sickness
Effect of altitude

# TABLE OF CONTENTS — PART ONE CONTINUED

Effect of Gravity
Effect of Oxygen deficiency
Pressurized cabins

That correct feeling

Be relaxed
Be alert
Make correct decisions
Be a doubting person

Ten commandments of fatigue

Ten hints for peace of mind

Lest we forget

Take it easy

Hold fast and clear

CHAPTER 5. TAXI – TAKE OFF & CRUISING
. . . . . . . . . . . . . . . . . . . . . . . . . . Page 58

The taxi

Take off procedure
Engine failure on take off
Angle of climb
Clearing an obstruction
Airport traffic
Light signals
Radio
Takeoff distance & rate of climb

How to use the table

Cruising
Mixture setting
Carburetor heat control
Oil temperature and pressure
Fuel tanks and pressure check
Trimming the ship

CHAPTER 6. LANDING . . . . . . . . . . Page 65

Before landing
Fuel mixture
Carburetor heat
Landing gear
Glide in
Engine
Propeller and flap

Landing
Landing speeds
Accuracy landing
Power-off full-stall
Power-on full-stall
Wheel landing

After landing
Taxi
Tie down
After flight inspection
Close flight plan

# PART TWO – – WEATHER–FRIEND OR ENEMY

CHAPTER 7. BASIC WEATHER SCIENCE
. . . . . . . . . . . . . . . . . . . . . . Page 71

Temperature

Moisture

Cloud base problems

Pressure

Wind

Wind and weather
Highs and lows

Fronts and weather

Kinds of fronts
Stationary fronts

Flying through a front

Characteristics of a cold air mass

Characteristics of a warm air mass

Thunderstorms

Thunderstorms and airplanes in flight
Drafts
Gusts
Lightning
Hail

Ceiling and clouds

Visibility

Fog
Advection fogs
Radiation fogs

Dust

Icing

Stability of the air
Lapse rates

CHAPTER 8. WEATHER INFORMATION & HOW
TO USE IT . . . . . . . . . . . . . . . . . Page 98

Weather sense

Weather information sources
Newspapers
Television
Telephone
Radio broadcasting stations

Weather bureau information
Weather maps
Observation
Radio range weather reports

Factors affecting the weather

# TABLE OF CONTENTS — PART TWO CONTINUED

Latitude
Local topography
Seasonal weather pattern
Receiving the information

Pre-flight weather planning

Weather map

Station model
Weather symbols
Daily weather maps
Weather reports sent by teletype
Aviation weather reports
Upper wind reports

In-the-air

## PART THREE — — ON COURSE

CHAPTER 9. WHERE AM I? . . . . . . .  Page 111

Position on the earth

Direction on the earth
Variation
Deviation

Distance on the earth

Time on the earth

Mapping the earth
The mercator projection
The lambert projection
The polar gnomonic projection

Aeronautical charts
Local aeronautical charts
Sectional aeronautical charts
World aeronautical charts

The wind triangle
The compass work form for wind
drift correction

The mathematics of navigation

CHAPTER 10. KIND OF NAVIGATION  Page 137

Pilotage
Laying out the course
Procedure when lost

Air markers

Dead reckoning

CHAPTER 11. PLANNING THE FLIGHT Page 144

Pre-flight planning

Steps in planning the flight

The flight plan

CHAPTER 12. IN-FLIGHT NAVIGATION Page 148

In-flight checking

Flight assistance service
Pre-flight assistance
In-flight radio assistance
Emergency flight assistance
Search and rescue action
Airport information service

CHAPTER 13. RADIO-NAVIGATION      Page 150

The VHF omnirange
VOR receivers

The low frequency range

The automatic direction finder

An illustration of VFR flight using radio
aids

## PART FOUR — — ATTITUDE INSTRUMENT FLYING

CHAPTER 14. THE BASIC SIX INSTRUMENTS
. . . . . . . . . . . . . . . . . . . . . . . Page 159

Pitot-static instruments
Pitot-static tube
Operation of the pitot-static system

Airspeed indicator
Corrections to indicated airspeed
Use of the airspeed indicator
Airspeed and mach number indicators

Vertical speed indicator

The altimeter
Reading the altimeter
Determining altitude
Setting the altimeter

Temperature correction
Altimeter errors
Using the altimeter
Don't ignore density altitude.

Gyro-suction instruments

The gyroscope
Properties of gyroscopic action
Rigidity in space
Precession
Drift
Gyro instruments

Turn-and-bank indicator
The ball
The turn needle

# TABLE OF CONTENTS – PART FOUR CONTINUED

Gyro heading indicator

Suction-operated horizon indicator
  Errors
  Using the horizon indicator
  Caging the instrument

Magnetic instruments
  Magnetism and magnetic fields

Panel-type compass
  Compass errors
    Variation
    Deviation
    Magnetic Dip
    Acceleration error
    Oscillation error
  Uses of the panel compass

CHAPTER 15. ATTITUDE INSTRUMENT FLYING
FOR PROPELLER AIRCRAFT . . . . .   Page 185

Attitude instrument flying
  Attitude instrument flying skills
    Instrument coverage
    Instrument interpretation
    Aircraft control

Instrument cockpit check
  Suction gauge (or inverters)
  Airspeed indicators
  Heading indicator
  Horizon indicator
  Altimeter
  Turn-and-bank indicator
  Vertical-speed indicators
  Panel magnetic compass

The instrument take-off
  Common foults in instrument take-off

Pitch control for level flight
  Horizon indicator
  Altimeter
  Vertical-speed indicator
  Airspeed indicator
  Scanning
  Trim

Bank control to produce coordinated straight
flight
  Horizon indicator
  Heading indicator
  Turn-and-bank indicator
  Scanning

Power control in straight-andlevel flight

Constant airspeed climbs, descents and
  level-offs

Rate climbs and descents

Turns: entry, turning, and recovery
  Steps in executing turn

Heading indicator turns

Use of the magnetic compass
  Characteristics of the magnetic
  compass

Steep turns

Recoveries from unusual attitudes
  Rules to recover from unusual attitudes
  attitudes

GLOSSARY OF AERONAUTICAL TERMS . . . . . . . . . Pg. 213

LIST OF SELECTED AERONAUTICAL BOOKS . . . . . . . . . Pg. 216

# INTRODUCTION

We can guess that ancient man observed the flight of birds and became interested in his desire to fly. No records of very early attempts to fly have been found although ancient writings and paintings show his interest in flying animals.

Somewhat later winged animals, other than birds, appeared in ancient religions and beliefs. Such were winged serpents, horses, and other animals.

Still later winged human beings such as certain gods or dieties were carved into statues and figurines. All of this leaves no doubt that man has long been interested in flight, with an ever welling desire, to build some kind of device by which he could travel from place to place by air.

Leonardo da Vinci's helicopter

Leonardo Da Vinci (1452) drew sketches of flying devices, some of which showed remarkable understanding of the principles of flight. He actually flew model helicopters, similar to those illustrated, which were powered with springs.

Mythology

Many pages could be written of man's early attempts to fly and become airborne; however a very brief summary follows.

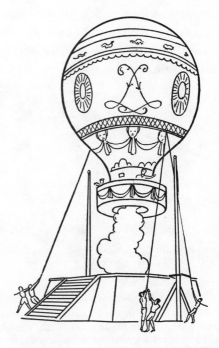

Montgolfier brothers' hot-air balloon

# INTRODUCTION

During the eighteenth century the Montgolfier brothers built animal-carrying hot air balloons for numerous successful flights. Others designed and built lighter than air devices but all of these machines were very difficult to guide and control. Nevertheless, they were all steps toward successful flight.

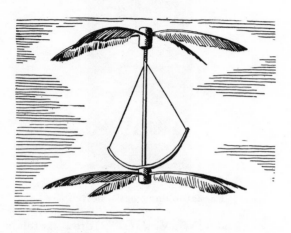

Chinese Top: Power source in this ancient top was a bow which unwound a string and whirled the feather blades. As boys, the Wrights experimented with this primitive helicopter.

Interest has never lapsed in man-carrying flapping wings, such as the bird in flight. Attemps to construct such machines in France and Germany during the 18th century were not successful.

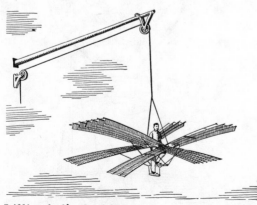

Lillienthal's Ornithopter: Leg muscles powered this early attempt to fly. With counterbalances offsetting the operator's weight, he managed to lift the machine several inches.

Gliders took over the interest of several scientists during the 19th century with Otto Lilienthal of Germany gliding several hundred feet when the wind was favorable. The Wright Brothers, Montgomery and others were making short gliding flights in this country.

The era just before Kitty Hawk - - 1902

Orville Wright

Wilbur Wright

# INTRODUCTION

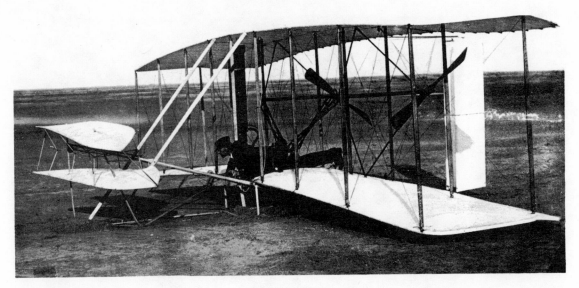

Wright biplane

Modern day flying done by the tremendous air fleets of today started at Kitty Hawk N.C. on December 17th, 1903, at 10:30 A.M., when Orville Wright piloted the Wright biplane a distance of 120 feet at a speed of 31 M.P.H. The original plane is well preserved at the Smithsonian Institute, a government museum, at Washington D.C. A fine full scale replica was built in 1952-53 at Los Angeles and is hung in the auditorium of the Institute of The Aeronautical Sciences.

From that time until the urgencies of World War I very little was done or known of the scientific and engineering problems of flight.

During World War I the airplane became an instrument of war for the first time. First used for observations of the enemies position and movements, it was not long before the pilots began throwing bombs and shooting. Many stirring stories came out of the war about dog fights, balloon bursting, and other exciting events.

After the first world war many aviation pioneers such as Boeing, Curtiss, Martin, Richenbacher, Loening, Towers, Stout, and others saw the great future of aviation and prepared to develop civil aviation as well as military aviation.

The science and engineering of Aeronautics developed by leaps and bounds to produce the forerunners of our modern aircraft. Douglas, Lockheed, Boeing, Curtiss, Martin, Cessna, Piper and others all led in the development of suitable aircraft for the coming air age.

World War II again saw the need for a very rapid expansion of military aviation. Thousands and thousands of aircraft were built each year that were great credit to the earlier scientific and engineering accomplishments which began with the Wright brothers. Vast fleets of war planes fought all over the world and defeated the best the enemy had to offer. During this period much was learned about aircraft design, control, engines, instrumentation, radio, radar, etc. by the hard road of experience.

Immediately after World War II, our aviation industry entered into a period of low construction of aircraft. Great factories were closed when military designs were laid aside. However, the air age had arrived and the great fleets of the future had to be designed, with the effort being carried on largely by civil aviation.

A few short years later, the Korean War and the "cold war of nerves" that

# INTRODUCTION

1920—Converted World War I DeHaviland carried U. S. Mail.

1940—Douglas DC-3. Forerunner of our modern commercial air fleets.

1960—Douglas DC-8. One of our great new commercial jet liners.

followed, indicated that world peace was far away and again our expanded military and civilian aviation industry sprang into action, producing large numbers of fine combat and transport type airplanes.

Today the aviation and missile industry is so massive, it parallels the automotive industry in size; thus these two industries constitute the largest manufacturers in the United States.

# PART ONE
# THE AIRPLANE

Grumman Gulfstream

# CHAPTER 1

# WHAT HOLDS THE AIRPLANE UP?

## TWO THEORIES OF FLIGHT

*Bernoullis Theory*

An accepted Theory of Flight is based on discoveries made by Daniel Bernoullis (Ber-new-ye) 1700-1782, who lived in Italy and Switzerland and experimented with the flow of liquids through various shaped tubes. He came from a very scholarly family and wrote up his findings so carefully that his theories are accepted today as outstanding.

Bernoullis' discoveries or theroums can be stated as follows: If in a stream tube the velocity of a fluid is increased at a particular point the pressure will decrease at that point.

The particular tube used by Bernoullis was similiar to a Venturi tube, which is a device to measure the flow of water in pipes. The device consists of a pipe-A, a conical reducer-B, and a smaller section-C, another conical reducer which in this case increases the pipe size-D.

Bernoullis' principle or theorum states that, a quantity of fluid, air or water, (Fig 1) entering pipe A will be discharged through the same sized pipe E at the same velocity. Therefore, the fluid must, on reaching the smaller section of the tube C, flow faster as it is drawn through the inlet cone B and then slow down again in cone D. The result is that the static pressure is less in section C. (Fig 1).

Restating Bernoullis theorum "If in a stream tube the velocity of a fluid is increased at a particular point (as in C, figure 1) the pressure will decrease at that point." Greater simplifications can be: "If the velocity is increased at a point the pressure is less". All aircraft concerned with horizontal flight have wings designed to increase the velocity of the air over the top of the wing to produce lift.

*Action and Reaction Theory*

There are several other theories as to how an airplane wing lifts. One of the more acceptable theories is based on Newton's Law of Action and Reaction which states that (For every action there is an equal and opposite reaction), (Fig 2).

With reference to lift, this theory states that basically the "wing keeps the plane up by pushing the air down". By pushing the air down we have our action that is balanced by our upward reaction or lift.

This theory can also explain lift at different speeds because increased speed will push down more air, (action) with a consequent greater lift, (reaction).

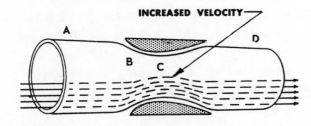

Fig. 1. Fluid flow.

Fig. 2. Basic airfoil.

Close examination of the basic airfoil (Fig. 3) shows that the air moving over the top of the airfoil has a longer path to travel than the air passing under the airfoil. That being so, the top air must move faster than the bottom air.

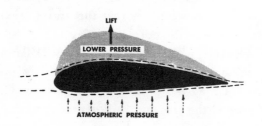

Fig. 3. Basic airfoil.

The result of the above condition is the lowering of the pressure on top of the airfoil in the manner stated by Bernoullis principle.

The faster the air moves over the top, the lower the pressure.

Actually the atmospheric or normal pressure is constantly pushing the wing up into the upper reduced pressure area. This is so because each air particle helps reduce the top lower pressure. Many pilots know the problems of take off from high altitude airports where the air is thinner with less lowering of the pressure.

Keeping in mind the foregoing explanation of the upward force called lift, any time we change the speed of the flow of air over the wing the upward push will be different.

If the engine speed (R.P.M.) is slowed, the forward push or thrust is decreased and the airplane will begin to loose altitude. Increase the speed and the airplane will go higher. Therefore altitude changes are made with the engine throttle.

In other words, to a large degree, the amount of lift is determined by the speed of the flow of the air particles over the wing. This is not quite all the story.

## ANGLE OF ATTACK

There is another very important fact to consider and that is angle of attack, (Fig. 4) which is the attitude of the wing to the relative wind.

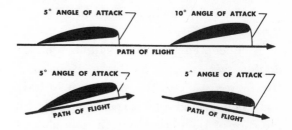

Fig. 4. Angle of attack.

At any given airspeed, this angle of attack determines the amount of lift which the wing will develop. At small angles the lift is at a minimum. The angle of attack, since it is a relationship between the attitude of the wing and the relative wind, cannot be measured as the angle of the wing with reference to the ground, but must be measured as the angle between the wing and the flight path.

If the pilot noses his plane up he will alter the attitude of the wing to the air. As the angle of attack is increased, the lift is also increased as long as the flow of air continues to be streamlines over the airfoil.

There is, however, a limit beyond which an increase in angle ceases to produce an increase in lift. For most airplanes this maximum effective angle is about 20 degrees. An increase beyond the maximum angle (sometimes called "stalling angle") produces a turbulent condition in the air above the upper wing surface, (Fig. 5), called burble, which reduces the effectiveness of the low-pressure area above the wing, and thereby causing a substantial loss in lift.

The flow of air may be changed to such an extent (Fig. 5) that lift is largely cancelled out. The air no longer flows over

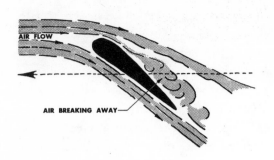

Fig. 6. Bottom push up.

Fig. 5. Burble.

the wing smoothly but breaks away caus-ing "burble". A negative or nose down angle of attack will also reduce lift.

During actual flight the plane will

"shudder" and shake when this breaking away (burbling) is pronounced.

When the angle of attack is increased, (Fig. 6) the under side of the wing adds to the push up as the air particles strike the under surface. This is, however, a small part of the total lift, (20-25%) and is somewhat like skiing on water.

Fig. 7. Forces in flight.

## FORCES IN FLIGHT

The primary purpose of every airplane is to fly, that is to have enough of the lift force to get the craft into the air.

Three other forces are involved in flight. (Fig. 7) One to produce the forward motion to get the air moving around the wing and is called THRUST. Another force starting immediately, called DRAG,

is the resistance built up by the air parti-cals as they pass around and over the air-craft. Another, called GRAVITY, is by nature an exceedingly strong force toward the center of the earth.

*Thrust*

Thrust is the forward force that is produced by some sort of a power plant. The Wright brothers used a home made

12 H.P. piston engine that turned two pusher type propellers for thrust in their airplane, as compared to the huge jet engines used by large aircraft of today.

Thrust is directly produced by the propeller which in itself is an airfoil, acting according to the same principles as the wing but producing a force at right angles to the wing. Propellers will be discussed at some length with the study of engines.

*Drag*

Drag as stated previously is the rearward force caused by the friction of the air particles on all parts of the airplane. At low altitude there is more drag because of the greater density of the air and less drag at high altitudes where the air is thinner. That is, there are far fewer air atoms and molecules to set up the frictional force of drag when it is realized that at 18,000 feet the density is about one half that of sea level and at thirty-six thousand feet the value is about one fourth.

Fig. 8.   Old time airplane—Large amount of parasite drag.

Aircraft designers (Fig. 9) are constantly trying to design wings, fuselages and all other parts to reduce the rearward force of drag. Surfaces are made smoother than glass, protruding parts are changed or faired to cut down the amount of wing and parasitic drag.

An examination of the foregoing figures (8 and 9) shows the great problems en-gineers encounter and the improvements made in reducing PARASITE (or profile or skin) DRAG. Note the abundance of spars, wire braces, and other surfaces contributing to drag in figure 8. This rearward drag force is actually skin friction produced by the air particles as they pass over all parts of the airplane structure. It must have been quite an experience to fly out in the open in the old time biplane (about 1912) of this era. As long as flying devices are flying in the earths' atmosphere the problem of drag will be ever present and aeronautical engineers are constantly trying to lower the amount of drag in proportion to the amount of lift.

There is another type of drag called INDUCED or WING DRAG which is produced by the fact that the airfoil causes the upward lift force. Air has viscousity which is the tendency to resist an instant change of shape. Therefore as the air passes over and under the airfoil a drag force is produced which depends on the size and shape of the airfoil, the amount of lift and the velocity.

*Gravity*

Gravity, (Fig. 7) the fourth force to be considered is always toward the center of the earth and must be overcome by the airfoil to produce flight.

Every object whether it be solid, liquid, or gas, that is every particle of matter, attracts every other particle of matter with the force called gravitation. The amount of gravitation force between two bodies of matter depends on how far apart they are and the amount of matter in each object. The greater the distance apart, the weaker the force which is inversely proportional to the square of the distance. In other words, if the distance is doubled between the two objects the gravitational force is reduced to one fourth. Thus it can be seen that the farther an object is from the center of the earth the less will be the attraction.

Fig. 9. Modern design.

Gravity is not constant over the world, being stronger at the poles and somewhat less at the equator with the nature of the earths crust influencing the attraction in some areas. When considering the gravitational attraction between an object and the earth the force is called weight, a common term used for many purposes.

## FACTORS AFFECTING FLIGHT

*Speed*

First of all, there is the factor of speed. How does speed effect lift, drag, thrust, and gravity? The faster the aircraft flies the greater the effect of Bernouill's principle of decreased pressure on the top of the wing. Also there is a greater

LOWER PRESSURE

LIFT

ATMOSPHERIC PRESSURE

PUSH UP

SKIING EFFECT

Fig. 10. Lift.

impact of air molecules on the underside of the wing. Thus, speed will increase the lifting power of the airfoil.

Now a consideration of drag brings up the fact that the air molecules by traveling faster over the surface of the wing and the rest of the aircraft structure cause an increase of air friction. Therefore, speed does increase drag. (Fig. 7).

*Angle of Attack*

Another factor that effects flight is the angle of attack. At a zero (Fig. 11) angle

Fig. 11. Zero angle of attack.

of attack there is very little impact of air molecules on the underside of the wing. Therefore, lift is less with a zero angle of attack.

An increase of angle of attack (Fig. 12) brings into full use the impact of these air molecules, thereby creating additional lift.

Fig. 12. Increased angle of attack.

There is however, a limit to the amount of angle of attack before considerable trouble is encountered. A very high angle of attack causes a breaking away of the air molecules at the top of the wing. (Fig. 13). This of course, decreases lift and when in the extreme causes a stall which is a condition of very greatly reduced lift.

*Altitude*

Another very important factor (Fig. 14) for consideration by the pilot is altitude. At sea level the air is denser due to

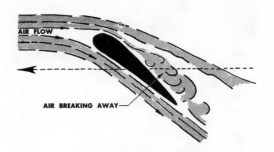

Fig. 13. Burble

Fig. 14. Altitude about 3500 feet.

gravitational pull towards the center of the earth. Consequently, the airfoil has greater lift on the top due to lowering of pressure and likewise a greater pushup underneath the wing by the impact of more air molecules. At higher altitudes the air molecules and atoms are fewer. There is less lift effect on top of the wing and also on the underside of the wing.

An interesting observation of how pilots can take advantage of the air density situations can be seen when a large transport type airliner fully loaded with fuel and passenger load will seek fairly low altitudes for the first two or more hours of flight. As the fuel load decreases the pilot will climb the plane higher thereby getting to altitudes where there will be less drag with the resulting increase of ground speed.

Another interesting observation is that when taking off from an airport with an altitude of say, 5,000 feet, a longer runway will be required, or less load to counterbalance and make it possible for the plane to fly where the air is thinner.

## Temperature

Another interesting fact is that weather changes can have considerable effect on flight. When we have warm days the air molecules and atoms are rising due to expansion caused by heating, thereby creating a lower atmospheric pressure near the ground. This thin air can be quite a factor when taking off or landing.

Cold days when there is little heating, the air molecules and atoms will not rise due to expansion caused by heating, but will become quieter and therefore the air will be denser near the ground. Thus, take off on a cold day can be done with much less runway and power and can result in a possibly increased payload.

Another factor which influences lift will be the size of the wing and its shape. Of course present planes do not have devices by which a pilot may change the size and shape of the wing. However, no doubt sometime in the future such things will be possible.

## Weight and Balance

Another factor, or group of factors, which are carefully watched today are weight, balance, and loading. The pilot flying an aircraft is quite aware that the plane must not be overloaded. If it is, the flying characteristics of the aircraft will be greatly changed and become quite hazzardous. Careful attention to weight must be observed, as can be seen at any airport where the baggage is carefully weighed before the plane take off.

Another important factor is balance, in other words, where will the load be placed aboard the aircraft. It is not difficult for one to imagine what the flight character-istics of an aircraft would be if the load is placed too far forward. The plane, of course, would be nose heavy and this would create many problems of take off, flight in the air, landing, and would be a condition of great hazard to all aboard. Likewise, the condition of unbalancing the aircraft by placing the load too far aft, or to the rear, producing a tail heavy aircraft with again much hazard in flight.

An interesting observation is noted that one of the small, older, two place tandem training planes must be flown, when solo, from the rear seat. A pilot sitting in the forward seat would unbalance the aircraft and produce again a serious condition. Therefore he flys solo from the rear seat.

Weight and balance can best be explained when we look back at the original airfoil, or aircraft wing, and realize that its ability to lift is not unlimited. As noted before, its ability to lift depends on the size of the wing, the speed of the aircraft, the altitude it is being flown, and the angle of attack. However, all of these factors have their limitations. An excessive weight cannot be lifted from the ground under any conditions. Therefore every aircraft has aboard a plaque or a plate stating the weight limitations and placement of the aircraft under various conditions and cautions the pilot to never exceed the weight limitations and placement regardless of his desires.

In the early days of flying when pilots were trying to fly the oceans, the Atlantic and the Pacific, numerous crashes occured because the pilots wanted to get aboard every ounce of fuel possible. They would taxi down the runway full power and with every device set for takeoff and were still unable to leave the ground, thus resulting in loss of life and loss of aircraft. Today we have learned much more about loading aircraft and seldom, if ever, do we see such a thing occur.

## STRESSES

The aircraft is a complex structure (Fig. 15) made up of straight pieces here, curved pieces there, with very few duplications. This is because the aircraft is composed of curved parts required to construct the airfoil, or the wing, to streamline the fuselage and to make every part structurally adaptable to flight through the air.

Preliminary designs are made of the overall desired shape of the aircraft, always of course considering its use. A fighter aircraft has quite a different functional design than the light sports type aircraft and both again differ from the commercial airliner. Each requires its own set of plans based on its use.

After the preliminary design, each small segment and part of the aircraft structure must be detailed, drawn by competent engineers and draftsmen to produce a complete set of drawings showing the size, the shape, and the use of the entire aircraft. When building a large aircraft, like the new jet airliners and others to come, thousands and thousands of drawings are required before construction can start.

For intricate supersonic fighter airplanes the total weight of the drawings can exceed the first plane built to the plans.

In flight the airplane is almost constantly buffeted about by wind. Therefore, the parts of the structure are constantly subjected to several forces. The forces are combined during flight and become collective in nature. Every airplane is a compromise between the two factors of strength and weight. Each pound of added weight to the airplane lessens its flying efficiency. This relationship is frequently called the stress weight ratio.

*Compression*

The stress called compression, (Fig. 15) which is the result of two forces acting toward each other, or the resistance to a crushing force, occurs in many places in the aircraft structure and can be well illustrated by noting the shock of landing as the aircraft wheels touch the ground. Considerable compressive force occurs from the ground to the structure of the aircraft.

Fig. 15. Stresses.

*Shear*

Another stress called shear (Fig. 15) occurs when one layer of material tends to slide over an adjacent layer of metal. Two rivited plates in tension subject the rivits to the shearing force.

*Tension*

Then there is tension, (Fig. 15) the result of two forces acting away from each other, pulling apart. This is also measured in pounds per square inches required to pull the material apart at any particular place.

*Bending*

The bending force, (Fig. 15) a force applied to a beam other than at the supporting ends, occurs in many places. It may be described as the deflection or curving of the member, due to the other forces acting upon it.

*Torsion*

Still another stress (Fig. 15) is torsion or torque, which is the twisting force, such as would occur if a member is fixed at one end and is twisted at the other.

Airplanes are flexible, that is, a certain amount of movement in the aircraft frame is expected and desirable. The aircraft is constantly being subjected to air currents or bumps of varying intensity and direction and must be so designed and built as to withstand these sudden changes of force that occur. A rigid air frame would certainly crack and come apart during flight and could not be considered desirable by the engineers and pilots.

### STABILITY OF THE AIRPLANE

No matter how well a plane is constructed, powered, and equipped, there is still a very important question to be answered. Will the plane fly right? Will it be the pilot's friend so that the flight can be enjoyed? Does the plane have the correct amount of stability? Aircraft are constantly being subjected to air currents because the air itself is a moving mass shifting this way and that with varying wind velocities.

From studying previous sections, the facts should now be clear concerning the lift action of the wing and the other forces on the airplane while in flight.

If all the upward (Fig. 16) lift forces are collected in one place, there will be established a center of lift, which is usually called center of pressure. (C.P.)

Fig. 16. Stability in pitch.

Also if all of the weight (Fig. 16) of the parts of the ship are collected in one place, there will be established a center of weight, usually called center of gravity (C.G.).

The locations of C.P. and C.G. are very important to the stability of the aircraft. If the upward lifting force— center of pressure— is forward of the center of weight of the airplane— center of gravity— the airplane would always have a tendency to fly with the nose up. No pilot would like such a ship because it would always have a tendency to go into a stall. Therefore, airplanes are usually designed to have their C.G. located slightly forward of the C.P., so that the ship will tend to glide downward.

When loading an aircraft, it is important not to upset the center of gravity which has been established by the manufacturer, because his exhaustive tests indicate how loads should be distributed. Some aircraft have devices that permit a wide range of load shifting, but even these cut down the flying efficiency of the aircraft if too greatly disturbed.

*Stability in Pitch*

An examination of the horizontal stabilizers (Fig. 16) shows a small negative angle of attack or a minus lift tendency.

As the plane flies at normal speeds there is a downward force exerted on the horizontal stabilizers which offsets the nose heaviness of the plane that is purposely built into the plane to give it a downward gliding tendency. Therefore, the plane will fly straight and level. When the aircraft slows down the " down wash" on the horizontal stabilizers will be less, and the plane will go into a gliding tendency. During this glide the speed again increases and the downward push on the tail again is greater causing the nose to go up with a resulting climb. This same thing will happen again and if the aircraft is dynamically stable, there will be less motion up and down after several diminishing oscillations.

Most aircraft have movable stabilizers or trim tabs which allow the pilot to adjust the pitching tendency of the airplane, if needed.

Several types of aircraft have a movable horizontal stabilizer that can be operated by a hand crank which is located in the cockpit. Therefore, the pilot can "trim the ship" by adjusting the angle of the horizontal stabilizer. The plane can be made so stable that no pressure on the control stick or wheel is required for straight and level flight. For landing or

Fig. 17. Trimming the ship.

maneuvering the stabilizer must be re-adjusted to give greater flexability of control.

Another method of "trimming the ship" is by tabs on the elevators that can be adjusted during flight. By moving the tab up or down, the action is similar to moving the horizontal stabilizers.

Trim tabs that are located on the rudder produce a similar action by providing better stability in yaw and roll. They also may be adjusted by the pilot during flight.

*Stability in Yaw*

Stability in yaw (Fig. 18) is obtained by the vertical fin and from the sweepback of the wing.

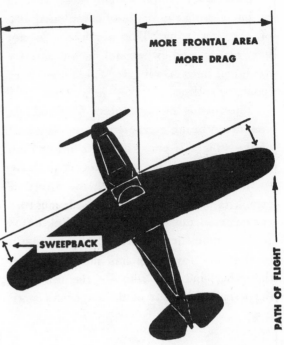

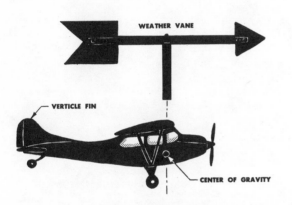

Fig. 18. Yaw stability.

It can readily be seen that the weather-vaning action of the vertical fin will help the aircraft in directional stability of yaw.

When sweepback (Fig. 19) is built into a plane's wing, a strong dynamic stability tendency results. As the plane starts to yaw or turn, one wing- the right one in the diagram- (Fig. 19) will have more frontal area. Frontal area creates drag and consequently the plane will tend to turn to the right. If the turn is past the flight path, the sweepback action will be somewhat to the left. A stabilizing effect results.

*Stability in Roll*

Stability in roll (Fig. 20) is obtained from the vertical fin, sweepback and dihedral.

Fig. 19. Sweepback for stability in yaw.

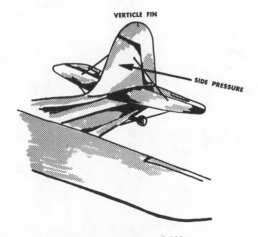

Fig. 20. Roll stability

The vertical fin exerts a side pressure as well as a directional tendency. The fin acts somewhat like the keel of a boat.

Sweepback helps to cut down rolling by increasing the angle of attack and lift- of the low wing. This tendency is not very strong, and sweepback is not usually designed into a wing for the purpose of reducing rolling.

The rolling of an airplane (Fig. 21) is constantly being corrected by the dihedral of the wings. If one wing gets lower than the other, it will have a different attitude to the wind; in other words, the angle of attack is unlike the other wing. It must be remembered that the angle of attack helps to determine the amount of lift. The result is that the low wing has more lift than the other and will rise. In the drawing, the wing to the left of the page has more

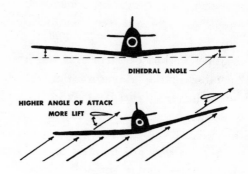

Fig. 21. Dihedral for stability in roll.

lift and will rise. If this action goes past the horizon, the other wing will have more lift. A dynamically stable plane will oscillate less and less and finally come back to its original position.

### PARTS OF AN AIRPLANE

A thorough knowledge of the parts of the plane (Fig. 22) is very essential for the study of flying. The same airplane vocabulary, is incidentally used world wide.

### AIRPLANE CONTROLS

Flying most aircraft is a real pleasure. The controls usually work smoothly and accurately, permitting the pilot to have complete control. Therefore, he is confident at all times of his ability to fly the aircraft safely.

The development of good control systems was a major problem of early aircraft builders, and it took a long time with much experimentation to develop the smooth operating aircraft of today.

The inside or cockpit controls (Fig. 23) are the rudder pedals and the stick or wheel. The instruments show flight conditions.

*Control Surfaces*

ELEVATOR: The elevator (Fig. 24-25) is a horizontal hinged surface attached to the tail. Its function is to control the angle of attack- the angle at which the wings move forward along the flight path.

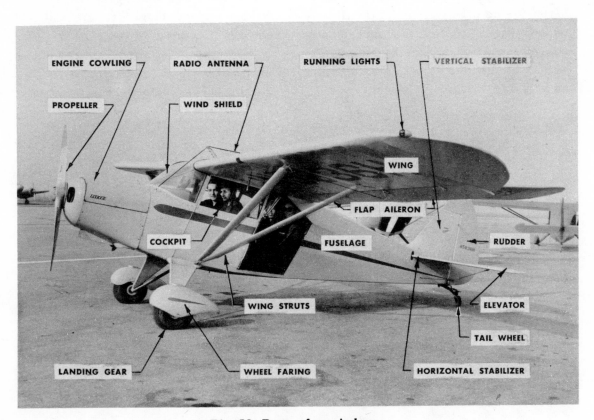

Fig. 22. Parts of an airplane.

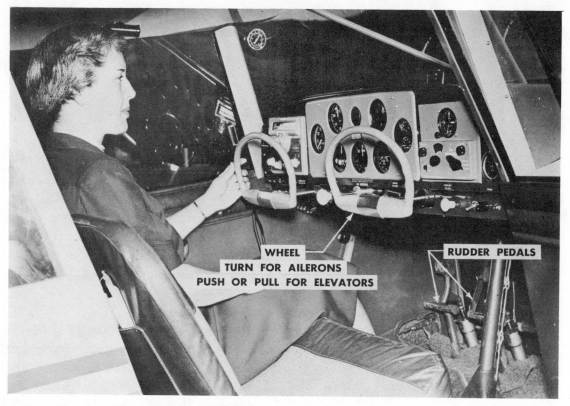

Fig. 23. Inside controls.

For the greatest safety in flight it is better for the pilot to think of the throttle as an altitude control, and the elevator as merely a device to govern the angle of attack. The elevators control the speed of an (Fig. 26) airplane.

RUDDER: The rudder (Fig. 24-25) is a vertical surface hinged to the tail and generally operated by foot pedals. Its function is to swing the tail to the left or right, just as the elevator forces the tail up or down. The proper use of the rudder

Fig. 24. Outside control surfaces.

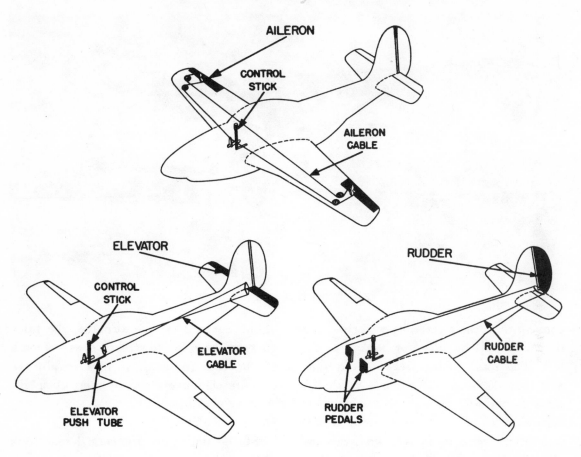

Fig. 25.  Control linkage system.

is often confusing to beginners. On the ground it is used to make the airplane turn, like the rudder on a boat or the steering wheel of an automobile. In flight, however, its primary function is not to make the airplane turn, but to assist it in entering and recovering from turns and to make minor adjustments for directional control or to execute maneuvers involving abnormal attitudes of the airplane. The rudder is perhaps the most frequently misused control on the airplane, but when properly applied it is a valuable aid to precision flying, however, its misapplication during a turn may lead to dangerous slips, skids, stalls, and spins.

AILERONS: Turns in flight are accomplished by tilting the wing through the use of ailerons (Fig. 24-25). To enter and recover from turns, use of the rudder is temporarily coordinated with the ailerons.

Ailerons are small sections of the trailing edge near the wing tips, which are hinged and so connected that a sidewise movement of the control stick, or turning of the control wheel will lower one aileron and raise the other simultaneously. If the control stick is moved to the left, while the airplane is flying level, the left aileron will tilt upward, increasing the lift. In

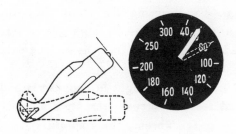

Fig. 26.  The elevators control the speed of an airplane.

FLAPS

Fig. 27. Flaps in operation.

consequence, the right wing will rise, and the plane will be tilted or banked to the left. The total lifting force of the wing will then no longer be exerted vertically upward, but will be pulling the airplane somewhat to the left, producing a left turn. Phrasing it in another way, the airplane is "lifted" around the turn.

*Flaps*

All but the smallest airplanes are equipped with flaps, which are attached to the trailing edges of the wings, between the ailerons and the fuselage. These serve to change the lifting capacity of the wing by changing the shape or area of the wing surface. An increase lifting capacity permits slower landing and take off speed. On the other hand, increased lift causes greater drag, with consequent loss in top speed. By lowering the flaps the pilot gains the advantage of high lift at low speed; by retracting them he reduces the drag at high speed.

An airplane in flight is constantly subjected to four forces— thrust, drag, lift, and gravity. Thrust, the forward pull of the propeller, is opposed to drag, the retarding force which resists forward motion. Lift, the upward force on the wings is normally opposed to gravity. By the use

of the controls on the airplane, the pilot governs the relative effectiveness of each of the four forces, and thus is able to execute maneuvers and to exert complete mastery over his airplane.

*Stalls and Spins*

Stalls and spins are normal reactions of the airplane to the pilot's use of controls. Left to its own recources, an airplane will avoid these maneuvers or, if

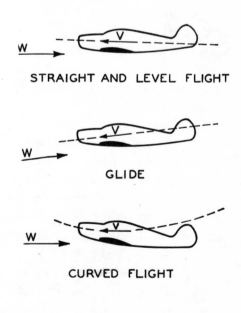

STRAIGHT AND LEVEL FLIGHT

GLIDE

CURVED FLIGHT

Fig. 28. Airplane in flight.

forced into them, will recover of its own accord. Unintentional stalls and spins occur only when an airplane is mishandled and made to violate its normal tendencies.

When an airplane stalls, the wings lose lifting power, the controls lose effectiveness, the nose drops, and the airplane falls rapidly toward the ground.

The loss of lift which produces a stall is caused by an excessive angle of attack. For most airplanes, the maximum effective angle of attack is about 20 degrees. If, then, the pilot, by back pressure on the elevator control, forces the wings to exceed this angle, the top low- pressure area above the wing which produces most of the lifting force will be destroyed by the turbulent eddies called burble. Then the airplane, losing much of its supporting force, will stall.

Most pilots associate stalls with slow air speed. Generally there is a close relationship between the two, but pilots should know that an airplane can stall at any speed from its minimum to its maximum. The controlling factor is the angle of attack, and not the air speed. Stalls occuring at relatively high speeds are likely to be more dangerous because they may be unexpected and are more violent.

Student pilots will be shown the kinds of stalls, spins, and how they are caused,

and how to prevent them. Most newer airplanes are so constructed to resist spins and recover from the stall situation by a long glide. Excessive angle of attack is the only cause of stalls. Many airplanes are now equipped with stall-warning devices which warn the pilot of an approaching stall.

### Making A Turn

During a turn all three control surfaces are used. The ailerons start the banking by lowering the wing on the inside of the turn. The rudder assists by cutting down adverse yaw, (a drag force caused by the ailerons, but which is in the opposite direction of the turn). The elevators help prevent a loss of altitude by increasing the angle of attack.

When turning, the wings are not as efficient as during level flights; therefore back pressure on the stick will change the angle of attack enough to keep the plane at the same altitude.

### Lift Force During A Turn

During a turn the lift force is no longer straight up but is slanted toward the center of the turning circle, therefore, more power is required to keep the plane at the same altitude.

### Losing Altitude

A pilot can lose altitude by closing the throttle then the airplane will begin to settle earthward.

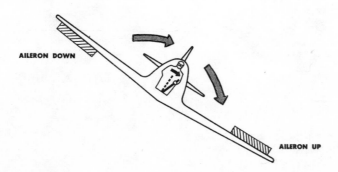

AILERON DOWN

AILERON UP

Fig. 29. Making a turn.

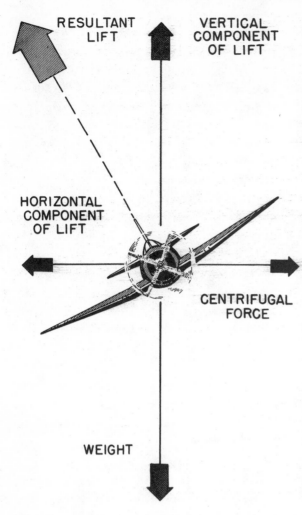

RESULTANT LIFT

VERTICAL COMPONENT OF LIFT

HORIZONTAL COMPONENT OF LIFT

CENTRIFUGAL FORCE

WEIGHT

gaining or losing of altitude'', and ''The elevators control the speed of the aircraft''.

Forward pressure on the stick or wheel will move the tail surface upward, nose the airplane downward and increase the speed but not contribute markedly to the altitude changes.

*Climbing Flight*

Lift can be increased by lowering the pressure above the wing and using full play of the underside of the wing. Therefore, increase the angle of attack to less than 18°-20°, and push the throttle in for more power. The plane will rise.

*Flight Instruments*

AIRSPEED INDICATOR: Fortunately, there are several easily learned instruments that assist the pilot in determining how well he is flying.

The airplane has no speedometer such as on an automobile because there is no direct contact during flight with the ground.

The airspeed indicator (Fig. 31-32) is a diaphram operated device (Fig. 33) actuated by ram air pressure into the pitot tube.

It should be remembered that the airspeed indicator (Fig. 31-32) shows the approximate airspeed and therefore will require correcting. The air speed indicator

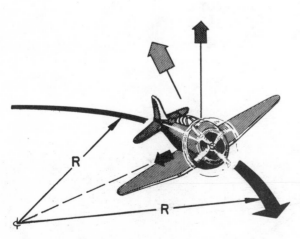

Fig. 30.  The forces acting on an airplane in a normal turn.

Two general statements stand out about flying. ''The engine controls the

Fig. 31. MPH.

Fig. 32. Knots.

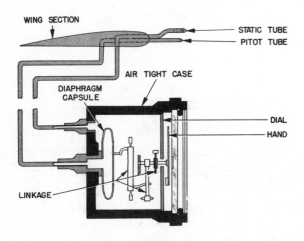

Fig. 33. The pitot-static tube showing the connection to the airspeed indicator.

Fig. 34. Pitot tube.

is operated by air pressure from outside the cockpit, through the pitot static tube, (Fig. 33) and any change in altitude will produce an error in airspeed. This is because the air is thinner and less air goes into the pitot tube to operate the instrument. The instruments read accurately at sea level. A general rule for obtaining true air speed (T.A.S.) is: Add 2% of the indicated airspeed for every 1000 feet of altitude. (To be more accurate, a computer should be used.)

ALTIMETER: The altimeter (Fig. 36) is a device that indicates to the pilot how high, in feet, the airplane is above sea level. The construction of the altimeter is such that it operates according to atmospheric pressure. In reality the altimeter is a mechanical barometer (A pressure device to measure atmospheric pressure).

The atmosphere is held to the earth by the gravitational pull towards the center of the earth. Therefore, most of the air is near the earth's surface, with about one half of the entire atmosphere below 18,000 feet.

A discussion of the barometer and how it works will lead to a much better understanding of the altimeter and its correction. A knowledge of the barometer is necessary to understand weather forcasting discussed in a later section.

Weather changes are associated with atmospheric pressure and temperature changes, thus the altimeter can give wrong altitudes unless a correction is made by the pilot.

During a period of cold weather, (Fig. 37) the atmospheric pressure at the earth's surface is usually higher than average, with the air being heavy and settling. The result is that more air is near the surface of the earth and less at higher altitudes. The opposite is true during warm weather, because rising, expanding air causes

Fig. 35. Unheated pitot static tube.

Fig. 36. Altimeter.

Fig. 38. Magnetic compass.

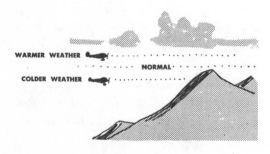

Fig. 37. Altimeter errors.

lower surface atmospheric pressure. Therefore, the altimeter, being a pressure instrument will be wrong in both cases, unless it is corrected.

The sensitive altimeter (Fig. 36) can be set before flight to a known altitude, thereby determining atmospheric pressure; or while in flight, the pilot can listen to the weather report over a radio range system or control tower and determine his altitude by turning the altimeter setting knob.

Before and during flight, the pilot can determine the corrected altitude by reading a graph, or by use of a computer (modified slide rule). The latter device is very useful to the pilot because many flight problems can be solved simply and quickly.

The important points to remember are that during cold weather the altimeter reads too high and during warm weather it reads too low. Therefore, the greater danger is during the winter months when the altimeter indicates an altitude greater than it really is.

COMPASS: The magnetic compass, (Fig. 38) that very useful, navigation instrument is very important because it indicates how much turning is being done.

TURN and BANK: Another very useful flight instrument is the turn and bank indicator (Fig. 39) which assists the pilot in determining the direction, amount, and how well the turn is being made. If the ball remains in the center during a turn, the bank is perfect. If it is on the inside

Fig. 39. Turn & bank.

The gyro has a tendency to "creep" off heading very slowly. This makes it necessary to check and reset the reading as required at approximately fifteen-minute intervals. During acrobatics the gyro ceases to yield correct indications and must be reset upon returning to straight and level flight.

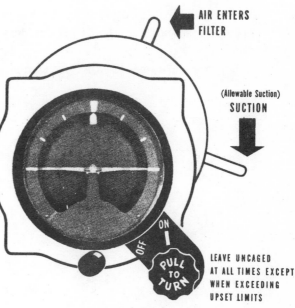

Fig. 41. Gyro horizon.

of the turn, the turn is too steep. If the ball flies outside on a turn the bank is too flat.

DIRECTIONAL GYRO: The directional gyro (Fig. 40) makes it possible for a pilot to steer a given course easily. Indications on the graduated card remain steady during straight flight and show the smallest changes when heading is changed.

Fig. 40. Directional Gyro.

The card, around which the airplane rotates, is attached by suitable means to an air driven gyroscope. Unlike the compass, the directional gyro does not show magnetic heading unless the card is set, by means of the caging knob, to agree with the compass.

GYRO HORIZON: The gyro horizon (Fig. 41) is a flight instrument which shows attitude at a glance, thus simplifying flight on instruments. The horizon bar is attached to an air driven gyroscope which spins in a horizontal plane and remains parallel to the earth's surface under all normal flight conditions. The index airplane is attached to the instrument case and appears above or below the bar when the airplane is in a climbing or gliding attitude. When the airplane is banked to the left or right, the index airplane appears banked to the left or right, thereby indicating to the pilot the attitude of the airplane.

An adjustment knob is provided for raising or lowering the index airplane for a given set of flight conditions.

Because the illustrated type instrument fails to yield correct indications during acrobatic maneuvers, a caging knob is provided on some models to keep the bar rigid.

### Torque

Every pilot is well acquainted with that nuisance left hand turning tendency called torque. It is ever present to a small degree and should be thoroughly understood.

There are two probable causes of torque, the most important one being caused by the rotation of the propeller and engine parts. This rotation force causes the airplane to want to turn to the left. The force is stronger when increasing speed and when the engine is pulling hard.

Another cause of a torque is the spiraling flow of air from the propeller wash back over the fuselage and tail.

To control the left hand turning tendency, opposite rudder is applied in varying degrees depending on the conditions at the time.

# CHAPTER 3

# THE POWER PLANT AND HOW TO USE IT

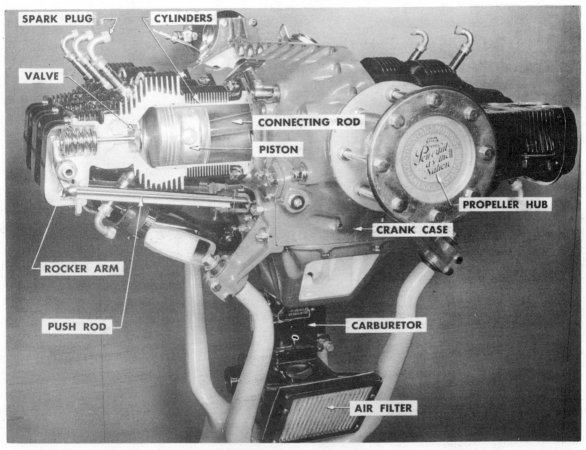

Fig. 42. Parts of engine.

## PARTS OF AN ENGINE

The engine (Fig. 42) is a very important part of the airplane and if properly serviced and maintained is a marvelous piece of machinery. It will respond to the pilots wishes and serve him well.

The knowledge of a few principles of engine operation will help the pilot to understand its nature and will reward him with dependable and efficient service.

## THE FOUR-STROKE CYCLE ENGINE

*Intake Stroke*

The piston has just left the top of its stroke as the intake valve opens and lets in a fuel mixture of about sixteen parts air to one part gasoline. The mixing is done in the carburetor.

*Compression Stroke*

The crank has gone nearly around and the piston is again near the top. Both valves are closed, with the air and the fuel now under compression (The act of pressing together). A spark occurs on the end of the spark plug which starts the fuel mixture burning. The spark was produced by the magneto (a device for making electricity). (Fig. 44).

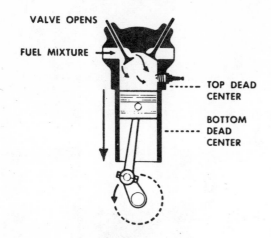

Fig. 43. Intake stroke.

Fig. 45. Power stroke.

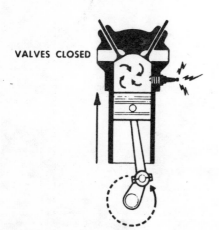

Fig. 44. Compression stroke.

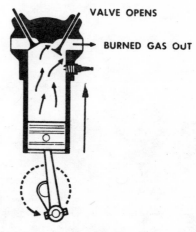

Fig. 46. Exhaust stroke.

*Power Stroke*

(Fig. 45) The piston starts another trip down the cylinder caused by the fuel mixture burning-not exploding. During the process of burning, heat is produced, and the gases are expanding. This produces a downward thrust which will turn the crank shaft, and the propeller.

*Exhaust Stroke*

The piston is on its fourth trip up or down the cylinder. The exhaust or exit valve now opens to let out the useless gases, and a new series of strokes can now begin.

This process-INTAKE STROKE, COMPRESSION STROKE, POWER STROKE, EXHAUST STROKE happens many times a minute. An airplane motor with an R.P.M.

of two thousand-two hundred and fifty will have four thousand-five hundred strokes up or down.

## COOLING OF THE ENGINE

The burning of fuel within the cylinders produces intense heat, most of which is expelled through the exhaust. Much of the remaining heat, however, must be removed to prevent the engine from overheating. In practically all automobile engines excess heat is carried away by water circulation around the cylinder walls. Most airplane engines are built with fins projecting from the cylinder walls so that heat will be carried away by air flowing past the fins.

When an engine is operating on the

ground, very little air flows past the cylinders (particularly if the engine is closely cowled) and overheating is likely to occur. Overheating may also occur during a prolonged climb, because the engine is usually developing high power at relatively slow air speed, and the airflow may be insufficient to provide adequate cooling.

Operation of the engine at a temperature in excess of that for which it was designed will cause loss of power, excessive oil consumption, and knocking. It will also lead to serious permanent injury, scoring the cylinder walls, damaging the pistons and rings, burning and warping the valves.

For engines equipped with a cylinder-head temperature gage, the proper operating temperature can readily be determined. Many light engines, however, do not have such a gage, and the pilot must rely on the oil-temperature gage to indicate engine temperature.

Oil is used primarily to lubricate the moving parts of the engine. It also serves, however, to help reduce engine temperature by removing some of the heat from the cylinders. The pilot should keep a constant check on oil gages (Fig. 47) because a variation beyond normal limits indicates engine trouble which calls for an immediate adjustment or landing to prevent serious damage. Use of the kind of oil specified by engine manufacturer will prevent expensive repairs which inevitably result from improper lubrication. Different brands of oil should not be mixed. Such mixture may produce gum and sludge which will cause sticking valves and piston rings.

## PROPER FUEL ESSENTIAL

The engine requires the proper fuel if it is to operate satisfactorily. Automobile gasoline should not be used because it is likely to contain gums and harmful substances which make it unfit for airplane

Fig. 47. Oil gauges.

engines. Furthermore, automobile gasoline has a much higher vapor pressure than aviation gasoline, which may produce "vapor lock," the vaporization of gasoline in the fuel lines preventing the flow of fuel to the carburetor.

Aviation gasolines are classified by "octane ratings" and "performance number" power ratings. The proper fuel rating for the engine (specified by the manufacturer) is always found in the operating limitations and usually is placarded at the fuel filler opening. The use of aviation gasoline with a rating higher than specified does not improve the engine operation, and it may, in some cases, prove harmful. The use of aviation gasoline with a lower rating is definitely harmful, because it causes loss of power, excessive heat, burnt spark plugs, burnt and stuck valves, high oil consumption, and knocking.

The fuel mixture in most engines can be changed from "rich" to "lean" by an adjustment in the cockpit. Inexperienced pilots need a word of warning about the use of this control. At high altitudes, where the air is less dense, the mixture may be "leaned out" somewhat to reduce fuel consumption and obtain smoother engine operation. At altitudes of less than 5,000 feet, a lean mixture may cause serious overheating and loss of power. The fuel mixture should never be "leaned out" unless the leaning produces an increase in r.p.m. at the same throttle setting.

Knocking, which is easily detected in an automobile engine by a "pinging" sound, cannot be heard in an airplane engine because of other noises. When the engine is operating normally the spark plug ignites the fuel at the proper instant, and the fuel burns and expands rapidly, exerting an even pressure on the piston. Knocking occurs when the fuel is ignited too soon (preignition) or explodes instead of burning (detonation). The resulting shock causes loss of power and frequently leads to serious engine trouble. As already stated, knocking may be produced by over-heating, low grade fuel, or too lean a mixture. It may also be caused by opening the throttle suddenly when the engine is running at slow speed. To prevent knock-ing, therefore, the pilot should use the correct grade of fuel, maintain a suffi-ciently rich mixture, open the throttle slowly, and keep the temperature of the engine within recommended operating limits.

## CARBURETOR ICING

Carburetor icing is a frequent cause of engine failure. The vaporization of fuel, combined with the expansion of air as it passes through the carburetor, causes a sudden cooling of the mixture. The tem-perature of air passing through the car-buretor may drop as much as 60° F. within a fraction of a second. Water vapor in the air is "squezzed out" by this cooling and, if the temperature in the carburetor reaches 32° F. or below, the moisture will be deposited as frost or ice inside the carburetor passages. Even a slight ac-cummulation of this deposit will reduce power and may lead to complete engine failure, particularly when the throttle is partly or fully closed. (See Fig. 17).

The carburetor heater is an anti-icing device which preheats the air before it reaches the carburetor, thus melting any ice or snow entering the intake and keep-ing the fuel mixture above freezing point. On dry days, or when the temperature is well below freezing the moisture in the air is not sufficient to cause trouble; but if the temperature is between 20° and 70° F., with visible moisture or high humidity, the carburetor heater should be turned on to forestall icing. The heater is adequate to prevent icing, but it will not always clear out ice which already has formed.

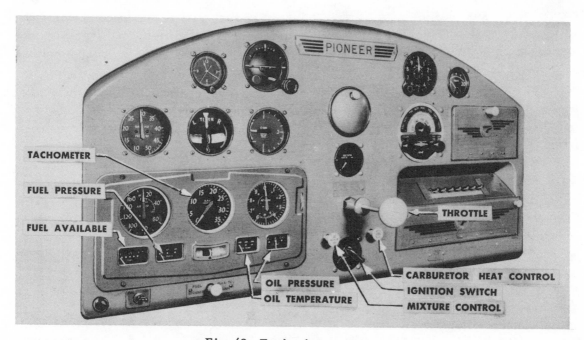

Fig. 48. Engine instruments.

The first indication of icing usually is a roughness in engine operation, together with loss of r.p.m. If this occurs, heat should be turned full-on immediately to prevent rapid accumulation.

During prolonged glides with closed throttle the carburetor heater may not provide sufficient heat to prevent icing unless the throttle is opened periodically to keep the engine warm. Preheating of the air tends to reduce the power output of the engine and to increase the operating temperature. Therefore, the carburetor heater should not be used on warm, dry days (when the engine may overheat), nor used on take off (when full power is required) unless weather conditions are such as to make the use of preheat desirable.

If, during a cross country flight, carburetor icing is evident by a loss of R.P.M., apply full carburetor heat even though the engine is sputtering. There is broken loose ice present in the Venturi or the manifold.

If the plane is equipped with manifold pressure gauge, a decrease of the manifold pressure will indicate carburetor icing.

Carburetor icing does not usually occur at very low (20°), or very high (80°F.) temperatures.

Apply carburetor heat about 30 seconds before reducing power.

## FUEL SYSTEM

A fuel strainer is incorporated in the fuel line near the carburetor for the purpose of collecting sediment and water which may drain from the fuel tanks. This should be inspected before flight and drained whenever there is indication of impurities in the fuel. The fuel tanks should be filled at the conclusion of a day's flying, so that the air in the tanks will be eliminated, thus preventing condensation of moisture which would cause an accumulation of water in the fuel.

Static electricity, formed by the friction of air passing over the surfaces of an airplane in flight, creates a fire hazard when refueling. To guard against the possibility of a spark igniting the fuel, a ground wire should be attached to the aircraft before the cap is removed from the tank. The refueling nozzle should be grounded by being kept in contact with the plane's fuel tank. Any fuel which is spilled in filling should, of course, be wiped off immediately. Vent holes in the tank caps must be open to permit fuel to flow from the tanks without creating suction which would prevent the flow and cause the engine to stop.

## IDLING PROCEDURE

Whenever the throttle is closed during flight, the engine cools rapidly and vaporization of the fuel is less complete than if it were warm. Furthermore, the airflow through the carburetor system under such conditions is not sufficiently rapid to assure a uniform mixture of fuel and air. Consequently, the engine may stop because it is receiving too lean a mixture ("starving") or too rich a mixture ("loading up").

## SWINGING THE PROP

If the airplane has no starting device, the person who is going to turn the propeller will call "gas on, switch off, throttle closed, brakes on," which the pilot will check and repeat. The switch and throttle must not be touched again until the person swinging the prop calls, "contact". The pilot will repeat "contact" and then turn on the switch. NEVER turn on the switch and then call "contact".

If you are swinging the prop yourself, a few simple precautions will help you avoid accidents.

When touching a propeller, always assume that the switch is on, even though the pilot may confirm your statement "switch off". The switches on many engine installations operate on the principle of short circuiting the current. If the switch is faulty, as sometimes happens, it can be in "off" position and still permit the current to flow to the spark plugs just as if it were "on".

Be sure the ground is firm. Slippery grass, mud, grease, or loose gravel might cause you to slip and fall into or under the propeller.

Never allow any portion of your body to get in the way of the propeller. This applies even though the engine is not being cranked; occasionally, an engine which is warm will backfire after it has been stopped for a minute or two.

Stand close- but not too close- to the propeller and step away as it is pulled down. If you stand too far away from the propeller, you must lean forward to reach it. This throws you off balance and you may fall into the blades as the engine starts. Stepping away after cranking provides a safeguard in case the brakes give way.

In swinging the prop, always move the blade downward by pushing with the palms of the hands. If you push the blade upward, or grip it tightly with your fingers, backfiring may break your fingers or draw your body into the path of the blades. (See Fig. 18).

If you are to remove blocks from in front of the wheels, remember that the propeller when revolving is almost invisible. Cases are on record where a person intending to remove the blocks attempted to walk directly through the propeller.

## PROPELLERS

*Parts of a Propeller*

Power to drive the airplane through the air is furnished by the engine, the brake horsepower of which is transformed into thrust by the propeller. (Fig. 49 & 50) The propeller may be described as a twisted airfoil of irregular plan form. To analyze the blade element, each blade is divided into 6-inch sections and each section is set at the proper angle to the relative air (Fig. 37). The sections near the tip of the propeller travel at a higher

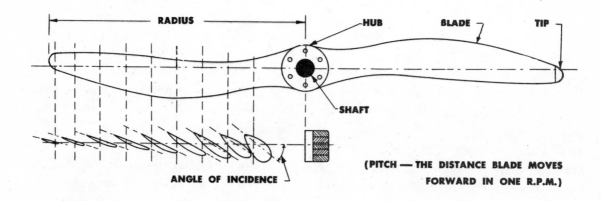

Fig. 49. Propeller.

Fig. 50. Thrust.

peripheral speed than those near the hub; consequently the blade angles become less as the tip is approached. On wood propellers the sections 12 to 18 inches from the hub are thick to give strength to the propeller; they deliver little or no thrust. Modern metal propeller blades either have cuffs or airfoil sections extending close to the hub. In general, each section is designed and set at an angle to obtain its maximum efficiency when the propeller is being operated at a given rotative and forward speed.

When the aircraft propeller starts rotating. (Fig. 50) the flow of air drawn around the blade creates a force which is similar to that created by the flow of air upon the wing, except that the wing is lifted upward, while the rotating wing (the propeller blade), is pulled forward. In order to obtain this forward pull, or thrust, the blade must be set at a certain angle to its plane of rotation.

*Types of Propellers*

FIXED PITCH: The pilot cannot change the pitch of this kind of propeller. (Fig. 51) Its action remains the same under all flying conditions.

ADJUSTABLE PITCH: The adjustable pitch type of propeller, (Fig. 52) permits the blade to be rotated to meet varying flying conditions. For example, the pitch can be increased when flying from a high altitude airport where the air is less dense. The adjustment is made while on the ground.

VARIABLE PITCH: The variable pitch type of propeller (Fig. 51) can be controlled by the pilot while in flight. When a greater bite of air is needed for thrust, the propeller blade can be rotated. When an airplane is moving at relatively low speed during take off and climb, the pitch

Fig. 51. Fixed pitch.

Fig. 52. Variable pitch.

of the blades should be lower- permitting more revolutions per minute- than during level cruising flight.

## ENGINE WARM UP

As soon as the engine starts, the throttle should be advanced to obtain the recommended warm-up r.p.m. (usually 700 to 1,000) and the oil-pressure gage checked immediately. Unless the gage indicates oil pressure within a few seconds, the engine should be stopped, and the cause discovered. If the oil is not circulating properly, the engine can be seriously damaged within 2 or 3 minutes.

The engine must reach normal operating temperature before it will run smoothly and dependably. Many accidents are attributable to attempts to take off with a cold engine. The correct temperature will be indicated, of course, by the cylinder-head temperature gage. However, if the engine is not equipped with such a gage, the pilot is dependent upon the oil-temperature gage. He will find that the oil warms very slowly in cold weather, and the engine will be ready for take off before the oil-temperature gage indicated normal operating temperature. Under these conditions, he may assume that his engine is

sufficiently warm when (1) the oil-pressure gage has moved close to a proper reading and (2) the throttle can be advanced to full power and back without causing missing or backfiring.

Just before take off, the engine operation should be thoroughly checked, including full-power output, operation on each magneto separately (the drop in r.p.m. should not be more than 100 when switching from two magnetos to one magneto). Idling speed should not be less than 550 to 600. The exhaust smoke should be light gray, or colorless. If blue, it indicates that too much oil is being burned; if black the mixture is too rich.

To enable the pilot to check operation quickly and easily, engine instruments are marked in much the same way as the air speed indicator. A red line indicates maximum or minimum limits, and a green arc indicates normal operating range.

With the switch in "off" position, rotate the propeller through two complete revolutions of the crankshaft to detect any oil that may have accumulated in the cylinders and to "prime" the engine by drawing a charge of fuel into the cylinders. The exact procedure for starting differs with various engines, and the pilot should be familiar with the operating manual for his particular engine.

If the engine has a starting device, the pilot should make sure that no one is in front of the propeller. He should always call "all clear," wait for a response, and then call "contact" before engaging the starter.

## ENGINE MAINTENANCE

If an airplane is to remain safe for flight, it must be properly maintained. Civil Air Regulations require that an aircraft shall not be flown unless, within the preceding 12 calendar months, it has been given a periodic inspection conducted by an appropriately-rated certificated mechanic who holds an inspection authorization, a FAA-approved repair station rated for the aircraft, or the manufacturer of the airplane. (Airplanes used, for hire, to carry passengers or to instruct students must be given additional inspections.) With proper care, the airplane will normally remain airworthy until next inspection period.

Any unusual conditions, such as excessive strain incurred in flight, hard landing, or abuse in the hangar, may make additional inspections advisable. Frequent additional inspections give the pilot assurance that his airplane is thoroughly airworthy, and often reduce cost of operation by revealing small indications of malfunctioning which may be remedied cheaply. and quickly before developing into serious defects calling for major repairs.

# CHAPTER 4
# BEFORE TAKE OFF

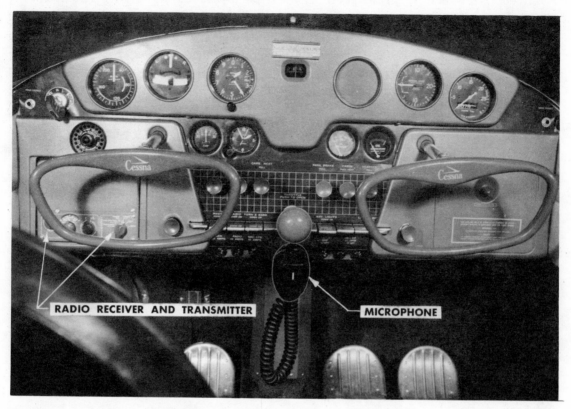

Fig. 53. Radio equipment in a small plane.

## RADIO EQUIPMENT

By this time, the student pilot knows the airplane, how and why it can fly, how to control it and has a knowledge of its power plant. He is ready for the final preparations before take off to experience that never to be forgotten feeling of being, poetically, out-of-this-world.

First of all, a knowledge of communication is so vital for successful and safe flight. (Fig. 53).

## RADIO COMMUNICATIONS

*Communications Terms*

| Word or Phrase | Meaning |
|---|---|
| ACKNOWLEDGE | "Let me know that you have received and understand this message." |
| ROGER | "I have received all of your last transmission". (It is used to acknowledge receipt, and should not be used for other purposes.) |
| AFFIRMATIVE | "Yes" |
| NEGATIVE | "That is not correct." |
| I SAY AGAIN | Self-explanatory. |
| SAY AGAIN | Self-explanatory. |
| STAND BY | Self-explanatory. |
| VERIFY | "Check with originator." |

| OVER | "My transmission is ended and I expect a response from you." |
| OUT | "This conversation is ended; and I do not expect a response from you." |
| CORRECTION | "An error has been made in this transmission (or message indicated)." |

## NUMBER STATEMENT
one-wun
two-too
three-thuh-ree
four-fo-wer
five-fi-yiv
six-six
seven-se-ven
eight-ate
nine-niner or ni-yen
zero-ze-ro

## THE PHONETIC ALPHABET

| | |
|---|---|
| A-Alpha | N-Nectar |
| B-Bravo | O-Oscar |
| C-Coca | P-Papa |
| D-Delta | Q-Quebec (Kibbeck) |
| E-Echo | R-Romeo |
| F-Foxtrot | S-Sierra (see-erra) |
| G-Golf | T-Tango |
| H-Hotel | U-Union (or oonion) |
| I-India | V-Victor |
| J-Juliett | W-Whiskey |
| K-Kilo (kee-lo) | X-Extra |
| L-Lima (lee-ma) | Y-Yankee |
| M-Metro (may-tro) | Z-Zulu |

*Using an Aircraft Radio Transmitter*

As already indicated, FAA recommends, and good operating practice demands that pilots use their two-way radios for (Fig. 53) air-ground communications. In order to use a transmitter, however, two licenses must be obtained through the Federal Communications Commission (FCC). A radio station license is required for the aircraft transmitter itself, and the pilot must have a restricted radiotelephone operator permit.

When an aircraft is equipped with a VHF transmitter, the pilot should be sure that he is transmitting on the proper frequency (122.1 mc. for communications stations, and 122.5 mc. for towers). Because low frequency transmitters use 3023.5 kc. with both towers and communications stations, no selection of transmitter frequencies is necessary with this type of equipment.

When ready to transmit, the pilot should hold the microphone close to his mouth. After giving thought to what he is going to say, he should speak in a normal tone of voice, using as few words as possible for correct meanings.

*Airport and en route communications procedures*

To illustrate two-way radio communications, an imaginary flight will be made from Los Angeles International Airport, Calif., to Phoenix, Arizona, flying direct. The appropriate sectional chart will be used.

The pilot goes in person to the Weather Bureau Airport Station where he checks the weather. Next, he files a VFR or IFR Flight Plan via interphone with Phoenix. He then completes all preparations and loads his airplane for the flight:

When ready to taxi, (Fig. 53) he calls the control tower giving the following information: Aircraft identification, position, the type of operation planned (VFR or instrument), and the point of first intended landing.

Example: (Some pilots and control tower operators vary this somewhat.)

Pilot: LOS ANGELES TOWER THIS IS PIPER FIVE SIX THREE TWO ALPHA AT HANGER TWO, READY TO TAXI, VFR FLIGHT TO PHOENIX, OVER.

Tower: PIPER FIVE SIX THREE TWO ALPHA, CLEARED TO RUNWAY ONE FOUR, WIND SOUTHEAST ONE SIX. ALTIMETER TWO NINE NINE NINE. TIME ZERO EIGHT THREE ONE.

Pilot: THREE TWO ALPHA, OVER

After taxiing up to position and completing his pretake off check-list, the pilot calls the tower.

Pilot: LOS ANGELES TOWER PIPER THREE TWO ALPHA, READY FOR TAKEOFF OVER

The tower controller determines that there is no conflicting traffic and replies.

Tower: PIPER THREE TWO ALPHA CLEARED FOR TAKEOFF

Pilot: THREE TWO ALPHA, ROGER AND OUT.

The pilot continues to guard the control tower frequency until leaving the control zone, or until cleared to leave the tower frequency.

While proceeding along the airway, he gives a position report to the FAA Air Traffic Communications Station at Riverside, and asks for the latest weather information at Phoenix.

*Radio Frequencies*

To take advantage of the communications and navigational features of the Federal Airways System, pilots should know something of the radio frequencies assigned for aviation usage by the Federal Communications Commission. Aviation frequencies may be checked in the Flight Information Manual, in the Airman's Guide, on aeronautical charts, or with the nearest FAA Air Traffic communications station, tower, or center.

Radio frequencies of normal interest to private pilots are here listed:

*Aircraft Receiving Frequencies*

Low and medium frequencies (Ranges, towers, beacons, etc.).....200 to 415kc.

Standard VOR stations (airway track guidance and en route communications.).....112.0 through 117.9 mc.

Air Traffic Control communications..... 118.1 through 121.3 mc., 122.2 mc.

Emergency.....121.5 mc.

Airport Utility (Ground Control).....121.9 mc., 121.7 mc.

Private flyer's frequency (UNICOM)..... 122.8 mc. (Aeronautical advisory stations which use this frequency are operated by private agencies such as Airport Operators.)

Note—Private aircraft so equipped may receive and transmit on this frequency.

*Aircraft Transmitting Frequencies*

Private aircraft to Towers.....122.5 mc., 122.7 mc. and 122.9 mc. (The Airman's Guide should be checked to determine frequencies which each tower guards.)

Private or commercial aircraft to FAA Communications Stations.......122.1 m.c., 126.7 mc.

Private aircraft to towers and communications stations. .....3023.5 kc.

Low and medium frequencies are subject to considerable interference from static, while the very high frequencies give relatively static-free radio communications. VHF reception distances vary with distance from the station and altitude of the aircraft.

Examples of normal VHF reception distances are shown in the following table for aircraft at several altitudes:

| Altitude of Aircraft (Above ground station) | Reception Distance (Statute miles) |
|---|---|
| 1,000 feet | 45 miles |
| 3,000 feet | 80 miles |
| 5,000 feet | 100 miles |
| 10,000 feet | 140 miles. |

Note—This table is based on zero elevation of the radio facility. Altitudes and distances shown are theoretical for flat terrain and assume that no physical obstructions intervene.

*Tuning a Radio Receiver*

An aircraft radio must be tuned to the station just as an ordinary home set is tuned. However, certain peculiarities must be recognized if we are to obtain best reception.

As in reading other instruments, the pilot should view the frequency indicator from directly in front, thus preventing an error which might result in no signal or reception of the wrong station. Another source of error is inaccuracy in frequency calibration, which is often caused by continued vibration or hard landings. Thus, a station which should be received on 116.4 mc. may appear on the radio dial on 116.1 mc., 116.6 mc., or some other frequency. If no signal is received when tuned to a given frequency the selector should be turned in both directions until the desired station is tuned in.

## PRE FLIGHT PLANNING

Without doubt, more time spent in pre-flight planning, will contribute to a safe and successful flight. Laying out the course, checking the weather, selection of airports, filing a flight plan, etc. will give the pilot confidence.

## PRE FLIGHT CHECK

Never take off in an airplane that you have not thoroughly ground checked. Do not take the other fellow's word for it because he may be of the dumb and happy breed that never become old.

Start at the port (left side of the airplane and proceed as follows;

1-Port Wing
(a) Inspect for tip damage.
(b) Inspect for trailing and leading edge damage.
(c) See that all safety keys are in the hinges.
(d) Inspect the covering, if fabric, for weak and torn areas.
(e) See that the control cables are in good order and properly attached.
(f) Stand off a yard or two for a general inspection of the wing.

2-Tail
(a) Inspect the hinges starting counter clock wise.
(b) Inspect the surfaces for damage.
(c) Inspect the cables.
(d) Inspect the trim tabs.

3-Starboard Wing
(a) Inspect for tip damage.
(b) Inspect for trailing and leading edge damage.
(c) See that all safety keys are in the hinges.
(d) Inspect the covering, if fabric, for weak and torn areas.
(e) See that the control cables are in good condition and properly attached.
(f) Stand off a yard or two for a general inspection of the wing.

4-Wing Tanks
(a) Check with your fingers for full tanks.
(b) Inspect the gas tank caps and secure them firmly.

5-Propeller
(a) Examine the blades for nicks or dents.
(b) See that the propeller bolts and nuts are secure.

6-Sediment Bowl
(a) Reach beneath the nose, to the rear of the engine and open the fuel pet cock sediment bowl to clear, then close.

7-Gas Line Drain
(a) Locate the pet cock near the landing gear and drain water from the lowest part of the gas line, then close.

8-Engine
(a) Unlatch and lift the cowl on the right side.
(b) Check oil level with dip stick. Then return stick.

(c) Examine ignition harness.

(d) Inspect the exhaust manifold for cracks.

(e) Close the cowl on the right side and secure the cowl latches or snaps.

(f) Unlatch and lift the cowl on the left side.

(g) Repeat c, d and e.

(h) Check both sides for cowling snaps in the locked position.

9-Landing Gear

(a) Examine tires for correct inflation. Inspect wheels and brakes.

## LET'S GET ON-BOARD THE AIRPLANE

Put your left foot on the step and with your right hand, take hold of the brace behind the wind shield and swing into the seat. Do not take hold of the stick or wheel to pull yourself into the cockpit.

*Before starting the Engine*

The following procedure is correct for most small aircraft.

1. Gas on, ignition off, and throttle shut.
2. Prime, and lock primer
3. Carb. heat off.
4. Brakes chocked.
5. Clear cylinders with prop.

*Starting the Engine*

1. See that all is "clear", in otherwords that no one is near the prop. Call it out.
2. Crack the throttle.
3. Fuel mixture pushed in to rich. Leave it there for running and take off.
4. Engage the starter.
5. Ignition on both magnetos.
6. Check oil pressure and temperature.
7. Check fuel pressure.
8. Wind the flaps to neutral.
9. Set the carburetor heat to cold. Do not use the carburetor heat control for takeoff because it robs the engine of some of its power.

The temperature can drop as much as 40° to 45° in the throat of the carburetor, therefore anytime the outside temperature drops below about 60°F and the humidity is high, ice can form. When icing starts there will be a drop of r.p.m. and perhaps a stalled motor. Don't be dumb and happy about carburetor icing.

10. Warm up the engine at about 800 R.P.M.

*Before Take off*

1. Check seat belts.
2. Check controls for free movement.
3. Check magnetos, switch to L then R. If there is a drop of more than 100 R.P.M. don't go. Set magnetos to both.
4. Check trim tabs for neutral setting.
5. Set carburetor heat to ON, then to OFF.
6. Check for oil temperature of 120 to 220.

## EFFECT OF FLIGHT

Persons preparing for their first flight are usually quite concerned as to what it will be like, and how it will affect them. They want to know what physiological (Pertaining to the vital organs of the body) effect of flight will be.

*Effect of Speed and Motion*

Simple speed itself has little or no effect on humans. Persons taking off and landing are quite aware of speed because a comparison can be made with the ground. At higher altitudes the feeling is one of being suspended, like hanging from a cloud, except when passing another aircraft or actually flying near a cloud. However, sudden changes of speed may become quite a factor. For example, a sudden stop in a car may cause physical discomfort because of the deceleration (the rate of decreasing velocity). In an airplane, a sudden gust of wind or a vertical air current may cause discomfort because of the acceleration (the rate of increasing velocity). An airplane in a spin or making continuous turns may cause a passenger to suffer from vertigo (dizziness) and air sickness may result.

This is not caused by speed alone; however, the greater the speed the more vertigo.

*Effect of Changing Speed*

People who fly soon become aware that acceleration during dives and pull-outs causes the blood to flow to the hands and feet. The hands and feet then become heavy.

This feeling is caused by changing the path of flight. The plane and its passengers are traveling in a circular path, and centrifugal force forces the blood from the upper parts of the body to the hands and feet. Try holding your arm out at right angles to your body when you are at the bottom of a shallow dive.

By increasing the speed and the pull out, the force can be built up to greater than normal weight. A student who normally weighs 125 pounds will have a weight of 250 pounds during a two "G's" maneuver.

When the force equals about five "G's" during steep bands or power dives, the liquid parts of the human body are thrown away from the brain, causing a black out (Loss of sight, fainting, loss of mental processes in extreme cases, etc.). The effect may last only for a portion of a minute.

*Air Sickness*

Air sickness is caused by the swirling movement of the liquids in the semicircular canals that are located in each ear.

The canals (Fig. 54) are connected by nerves to the brain and produce balance for us. If the human body is subjected to whirling or any other unusual movement,

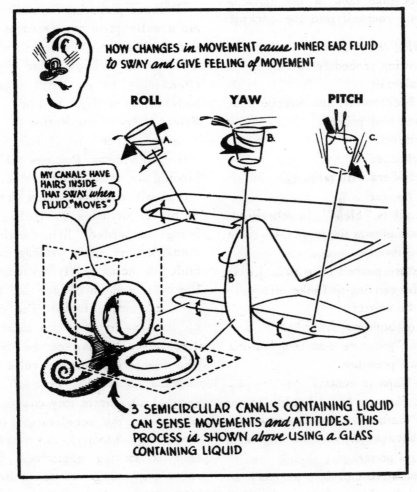

Fig. 54. Air sickness.

the semicircular canal fluids move too much. The brain receives rather confused signals and the result is airsickness which has the same result as seasickness. New harmless drugs are available, on prescription of a doctor, which can prevent and cure a very high percentage of airsickness.

### Effect of Altitude

Most persons have a dread of approaching the edge of a high cliff or a tall building. In an aircraft this feeling is almost lacking. Sudden banking the first time may cause some fear, but, if the turn is made at the correct speed and angle of bank, there will be practically no feeling of being thrown to one side or the other.

Change of altitude effects the ear because atmospheric pressure is lower away from the earth. Our ears have an equalizer tube called a eustachian tube, which helps balance those differences in pressure. By chewing gum, the motion of the jaws helps to keep the tubes open thus permitting an equalization of pressure. In any event, the ears will return to normal in a few minutes.

### Effect of Gravity

Gravity (The force towards the center of the earth) pulls solids, liquids, and gases (Atmosphere) toward the earth's center. This pull is stronger near the ground; thus it is that most of the atmosphere is concentrated there. Actually, one-half of the earth's atmosphere is below 18,000 feet.

The human body and all animals have structures suited for low altitudes, and at high altitudes the body is physiologically upset by low outside pressure. The pressure inside the body is higher than the pressure outside the body. This difference in pressure can cause death by the rupturing of some of the vital organs. Death or discomfort is also caused by a lack of oxygen (28% of the atmosphere).

### Effect of Oxygen Deficiency

Since most of the atmosphere is below 18,000 feet, there will be a lessening of the amount of oxygen as the plane climbs higher. Human beings can live only three or four minutes without oxygen and any lessening of the amount of oxygen in the air will cause discomfort or death. The altitude at which persons need extra oxygen depends on their physical make-up and condition of health. Some need oxygen at ten or twelve thousand feet, while others can get along at somewhat higher altitudes. A dog can stand altitudes somewhat higher than a man.

### Pressurized Cabins

The difficulties that arise from increased altitude and decreased oxygen may be corrected by some kind of pressure suits for the people aboard an airplane or by a tight cabin that has a pressure and oxygen content, which is controlled to produce a comfortable situation. Usually this is about the pressure of nine to ten thousand feet. Pressurized suits are too bulky, and would not be practical for normal use.

Airplanes fly at the higher levels because the air is smoother, winds are more reliable, and visibility is better.

## THAT CORRECT FEELING

There are several requirements of the pilot that makes him a good or a bad pilot. They are, be relaxed, alert, make correct decisions, and be a doubting person.

## BE RELAXED

If not relaxed, the nerves will affect the stomach muscles, heart beat, blood pressure and brain to reduce the flying ability of the pilot. He will no longer be able to exert his reflexes as well or make decisions quickly. Every pilot must be doing two things constantly, using reflexes and making decisions. This can be done only when relaxed and alert

*Be Alert*

A pilot may be relaxed and in a very dumb and happy mood and be a great hazard to himself and others. There is no substitute for awareness by the pilot, of his own aircraft and others.

*Make Correct Decisions*

At times, only a minute or two, or less time, is available for a very important decision. Remain relaxed, be alert and make the decision quickly. The chances are you will be safer on your first decision.

*Be a Doubting Person*

Never take anything for granted from the time you think of the flight, clear through the weather check, route planning, preflight check, while in flight, and landing. If you know the situation, your judgement will be far better.

## TEN COMMANDMENTS OF FATIGUE

From time to time, accident investigations have disclosed fatigue as a contributing factor. Generally speaking, fatigue is described as "weariness, usually from overexertion". Describing fatigue from a pilot's standpoint, the medical dictionary calls it "a progressive decrease of efficiency together with a feeling of control". In a recent TV interview, Dr. Nicholas Padis of Lanenau Hospital, Philadelphia, called fatigue the "number one disease of our civilization", and offered this list of Ten Commandments:

1. It is healthy to be active and to get pleasantly tired.
2. Remember that nature needs time for good repair work. You may forget about rest or sleep, but nature doesn't.
3. Prevent fatigue by periodic health examinations. You must be healthy to be happy.
4. Fatigue is the most common symptom of all diseases. If fatigue persists, seek medical care and prevent further wear and tear.
5. Choose your work according to your physical and mental powers and not according to your dreams.
6. Be prepared. Cultivate a philosophy of acceptance for any crisis, either success or failure.
7. Be very careful of the physical and social environment in which you work.
8. Take time to live. Don't just exist. Eat properly. Rest properly. Faulty diet can cause both physical and mental fatigue.
9. Life is short. Don't make it shorter by unnecessary fatigue.
10. Play and work and meditate with wonder and enthusiasm. And, paraphrasing some thoughts from the Good Book, remember that "all things work together for good to those who love freedom, truth, man and and God."

(Flight Safety Foundation)

## TEN HINTS FOR PEACE OF MIND

1. Do not exercise your right-of-way while flying— give way to the other fellow if circumstances require it. You may be dead right, and unable to argue in a wooden overcoat.
2. Always fly a prescribed traffic pattern when approaching or departing from an airport; do not make straight in approaches— others in the pattern may not see you. Above all, be courteous to others, both on the ground and while in the air.
3. Under light and variable winds conditions, double check the direction and pattern of other aircraft. Conform to the pattern unless safety dictates otherwise, in which case remain clear until a safe landing, or take-off, can be effected.

4. During winter months, never take off with frost or snow on the wings and control surface— it reduces lift and may prevent your becoming airborne.

5. Drain fuel tank sumps, as well as gascolators. Any low point in the fuel system collects moisture, which if not removed may result in engine stoppage.

6. Apply full carburetor heat at least 20 seconds before closing the throttle, prior to prolonged glides, in order to assure removal of any ice that may have accumulated in the carburetor.

7. Clear your engine periodically by use of the throttle to prevent the engine from loading or cooling off.

8. Have your cabin heater checked for exhaust leaks— carbon monoxide gives no warning.

9. Avoid flying through areas with known, or suspected icing conditions.

10. Always remember that the best safety device is located just above the ears— and after an accident, its not who is right that counts, but rather who is left.

(Montana Aeronautics Commission)

## LEST WE FORGET

If all the bent and bruised pilots who have crawled out of wrecked airplanes "I didn't think conditions warrented carburetor heat" were laid end to end, they would clutter up approach zones across the Nation. Any muggy or high humidity day, even in high air temperatures, calls for the prudent use of carburetor heat on final, and periodically enroute. To disregard this cardinal rule is to invite disaster when you nudge the throttle to clear that last obstacle between you and the runway.

## TAKE IT EASY

Successful air operation is largely the result of careful planning, coordination and timing. When something interferes with this, an otherwise perfectly synchronized operation becomes a hurried, hectic, disorganized one. An operation under pressure can lead to mistakes, omissions, forgetfulness and accidents. The Flight Safety Foundation reports— "When tempo increases, response begins to fall behind the required pace and people begin working, operating, and thinking faster than they can normally handle any given situation..." This applies particularly to pre-flight checks and operations in the cockpit when a flight becomes involved. Moral— A wise pilot will call a halt to hurrying, will take it easy until all factors are satisfied, and then proceed accordingly.

But, we are airmen; therefore, we respect the ones that will get us safely to our destination. Where practical we choose alternate airports on the sea side of nearby terrain because downslope winds warm adiabatically, causing evaporation of clouds and reducing precipitation which results in favorable ceilings. Who can quarrel with a nice big clear spot in an overcast? When receiving the latest weather dope at your destination, evaluate the height of ceiling reports by checking the temperature and dew point spread. Ceilings that have a spread of one degree for each 250 feet of ceiling may generally be trusted, but if the spread is less, it is dubious if the weather will hold. This is due to a difference between temperature, and dew point lapse in the mixing air causes 100% relative humidity at an altitude of about 280 feet for each degree of spread. Clouds will evaporate below that supporting altitude.

## HOLD FAST...AND CLEAR

Whether runways are wet or icy, their condition is the same--slippery. When you taxi out for take-off and the runway is wet, remember that braking may have little effect. Stop well clear of the active runway or well behind the aircraft holding ahead of you. Sliding into the plane in front of you or onto the active runway can be shattering as well as scattering.

IF YOU'RE GOING TO FLY IFR, FILE IFR. IF YOU'RE GOING TO FLY VFR AND THE WEATHER IS IFR--STAY ON THE GROUND!

What is it moulds the life of man-- The weather.

What makes some white and others tan--The weather.

What makes the Zulu live in trees— Eskimos wear furs and freeze--The weather

(Climatology and Weather Vagaries)

What makes the pilot cuss and wheeze-- The weather.

(California Aeronautics Commission)

# CHAPTER 5

## TAXI - TAKE-OFF & CRUISING

### THE TAXI

Before starting the taxi to check area and runway, call to control tower for taxi permission. Be a doubting person and determine that all is clear before moving the aircraft.

While at the engine check area, pull off to the prescribed angle to show others that the check is being made.

Set brakes, check controls, throttle on, and check magnetos, LEFT and RIGHT, and BOTH. Allow no more than a 100 R.P.M. drop of left or right magnetos. Set magnetos to both.

Call to tower for take off instructions (Refer to page 49 for a review of communications procedures). Set fuel mixture to rich. Set nose-up or nose-down trim to neutral. Set carburetor heat control to cold. Advance throttle for full power. Set altimeter for the airport height above sea level.

### TAKE OFF PROCEDURE

The take off should always be started at the extreme end of the runway. This will give the advantage of the entire length available, and will enable the pilot to discontinue the take off should he sense anything wrong in the early stages.

After receiving takeoff clearance, or rechecking the traffic if there is no control tower, the pilot should head the airplane down the runway and gradually open the throttle. When the controls become effective, place the airplane in an attitude corresponding to a shallow climb. The airplane will then leave the ground when it has acquired sufficient speed.

In a crosswind take off, the airplane should attain greater speed before leaving the ground. The excess speed will prevent it from settling back on the ground with possible damage to the landing gear due to drifting motion. For crosswind take offs, the pilot should place the airplane in level flight attitude, wait until it has attained the speed used for normal climb, and then "lift it off" by a slight backward pressure on the stick. To prevent drift, the windward wing should be lowered slightly by moving the aileron control in that direction. .

Takeoff performance- that is, the length of ground-run required and the rate-of-climb, is affected by several factors.

One of these factors is the design of the airplane, involving the "power-loading" (the ratio of gross weight to horsepower) and the "wing-loading" (the ratio of gross weight to wing area). A very little difference in weight makes a considerable difference in ability to take off quickly, and therefore is particularly significant when flying from short fields or at high altitudes. If there is any question as to ability of the airplane to make a safe take off and climb, the weight should be reduced to a minimum by limiting the amount of baggage, the number of passengers, and the quantity of fuel.

The condition of the runway surface also affects take off. Long grass, soft ground, mud, snow, or water will set up resistance. That necessitates a greater length of runway for the airplane to gain flying speed.

A take off under no-wind conditions, or into a very light wind, will require a longer runway than a take off into a moderate or strong wind.

Another factor, sometimes overlooked by pilots, is the effect of atmospheric conditions- temperature, humidity, pressure, and altitude.

On a very cold day an airplane may take off after a run of 800 feet and climb at the rate of 600 feet a minute, clearing obstructions close to the boundry without the slightest difficulty. The same airplane, flying from the same field on a very hot day may require 1,300 feet for take off (an increase in distance ranging from 50 to 75 percent) and may climb at only 450 feet a minute. Cold air settles while warm air rises.

Higher altitudes or lower atmospheric pressures also increase the take off distance and reduce the rate-of-climb. An airplane which requires 800 feet for take off from a field at sea level may require more than 1,600 feet to take off from a field at 5,000 feet elevation. The maximum rate of climb might be reduced from 600 feet per minute at sea level to 250 feet per minute at 5,000 feet altitude.

*Engine Failure on Take Off*

If engine failure should occur at low altitude, the pilot should immediately drop the nose to prevent a stall. While he is establishing a normal glide there will be a few seconds in which to decide on the next move. Unless he is positive that he has sufficient altitude for a 180° turn and downwind landing, the pilots best procedure is to continue straight ahead, landing into the wind or slightly crosswind. Even though the terrain may be entirely unsuited for landing, there is less probability of serious injury if reaching the ground in normal landing attitude than in a stall or spin while attempting to return to the field.

*Angle of Climb*

Upon leaving the ground, hold the plane level to gain additional speed before entering the climb. Sometimes a pilot will take off at minimum flying speed and immediately point the nose of his airplane upward at a steep angle, under the delusion that he is obtaining maximum climb. Actually, such a procedure is dangerous because it places the airplane in a critical stalling attitude in case of engine failure or sudden gust. (See fig. 20.)

Climbing steeply at slow speed is an inefficient way to gain altitude. The best rate of climb for airplanes with fixed-pitch propellers is attained when air speed is about 50 percent greater than normal stalling speed. An efficient take off method for an airplane with normal stalling speed of 40 m.p.h. is to leave the ground at 50 m.p.h., level off until speed reaches 60 m.p.h., and then enter the climb, maintaining a speed of 60 m.p.h. If the pilot reduces power during the climb, he should lower the nose sufficiently to maintain 60 m.p.h. air speed. If he increases power, he should raise the nose accordingly. The type of climb just discussed, known as the "best rate of climb", will enable the airplane to reach the greatest altitude in the least time at a given power setting.

*Clearing An Obstruction*

Another type of climb, called the "steepest climb" or "best angle of climb", is sometimes helpful in clearing an obstruction close to the field because it enables the airplane to gain the greatest altitude in the least horizontal distance. It is made at an air speed about 25 percent above stalling. If prolonged, however, the "steepest climb" is likely to cause overheating of the engine.

A type of climb, called "zooming" should perhaps be discussed briefly. It is executed by attaining considerable air speed, either in level flight or dive, and then pulling the nose up sharply into an excessive angle of climb, holding the airplane in this attitude until it has lost its upward momentum and is about to stall. The zoom merely translates air speed into altitude, and it leaves the plane at a critical angle of attack with insufficient flying speed. Recovery is made by nosing the plane down, thereby losing most of the altitude just gained. A common misconception among pilots is that a zoom is an effective method for gaining altitude to clear obstructions on take off. Actually, the zoom will not attain as much altitude in a given distance as a steady climb at the best angle of climb. Moreover, it is an exceedingly dangerous maneuver, because the slightest misjudgment may lead to disaster. The zoom entered from a dive is a show-off maneuver frequently attempted by irresponsible pilots to amaze their friends. Many of these attempts end in fatalities because the pilot miscalculates the loss of altitude necessary in changing the flight path from a downward to an upward direction, or because he stalls at the end of the zoom- with too little altitude for recovery- and consequently falls or spins to the ground nose-first.

*Airport Traffic*

At landing fields not equipped with control towers, the entire responsibility for avoiding accidents rests upon you- the pilot.

When taxiing go slow and, unless visibility is unrestricted, use a zig-zag pattern to see that the path is clear at all times. Before crossing any runway, make sure that no planes are approaching on take off or landing. Immediately before take off make sure that the runway is clear, and check incoming traffic. Aircraft approaching for a landing have right-of-way. A plane on the ground should face incoming traffic and delay take off until there is absolutely no danger of collision.

After take off, continue straight flight until the airplane has reached the airport boundary and has gained at least 500 feet of altitude. After checking for other air-

craft, then make a turn of 90° to the left (at airports using left-hand traffic), followed by a turn of 45° to the right to leave the traffic pattern. All turns in the vicinity of an airport must be to the left unless otherwise specified.

Before take off, observe traffic, to determine wind direction and velocity, and to note which runway is being currently used. The wind direction is indicated by a wind sock (Fig. 55) a wind tee, (Fig. 56) or tetrahedron. (Fig. 57)

Fig. 55.  Wind Sock.

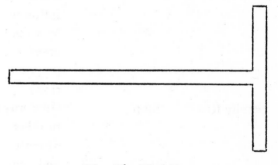

Fig. 56.  Wind Tee.

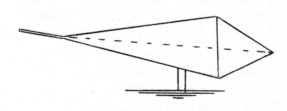

Fig. 57.  Tetrahedron.

At airports which have a control tower, the operator is able to assist pilots in avoiding collisions both on the ground and in the air. All pilots are required to observe and follow directions issued by light signals or radio, but this does not relieve them of the necessity of exercising due care and good judgement in carrying out the instructions.

*Light Signals*

Light signals from the control tower should be acknowledged by moving ailerons or rudder when on the ground, by rocking the wings when in the air, and by flashing the landing or navigation lights at night. The correct interpretations of signals from an airport traffic control light are given in the following table:

| Color and Type of Signal | On the Ground | In Flight |
|---|---|---|
| Steady Green | Cleared for take off | Cleared to land |
| Flashing Green | Cleared to taxi | Return for landing (to be followed by steady green at proper time). |
| Steady Red | Stop | Give way to other aircraft and continue circling. |
| Flashing Red | Taxi clear of landing area (runway) in use. | Airport unsafe- do not land. |
| Flashing White | Return to starting point on airport. | |
| Alternating Red and Green | General Warning Signal- Exercise Extreme Caution | |

Table 1.

*Radio*

Radio is the most effective means of traffic control, issuance of instruction by use of lights being very limited. Traffic is almost entirely controlled by radio at most airports where control towers are located; and a majority of light aircraft which fly the airways are equipped with two-way radio.

Civil Air Regulations require that pilots obey instructions given by either radio or lights from the control tower. When ready to taxi prior to departure, a pilot calls the control tower by radio for taxi and take off instructions. He follows the tower operator's instructions before and during take off, continuing to keep his set tuned to the tower frequency until he is out of the control zone.

A pilot approaching an airport under VFR conditions calls the tower when he is several miles from the field. He remains in radio contact with the tower and follows the approach and landing instructions given by the tower operator. Control by the tower continues until the plane has been parked.

In addition to being important in traffic control at airports, radio is a valuable aid in cross-country flying. In order to make flying safer and easier for pilots, the F.A.A.'s Federal Airways System also provides communications facilities, electronic aids to navigation and several other services.

Every pilot of light aircraft should familiarize himself with the use of two-way radio and with the convenience and security it affords. Valuable information on the subject will be found in "Pilots' Radio Handbook" and "Flight Information Manual", two Government publications suggested for further study.

*Take-off Distance and Rate of Climb*

The following table gives approximate

figures for take-off ground-run and rate-of-climb at temperatures from 0° F. to 100° F., and pressure altitudes from sea level to 7,000 feet. They do not take into consideration the extra performance which may be obtained from use of constant-speed or controllable-pitch propellers, supercharged or altitude engines, flaps, retractable gear, etc., which may permit a shorter take-off and faster rate-of-climb. The figures used are merely typical and may not be exact for any given airplane. However, they do represent an accurate measurement in terms of increase or decrease in performance.

The altitude used in the tables is "pressure altitude" which may be determined by setting the altimeter to the "standard atmosphere" of 29.92 and reading the altitude shown on the dial. The power-loading and wing-loading of any aircraft can usually be obtained from the manufacturer's specifications. Power-loading is the gross weight of the airplane divided by the rated horsepower of the engine. Wing-loading is the gross weight of the aircraft divided by square feet of wing area (on nontapered wings the product of the span times the chord).

## HOW TO USE THE TABLE

(1) Select the columns corresponding to the wing-loading and power-loading of of the airplane (if the values fall between those listed, select the next higher value). (2) Set the altimeter scale at 29.92, read the altitude indicated, and select the altitude grouping for the nearest 1,000 feet. (3) Select the temperature nearest the outside air temperature. (4) Opposite the temperature, in the appropriate columns, read the take-off distance in feet required on a hard-surfaced runway with no wind and the rate-of-climb in feet per minute.

For example, an airplane with a wing-loading of 10 and a power-loading of 15, taking off from a field at which the altimeter showed a reading of 4,000 feet (when the scale is set to 29.92), with air temperature 80° F., would require a take-off ground-run of approximately 1,135 feet. The rate-of-climb would be 700 feet a minute.

## CRUISING

The cruising speed (normal operating speed) is usually established by using sufficient power to provide relatively fast flight without undue wear on the engine or excessive fuel consumption. Most light airplanes with fixed-pitch propellers are operated at about 70 to 75 percent of the maximum horsepower. A simple way to determine this horsepower is to deduct 10 percent from the maximum cruising R.P.M. (Fig. 58) specified in the Operation Record.

Thus an engine with maximum r.p.m. of 2,000 would be operated at 2,000 minus 200, or 1,800 r.p.m. The advantages in using reduced power far outweigh the benefits of increased speed. For example: in a typical airplane with a 145-horsepower engine, the air speed when operating at 73 percent available horsepower is 110 m.p.h. At full throttle it is 121 m.p.h.- a gain of only 11 m.p.h. But, at full throttle, the engine consumes 50 percent more fuel than at 73 percent power, and its range is reduced from 4 hours to 2 hours and 40 minutes. Under no-wind conditions, its range in distance is reduced from 440 to 320 miles.

*Mixture Setting*

Adjust the fuel mixture to the most efficient setting. It will be somewhat leaner than for take off.

*Carburetor Heat Control*

Occasionally try using the carburetor heat control for better performance of the

## Table 2.
### TAKE-OFF DISTANCE AND RATE OF CLIMB
(CALCULATIONS SHOWN HERE APPLY TO SEA LEVEL ENGINES AND FIXED PITCH PROPELLERS)

Columns are grouped into two sections — TAKE-OFF GROUND RUN (Feet) and RATE OF CLIMB (Feet per minute) — each subdivided by Wing Loading (W) and Power Loading (P). Rows are grouped by Altimeter Reading and Temperature.

| Altimeter | Temp | GR W5 P5 | GR W5 P10 | GR W5 P15 | GR W5 P20 | GR W10 P5 | GR W10 P10 | GR W10 P15 | GR W10 P20 | RC W5 P5 | RC W5 P10 | RC W5 P15 | RC W5 P20 | RC W10 P5 | RC W10 P10 | RC W10 P15 | RC W10 P20 | RC W15 P5 | RC W15 P10 | RC W15 P15 | RC W15 P20 |
|---|---|---|---|---|---|---|---|---|---|---|---|---|---|---|---|---|---|---|---|---|---|
| Sea Level | 0 | 173 | 246 | 330 | 429 | 234 | 486 | 719 | 1,000 | 4,265 | 1,825 | 1,013 | 607 | 1,925 | 1,108 | 703 | 456 | 1,245 | 838 | 593 | 430 |
| Sea Level | 20 | 189 | 270 | 366 | 476 | 254 | 530 | 787 | 1,110 | 4,160 | 1,765 | 966 | 570 | 1,862 | 1,064 | 668 | 427 | 1,203 | 810 | 564 | 405 |
| Sea Level | 40 | 207 | 298 | 405 | 530 | 277 | 589 | 877 | 1,250 | 4,055 | 1,706 | 923 | 534 | 1,805 | 1,022 | 635 | 398 | 1,165 | 775 | 538 | 384 |
| Sea Level | 60 | 226 | 326 | 446 | 589 | 301 | 641 | 965 | 1,390 | 3,950 | 1,650 | 880 | 500 | 1,750 | 981 | 600 | 369 | 1,125 | 745 | 513 | 360 |
| Sea Level | 80 | 252 | 352 | 493 | 655 | 328 | 702 | 1,062 | 1,540 | 3,850 | 1,594 | 840 | 466 | 1,697 | 941 | 567 | 341 | 1,088 | 715 | 488 | 338 |
| Sea Level | 100 | 270 | 392 | 541 | 720 | 354 | 768 | 1,170 | 1,710 | 3,750 | 1,536 | 800 | 430 | 1,643 | 903 | 538 | 305 | 1,050 | 686 | 464 | 316 |
| 1,000 | 0 | 193 | 276 | 374 | 489 | 256 | 540 | 804 | 1,141 | 4,090 | 1,734 | 945 | 554 | 1,830 | 1,043 | 652 | 414 | 1,183 | 791 | 553 | 396 |
| 1,000 | 20 | 211 | 304 | 413 | 541 | 282 | 600 | 899 | 1,279 | 3,990 | 1,673 | 902 | 518 | 1,773 | 1,002 | 617 | 385 | 1,143 | 762 | 526 | 372 |
| 1,000 | 40 | 232 | 342 | 459 | 605 | 306 | 656 | 990 | 1,426 | 3,890 | 1,616 | 860 | 483 | 1,717 | 960 | 585 | 355 | 1,104 | 728 | 500 | 350 |
| 1,000 | 60 | 253 | 368 | 503 | 670 | 334 | 720 | 1,092 | 1,595 | 3,790 | 1,560 | 818 | 448 | 1,662 | 920 | 551 | 328 | 1,067 | 698 | 475 | 327 |
| 1,000 | 80 | 276 | 401 | 554 | 740 | 361 | 790 | 1,210 | 1,770 | 3,690 | 1,505 | 777 | 415 | 1,611 | 881 | 518 | 300 | 1,030 | 669 | 450 | 304 |
| 1,000 | 100 | 299 | 439 | 610 | 821 | 391 | 863 | 1,332 | 2,329 | 3,590 | 1,450 | 737 | 380 | 1,558 | 842 | 488 | 273 | 994 | 640 | 425 | 283 |
| 2,000 | 0 | 212 | 304 | 415 | 545 | 282 | 600 | 898 | 1,290 | 3,920 | 1,640 | 881 | 502 | 1,740 | 981 | 602 | 373 | 1,122 | 743 | 514 | 362 |
| 2,000 | 20 | 232 | 335 | 460 | 606 | 305 | 660 | 990 | 1,440 | 3,820 | 1,582 | 838 | 467 | 1,683 | 940 | 567 | 344 | 1,083 | 714 | 487 | 338 |
| 2,000 | 40 | 252 | 370 | 510 | 677 | 333 | 725 | 1,111 | 1,662 | 3,720 | 1,525 | 796 | 431 | 1,628 | 900 | 535 | 313 | 1,045 | 682 | 461 | 316 |
| 2,000 | 60 | 278 | 407 | 563 | 755 | 363 | 802 | 1,231 | 1,820 | 3,620 | 1,470 | 754 | 397 | 1,575 | 859 | 502 | 287 | 1,008 | 652 | 437 | 293 |
| 2,000 | 80 | 306 | 449 | 625 | 844 | 397 | 882 | 1,370 | 2,042 | 3,525 | 1,418 | 714 | 364 | 1,525 | 820 | 470 | 259 | 973 | 624 | 413 | 272 |
| 2,000 | 100 | 330 | 487 | 684 | 930 | 426 | 956 | 1,492 | 2,260 | 3,430 | 1,363 | 673 | 330 | 1,474 | 782 | 440 | 233 | 936 | 596 | 388 | 250 |
| 3,000 | 0 | 234 | 340 | 465 | 615 | 309 | 666 | 1,010 | 1,450 | 3,745 | 1,548 | 816 | 450 | 1,650 | 918 | 552 | 331 | 1,060 | 695 | 474 | 328 |
| 3,000 | 20 | 258 | 378 | 520 | 695 | 339 | 742 | 1,140 | 1,660 | 3,650 | 1,490 | 773 | 415 | 1,594 | 876 | 517 | 301 | 1,023 | 666 | 448 | 304 |
| 3,000 | 40 | 285 | 414 | 575 | 771 | 369 | 820 | 1,260 | 1,865 | 3,550 | 1,434 | 731 | 380 | 1,540 | 837 | 485 | 272 | 987 | 636 | 422 | 282 |
| 3,000 | 60 | 310 | 455 | 635 | 860 | 400 | 896 | 1,390 | 2,080 | 3,455 | 1,380 | 691 | 346 | 1,488 | 798 | 453 | 245 | 950 | 606 | 400 | 259 |
| 3,000 | 80 | 338 | 499 | 700 | 953 | 435 | 980 | 1,538 | 2,340 | 3,360 | 1,329 | 650 | 313 | 1,439 | 759 | 421 | 218 | 915 | 578 | 375 | 239 |
| 3,000 | 100 | 368 | 544 | 772 | 1,063 | 470 | 1,071 | 1,695 | 2,620 | 3,270 | 1,278 | 611 | 280 | 1,390 | 723 | 392 | 193 | 880 | 550 | 350 | 217 |
| 4,000 | 0 | 266 | 390 | 538 | 722 | 349 | 765 | 1,180 | 1,739 | 3,570 | 1,456 | 751 | 397 | 1,558 | 854 | 500 | 288 | 1,000 | 647 | 435 | 293 |
| 4,000 | 20 | 294 | 431 | 599 | 797 | 382 | 849 | 1,320 | 1,965 | 3,475 | 1,400 | 707 | 363 | 1,504 | 813 | 466 | 258 | 963 | 618 | 408 | 270 |
| 4,000 | 40 | 322 | 477 | 666 | 890 | 417 | 939 | 1,471 | 2,225 | 3,380 | 1,343 | 687 | 328 | 1,450 | 774 | 434 | 230 | 927 | 588 | 383 | 248 |
| 4,000 | 60 | 351 | 521 | 735 | 1,010 | 452 | 1,027 | 1,623 | 2,490 | 3,290 | 1,292 | 626 | 294 | 1,400 | 735 | 404 | 203 | 892 | 560 | 360 | 226 |
| 4,000 | 80 | 386 | 575 | 815 | 1,140 | 492 | 1,135 | 1,810 | 2,925 | 3,195 | 1,241 | 587 | 261 | 1,352 | 700 | 372 | 176 | 857 | 532 | 338 | 205 |
| 4,000 | 100 | 419 | 630 | 903 | 1,268 | 532 | 1,250 | 2,020 | 3,210 | 3,105 | 1,190 | 549 | 230 | 1,304 | 660 | 343 | 151 | 822 | 504 | 313 | 184 |
| 5,000 | 0 | 293 | 430 | 601 | 811 | 380 | 848 | 1,320 | 1,980 | 3,400 | 1,364 | 686 | 345 | 1,466 | 790 | 449 | 247 | 938 | 600 | 395 | 258 |
| 5,000 | 20 | 324 | 477 | 670 | 915 | 417 | 943 | 1,480 | 2,250 | 3,305 | 1,306 | 643 | 310 | 1,414 | 750 | 416 | 216 | 902 | 570 | 370 | 236 |
| 5,000 | 40 | 354 | 525 | 747 | 1,022 | 454 | 1,040 | 1,646 | 2,558 | 3,210 | 1,253 | 603 | 277 | 1,362 | 711 | 385 | 189 | 867 | 542 | 345 | 214 |
| 5,000 | 60 | 387 | 581 | 834 | 1,151 | 491 | 1,141 | 1,843 | 2,920 | 3,125 | 1,202 | 562 | 243 | 1,313 | 673 | 354 | 162 | 833 | 514 | 322 | 193 |
| 5,000 | 80 | 421 | 639 | 920 | 1,283 | 536 | 1,252 | 2,050 | 3,290 | 3,030 | 1,153 | 523 | 210 | 1,266 | 638 | 323 | 136 | 800 | 486 | 300 | 172 |
| 5,000 | 100 | 456 | 694 | 1,010 | 1,420 | 576 | 1,363 | 2,260 | 3,682 | 2,945 | 1,105 | 485 | 178 | 1,220 | 602 | 293 | 110 | 764 | 460 | 275 | 151 |
| 6,000 | 0 | 326 | 484 | 681 | 930 | 421 | 950 | 1,502 | 2,280 | 3,230 | 1,272 | 620 | 293 | 1,375 | 726 | 400 | 204 | 876 | 552 | 355 | 224 |
| 6,000 | 20 | 359 | 539 | 758 | 1,048 | 458 | 1,052 | 1,682 | 2,590 | 3,130 | 1,215 | 578 | 259 | 1,324 | 686 | 367 | 174 | 842 | 523 | 330 | 202 |
| 6,000 | 40 | 397 | 595 | 850 | 1,183 | 502 | 1,173 | 1,900 | 2,990 | 3,040 | 1,162 | 538 | 224 | 1,273 | 648 | 335 | 147 | 807 | 495 | 306 | 180 |
| 6,000 | 60 | 431 | 655 | 944 | 1,327 | 546 | 1,286 | 2,100 | 3,400 | 2,955 | 1,113 | 500 | 192 | 1,226 | 611 | 305 | 121 | 773 | 467 | 283 | 158 |
| 6,000 | 80 | 471 | 722 | 1,048 | 1,500 | 590 | 1,415 | 2,360 | 3,860 | 2,870 | 1,066 | 460 | 160 | 1,180 | 576 | 274 | 95 | 743 | 440 | 262 | 139 |
| 6,000 | 100 | 513 | 789 | 1,122 | 1,680 | 641 | 1,542 | 2,620 | 4,430 | 2,785 | 1,020 | 423 | 128 | 1,135 | 541 | 245 | 70 | 707 | 414 | 238 | 118 |
| 7,000 | 0 | 306 | 545 | 776 | 1,075 | 467 | 1,077 | 1,721 | 2,685 | 3,060 | 1,181 | 556 | 242 | 1,287 | 664 | 349 | 164 | 817 | 505 | 318 | 192 |
| 7,000 | 20 | 407 | 609 | 872 | 1,228 | 535 | 1,210 | 1,940 | 3,080 | 2,965 | 1,125 | 515 | 208 | 1,238 | 623 | 318 | 135 | 782 | 475 | 292 | 168 |
| 7,000 | 40 | 451 | 685 | 990 | 1,412 | 569 | 1,347 | 2,205 | 3,635 | 2,875 | 1,074 | 475 | 174 | 1,186 | 576 | 287 | 106 | 748 | 448 | 267 | 147 |
| 7,000 | 60 | 490 | 772 | 1,092 | 1,580 | 613 | 1,470 | 2,442 | 4,100 | 2,785 | 1,026 | 437 | 142 | 1,140 | 550 | 258 | 80 | 715 | 422 | 246 | 127 |
| 7,000 | 80 | 541 | 825 | 1,220 | 1,790 | 662 | 1,623 | 2,740 | 4,750 | 2,710 | 980 | 400 | 111 | 1,095 | 518 | 228 | 56 | 684 | 396 | 225 | 107 |
| 7,000 | 100 | 585 | 910 | 1,361 | 2,025 | 720 | 1,731 | 3,181 | 5,450 | 2,625 | 935 | 362 | 79 | 1,052 | 482 | 198 | 31 | 651 | 370 | 202 | 85 |

Fig. 58. Tachometer.

Fig. 59. Oil temperature gauge.

Fig. 60. Oil pressure gauge.

Fig. 61. Fuel gauges.

engine. The Tachometer (Fig. 58) will show the effect. **WATCH FOR ICING CONDITIONS**

During the cooler seasons and in areas of high humidity and low temperatures, icing can be a serious problem. There will be more discussion of icing in Part II "Weather—Friend or Enemy".

*Oil Temperature and Pressure*

Check the oil temperature range (Fig. 59) because it is the only means of indicating a warm or cold motor. The range of 40° C. to 80° C. shows safe operating temperatures for many aircraft engines. Oil pressure shows the proper forcing of oil to the moving parts inside of the engine. The pressure (Fig. 60) is provided by a small pump. Too high or too low pressures require an immediate return to the airport.

*Fuel Tanks and Pressure Check*

Make a final check of fuel available (Fig. 61) in each tank.

*Trimming the Ship*

Adjustment of the trim tabs, by turning the crank or small wheel located in the cockpit, with engine speed will give the airplane the most economical cruising speed. When properly trimmed the ship will literally fly itself.

# CHAPTER 6
## LANDING

### BEFORE LANDING
### (Check the Following)

*Fuel Mixture*

Adjust fuel mixture to rich.

*Carburetor Heat*

Adjust carburetor heat control to cold to prevent loss of power. If the humidity is high and the temperature below 60° F., carburetor icing can form rather quickly. Test for the formation of ice before entering the pattern.

*Landing Gear*

Gear down for an airplane equipped with retractable landing gear.

*Radio, Landing Instructions*

Call the control tower for landing instructions.

*Glide In*

Check for a glide-in-speed of m.p.h. or knots as it applies to the particular type of aircraft.

*Engine*

Clear the engine on the base leg.

*Propeller and Flap*

Adjust the propeller for designated pitch and put flaps to down.

### LANDING

*Landing Speeds*

In an approach for landing it is advisable to use a speed which gives a relatively slow rate of descent (long glide) and at the same time provides a sufficient safety margin above stalling. The speed recommended for approach is the same as for best climb-50 percent above stalling. Under gusty conditions, a slightly higher speed is desirable.

A competent pilot should be able to make three types of landings and to select

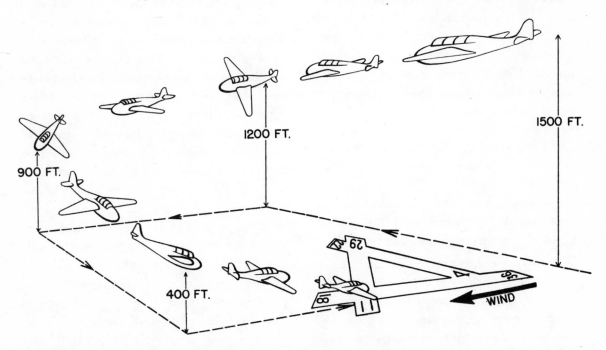

Fig. 62. A schematic drawing of an airplane descending in an airport traffic pattern.

the type most suitable for the conditions of wind and terrain.

### Accuracy Landing

The power-off full-stall landing is commonly used for light airplanes with tail wheels. F.A.A. flight tests require proficiency in "accuracy landings". In making such a landing, the pilot must close the throttle on the downwind leg, turn into base leg and make final approach without power, touching the ground at a predetermined "spot"

This type of approach and landing is an excellent maneuver for testing skill and judgement; it may also be of some value as preparation for forced landings. In some ways, however, it is the most difficult type to execute properly. Its success depends upon accurate calculation of wind effect, maintenance of a steady air speed and rate of descent, and careful manipulation of the controls while the airplane is flying slowly, near the ground, at a critical angle of attack. Down-currents may cause the airplane to descend too rapidly and fall short of the field; up-currents may carry the airplane beyond the intended landing spot; a gust may produce an unintentional stall; "dropping in" imposes a severe strain on the landing gear; bouncing or "ballooning" may cause loss of control and subsequent damage.

### Power-off Full-stall

When executing this type of landing, a pilot should not try to touch at the end of the runway, but should select a spot a few hundred feet from the boundary. He thus provides a margin of safety in the event of unexpected down-currents which frequently are encountered at the edge of landing field. He should keep one hand on the throttle, and never hesitate to use power to correct for errors or to go around the field again for another approach.

As a general practice most pilots employ a modification of the "accuracy landing," making the approach under reduced power, and closing the throttle for a full stall landing only after it becomes evident that the airplane will touch the runway at the desired spot.

### Power-on Full-stall

The power-on full-stall landing is executed by using partial power during the descent, putting the plane into stalling attitude just before it touches the ground, and reducing power still further or cutting it entirely after contact is made with the ground.

This landing is useful for soft terrain- snow, sand, or mud because the nose is slightly higher at the moment of contact and the forward speed is slightly less than in a power-off full-stall landing. If the plane shows any tendency to nose over, the throttle can be opened and the propeller blast on the tail will help to keep the plane in three-point position.

### Wheel Landing

The wheel landing is executed by using partial power during the descent, leveling off just before touching the ground, and making contact with the landing wheels while the tail is only slightly lower than in level-flight position. The throttle need not be fully closed until the plane has settled on the wheels in complete contact with the runway. The control wheel or stick should be moved forward slightly as the wheels touch the runway, in order to prevent the plane from bouncing and also to keep it firmly on the ground if the air is gusty during the landing roll. This landing is generally used for airplanes with tricycle landing gear (nose wheel), and for heavy aircraft. The level attitude of the airplane upon landing gives the pilot better vision over the nose than is possible with a full-stall landing.

The wheel landing is particularly useful for light planes whenever the wind is strong or gusty. The airplane makes ground contact while it is still maintaining flying speed, and thus passes from positive air control to positive ground control without the intermediate critical period characteristic of the full-stall power-off landing. There is no danger of an unintentional stall in this landing. If the tail is held high until all flying speed is lost, there is no tendency for a gust to lift the plane back into the air once it has touched the ground.

Obviously, the speed at the moment of contact is much greater in the wheel landing than in the other two landings just discussed. If the plane is of the nose-wheel type, brakes can be applied almost immediately after contact with the ground. For the tail-wheel type, the distance required to bring the airplane to a stop is greater. Therefore, the wheel landing is impractical for very short runways, or even runways of moderate length, unless the landing is made at the near end of the runway, and the wind is sufficiently strong to prevent possibility of running into the field boundary.

For take-off, climb, cruising, and land-ing, two flight instruments constantly used are the air-speed indicator and the altimeter. Because both of these instruments are affected by changes in atmospheric pressure, the pilot needs to know the corrections and adjustments necessary to obtain correct readings.

Special care is necessary on the final approach to see that the runway is clear and that no other plane is approaching from a slightly different angle or at a different altitude. Do not insist on your "right-of-way".

## AFTER LANDING

*Taxi*

Contact the control tower for taxi permission.

*Tie Down*

Set all switches to off. Get out of the aircraft and securely tie it down.

*After Flight Inspection*

Walk around the aircraft inspecting structure and surfaces for damages. If damage has occured, repairs can be made and the next flight will not be delayed.

*Close Flight Plan*

Reference — Part 3 Page 147.

# PART TWO

# WEATHER---FRIEND OR ENEMY

Piper Comanche

# CHAPTER 7
# BASIC WEATHER SCIENCE

Talk among private pilots frequently is as follows: "I wish I knew more about meterology", How much should I know about weather changes?", "Do I have to be a meterologist to fly safely?", etc.

The answer to all of this; and more too, is that a private pilot must study and learn about weather changes. He must use his judgement about when and where to fly. No weather station can tell the pilot what to do. Its function is to report the weather.

The meterologist's predictions are based on movements of large air masses and upon local conditions at specific points where weather stations are located. The air masses do not always perform as predicted, and the weather stations are sometimes spaced rather widely apart; therefore, it is necessary for the pilot to understand the weather conditions occuring between the stations, as well as conditions he encounters which are different from those indicated by the weather reports.

For private pilots, most of whose flights are conducted in smaller aircraft not equipped with elaborate and expensive instruments, a knowledge of the atmosphere and the behavior of weather is tremendously important to avoid hazardous flight conditions. The pilot should become acquainted with local weather changes. If he intends to fly to another region, he must study its weather changes in detail.

A good understanding of the basic facts that cause weather is necessary before analyzing weather changes.

## TEMPERATURE

Temperature (condition of a solid, liquid or gas as regards to heat or cold) information is very important to the pilot, meterologist, and others because a change in temperature may indicate a possible weather change.

Thermometers are instruments (Fig. 63) that show the condition of heat or cold in degrees (a unit for measuring heat or cold). Thermometers are constructed of hollow glass tubes closed at both ends, partially filled with mercury or colored alcohol. The upper part of the tube has the air removed producing a vacuum. This allows the liquids to expand (to enlarge the dimensions without increasing the substance). Then, when there is an increase of heat, the molecules and atoms increase their activity, causing the thermometer liquids to rise.

Cooling causes a quieting of the molecules - this action is called contraction.

Fig. 63. Mercury thermometers.

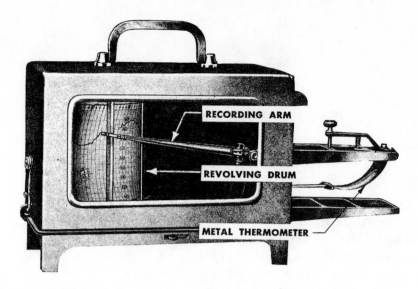

Fig. 64. Thermograph — recording thermometer

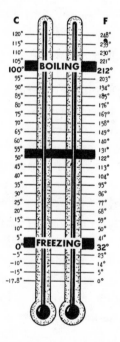

Fig. 65. Centigrade and fahrenheit scales.

There are two kinds of thermometers, centigrade and fahrenheit, (Fig. 65) which differ only in the scale markings. It will be noted that the centigrade thermometer has 0° for freezing and 100° for boiling as contrasted with the fahrenheit which has 32° freezing and 212° boiling. Fortunately, or unfortunately, depending on the viewpoint, it is sometimes necessary to convert from one scale to another. This can be done by using the above figure or by these formulas.

To find: $- °C = \frac{5}{9} \times (°F - 32) -$ subtract first, then multiply

To find: $- °F = (\frac{9}{5} \times °C) + 32 -$ multiply first, then add

Computers will also change fahrenheit to centigrade and visa versa.

The earth's heating by the sun is the source of most all of the earth's heat energy.

The earth receives most of this heat energy directly from the sun by a process of radiation (Transferring by wave motion) which is called insolation. All of the earth does not receive the same amount of insolation because the equator (Fig. 66) is more directly in the path of radiation waves and is therefore hotter than the poles.

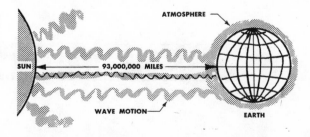

Fig. 66. Transfer of heat by radiation waves.

This fact is further complicated because of the seasons. During the winter the north pole is pointed away from the sun, thereby making still greater differences in the earth's heating. This difference in heating produces the two basic kinds of air — warm and cold. A small amount of the sun's radiation is absorbed directly by the atmosphere. However, most of the heat rays are absorbed by the earth.

The entire process is further complicated by the fact that some parts of the earth's surface absorb more heat while other areas reflect considerable radiation.

The earth's surface consists of light and dark areas, (Fig. 67) consequently there will be considerable reflection by the lighter areas. Water absorbs heat more slowly than land areas; therefore, the ocean never becomes very hot, while land areas become quite warm.

During the day, the outer crust of the earth absorbs large amounts of radiant energy. Some of the heat is then radiated from the earth to the air, producing warmer air. This depends on the kind of earth's surface.

After sundown, radiation ceases to come to the earth, but the radiation away from the previously heated earth's surface continues. The soil loses heat rapidly, depending on the kind of air next to it. If the air is dry, the ground cooling is very rapid. If the air is moist or cloud-covered, the loss of ground heat will be much slower. It can thus be seen that oceans and large bodies of water heat up slowly and lose heat slowly. Ocean temperatures will only change up or down about seven to ten degrees Fahrenheit during this year, while land temperatures may show changes of many degrees. Of course the kind of air, whether warmer or colder, passing over the land has much to do with temperature changes.

Another method of heating is by conduction (A transference of heat from a hot solid, liquid, or gas to a cold solid, liquid or gas.) During this process, air passing over a hot surface will gain some heat. As this air moves to another place, heating will be done by convection. (Transfer of heat by the movements of masses of a fluid.)

Warm air (Fig. 67) and cold air are quite different in behavior, basically because of the activity of the molecules and atoms.

Warm air will expand due to the increased activity and collision of the molecules which is caused by the heat. It will then rise as it expands, due to

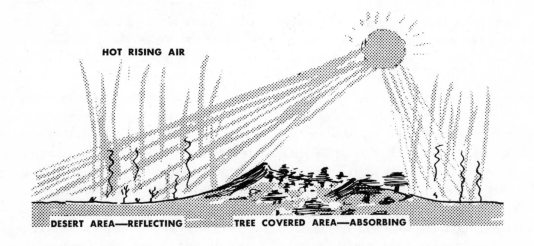

HOT RISING AIR

DESERT AREA—REFLECTING    TREE COVERED AREA—ABSORBING

Fig. 67. Local uneven heating.

weighing less. If warm air is near a body of water, it will pick up the water molecules that rise from the heated water. Therefore, the air will be warm and moist.

Cold air (Fig. 67 & 68) has less molecular activity and is contracting; therefore, it is sinking or settling air. It is not picking up moisture but may be squeezing it out.

Bumpy air (Fig. 68), unequal heating over local areas, can cause considerable difference in the vertical flow of air. The result is bumpy or rough air which causes the plane to oscillate, (move from side to side or up or down). This is a motion that can be very unpleasant. Over the ocean, there will be little rough air because local unequal heating of the surface is absent.

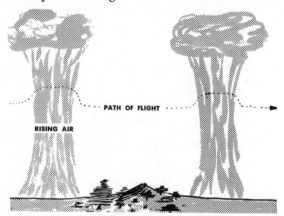

Fig. 68. Bumpy air.

## MOISTURE

Dew point (the temperature at which droplets of water begin to form in the air and on objects) is of particular interest because it gives an indication of the amount of moisture in the air.

Air contains varying amounts of water vapor depending on the temperature and atmospheric pressure existing at the time. From the previous study of temperature, the fact is known that in warm air the molecules are more active causing expansion. This being so, there is considerable space between the rapidly moving air molecules.

The mass or amount of air (Fig. 69) is the same but due to the increased activity of the molecules the volume is greater.

If there are any water (Fig. 70) molecules near by, they too will become more active when heated by a passing quantity of warm air or directly by the sun, and they will leave the water surface to become intermingled with the air molecules and atoms. The result is warm moist air.

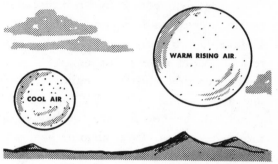

Fig. 69. Expansion of air.

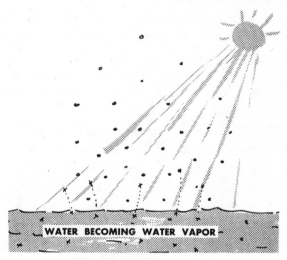

Fig. 70. Evaporation

As stated before, the temperature and pressure of the air determine the amount of moisture the air can hold. However, this process of evaporation only continues to the point when the air becomes saturated, (the maximum amount of moisture that the air can hold at a given temperature).

If at any time the temperature is changed, one of two things can happen. If it is warmed still more, the air can hold more moisture; but if it is cooled, (Fig. 71) the result is condensation (the return of water vapor to liquid).

The sling psychrometer (Fig. 71) is the common weather instrument used to determine the amount of moisture (Fig. 72) in the air. It consists of a dry thermometer and one covered with a cloth sack, which is kept wet and requires the use of a scale or table to find the dew point.

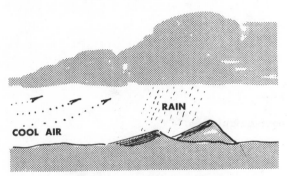

Fig. 71. Condensation.

To the pilot or weather observer, dew point determination can help indicate the weather to come. For instance, a low dew point of 10°F. shows that clouds probably will not form soon, since the air is dry. On the other hand, a dew point of 50° F. shows that clouds probably will form soon, since the air is moist. A dew point of 50° F. or above indicates that fog or clouds will form soon, even if none are present when the reading was taken.

To illustrate the point— at the base of a cloud the dew point and temperature are the same.

If the temperature is 56° F., no cloud will be visible but will form when the temperature drops to the dew point. The same is true with fog. A pilot sees a report of the dew point being 51° F., and say the temperature is 55° F. Therefore, just as soon as the temperature drops to 51° F., fog will form. Caution is advised for such a situation.

At times the dew point and temperature will be near 32° F., and ice may form on the aircraft. The pilot will want to fly at a lower altitude, if such is possible, to avoid the condition.

## CLOUD BASE PROBLEMS

When planning a flight, a pilot not always has all of the weather information available. However, under certain conditions of rising air it is possible for him to compute the approximate cloud base. (Fig. 73).

The answers that we will obtain from the following formula will be in thousands of feet. To determine the height of the clouds in feet, move the decimal point three places to the right.

$$\text{cloud base} = \frac{\text{surface temp.-dew point}}{4.5}$$

## PRESSURE

A barometer (Fig. 74) is the standard instrument used by the weather stations for the measurement of barometric pres-

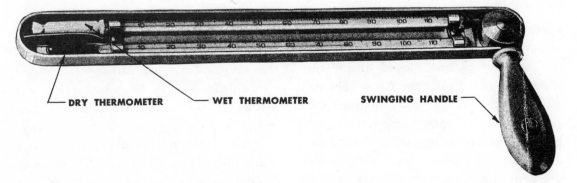

DRY THERMOMETER — WET THERMOMETER — SWINGING HANDLE

Fig. 72. Sling psychrometer.

|   | SURFACE TEMP. | DEW POINT | CLOUD BASE |
|---|---|---|---|
| 1 | 66°F | 52°F | |
| 2 | 50 | 50 | |
| 3 | 75 | 55 | |
| 4 | 69 | 51 | |
| 5 | 68 | 68½ | |
| 6 | 73 | 43 | |

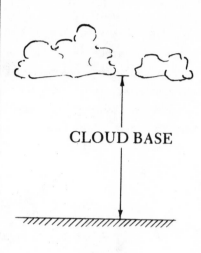

CLOUD BASE

Fig. 73. Cloud base calculation.

Fig. 74. Altimeter.

Fig. 75. Mechanical barometer.

sure, (Atmospheric pressure). It is constructed of a glass tube which is open at the bottom end and closed at the top. Mercury is used because its weight permits the use of a weather instrument of convenient size. The barometer is calibrated in inches of mercury and millibars, 34 millibars equal one inch of mercury), are convenient units of measure used by meteorologists.

As stated before, the altimeter (Fig. 75) is a mechanical barometer which must be set to a mercury barometer. There is little difference in the construction of an altimeter and a mechanical barometer other than the markings on the face.

The barograph is a recording mechanical barometer which actually draws the record of pressures for a period of about a week.

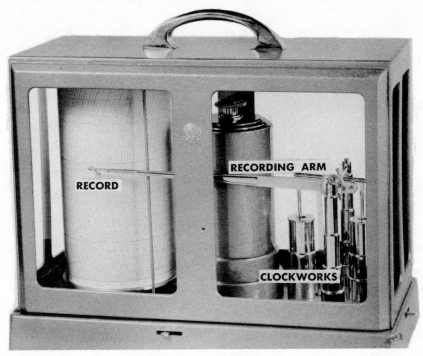

Fig. 76. Barograph.

Atmospheric or barometric pressure information is very important to the airman, because as stated previously, it permits a correction for altitude. The information also shows weather changes associated with high and low pressure areas, fronts, etc.

If the foregoing facts were as simple as they seem, the altimeter would be quite an accurate instrument, and would register altitudes according to a uniform pressure scale. However, the one big factor is that atmospheric pressure rarely is arranged in an orderly manner for very long periods of time.

Weather changes are associated with atmospheric pressure and temperature changes, thus the altimeter can give wrong altitudes unless a correction is made by the pilot.

During a period of cold weather (Fig. 77) the atmospheric pressure at the earth's surface is usually higher than average, with the air being heavy and settling. The result is that more air is near the surface of the earth and less at higher altitudes.

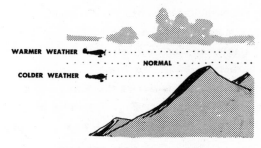

Fig. 77. Altimeter errors.

The opposite is true during warm weather, because rising, expanding air causes lower surface atmospheric pressure. Therefore, the altimeter, being a pressure instrument will be wrong in both cases, unless it is corrected.

The sensitive altimeter (Fig. 74) can be set before flight to a known altitude, thereby determining atmospheric pressure; or while in flight, the pilot can listen to the weather report over the radio range system or control tower and determine his altitude by turning the altimeter setting knob.

Before and during flight, the pilot can determine the corrected altitude by read-

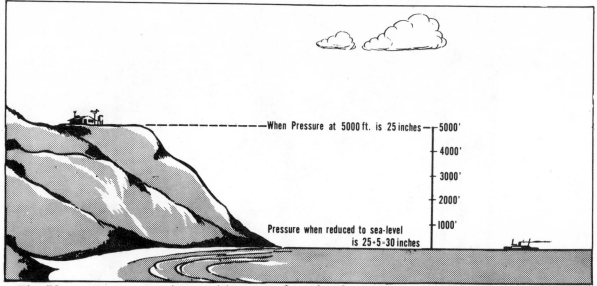

When Pressure at 5000 ft. is 25 inches — 5000'

4000'

3000'

2000'

Pressure when reduced to sea-level
is 25+5-30 inches — 1000'

Fig. 78. Station pressure is stated in terms of sea-level pressure to make comparisons possible.

ing a graph, or by use of a computer, (Modified slide rule). The latter device is very useful to the pilot because many flight problems can be solved simply and quickly.

The important points to remember are that during cold weather (Fig. 77) the altimeter reads too high and during warm weather it reads too low. Therefore, the greater danger is during the winter months when the altimeter (Fig. 74) indicates an altitude greater than it really is.

## WIND

A pilot is very much interested in whatever information can be obtained by radio or observation of wind direction and velocity. He needs the information to plan his navigation, to takeoff and land the aircraft, and to apprise possible weather changes. The effect of wind on navigation is discussed in part three of this book.

Wind and Landings— The larger air-ports have landing strips in several di-rections, making the take-off and landing problem a minor one. However, the smaller airports may have a single landing strip, thus making landings hazardous for smaller aircraft if a strong crosswind is blowing.

The pilot must know his airplane and

how strong a crosswind will be dangerous to him.

Wind directions obtained over the radio range system are satisfactory, providing the plane is landing at or near the source of the information. In general, the pilot must estimate wind direction and velocity.

Adjacent to each smaller airport will be a wind sock (Fig. 79) to indicate wind direction (a south wind blows from the south). To determine the direction, the observer will compare the wind sock di-rection with some prominent feature of known direction such as the landing strip or a highway, etc.

Fig. 79. Wind sock for wind direction.

| Beaufort Number | Miles per Hour | Knots | Terms Used in U.S.W.B. Forecasts | Wind Effects Observed on Land and at Sea |
|---|---|---|---|---|
| 0 | Less than 1 | Less than 1 | Light | Calm; smoke rises vertically; sea like mirror |
| 1 | 1–3 | 1–3 | Light | Direction of wind shown by smoke drift but not by wind vanes; sea ripples with the appearance of scales formed, but without foam crests. |
| 2 | 4–7 | 4–6 | Light | Wind felt on face; leaves rustle; ordinary vane moved by wind. At sea, small wavelets, short but pronounced; crests appear glassy, do not break. |
| 3 | 8–12 | 7–10 | Gentle | Leaves and small twigs in constant motion; wind extends light flag. Large wavelets with crests beginning to break; foam appears glassy, perhaps scatterred white horses (white foam crests). |
| 4 | 13–18 | 11–16 | Moderate | Raises dust and loose paper; small branches are moved. Small waves, becoming longer; frequent white horses. |
| 5 | 19–24 | 17–21 | Fresh | Small trees in leaf begin to sway; crested wavelets form on inland waters. moderate waves of a pronounced long form at sea; many white horses, possibly some spray. |
| 6 | 25–31 | 22–27 | Strong | Large branches in motion; whistling heard in telegraph wires; umbrellas used with difficulty. Large waves begin to form; white foam crests more extensive everywhere; probably some spray |
| 7 | 32–38 | 28–33 | Strong | Whole trees in motion; inconvenience felt walking against wind. Sea heaps up; some white foam from breaking waves blows in streaks with the wind. |
| 8 | 39–46 | 34–40 | Gale | Breaks twigs off trees; generally impedes progress. Moderately high waves. Edges of crests beginning to break into spindrift; well-marked streaks of foam blow along direction of wind. |
| 9 | 47–54 | 41–47 | Gale | Slight structural damage occurs (chimney pots, slates removed). High waves, dense streaks of foam along direction of wind; spray may affect visibility. |
| 10 | 55–63 | 48–55 | Whole gale | Seldom experienced inland; trees uprooted; considerable structural damage occurs. Very high waves with long overhanging crests; great patches of foam blow in dense white streaks along direction of wind. Sea surface takes on a white appearance; visibility affected. |
| 11 | 64–72 | 58–63 | Whole gale | Very rarely experienced; accompanied by widespread damage. Exceptionally high waves; sea completely covered with long white patches of foam lying along direction of wind; edges of wave crests everywhere blown into froth. Visibility affected. |
| 12 | 73 or more | 64 or more | Hurricane | Very rarely experienced; accompanied by widespread damage. Air filled with foam and spray; sea completely white with driving spray. Visibility very seriously affected. |

Table 3. Beaufort scale for estimating wind velocities.

Wind velocity can best be estimated by the Beaufort sacle.

With a little practice, this scale becomes a very useful guide.

## WIND AND WEATHER

Considerable discussion is necessary to understand the importance of wind and its relationship to weather.

By referring to temperature, (Fig. 66) it will be noted that the earth is unequally heated by insolation thereby creating a warm belt of air and two cold belts of air. It will also be remembered that warm air in expanding, (Fig. 69) is lighter in weight, and is rising. Again, cold air is contracting and is sinking or settling. Thus, there is a band of rising air and two areas of sinking air over the earth. (Fig. 80).

Air seeks its own level just like water thereby setting up a basic air circulation (winds) over the surface of the earth. However, the earth is turning, (Fig. 81 and Fig. 82) which complicates the basic flow by the fact that the equator is spinning much faster than the polar regions.

The result of all this (Fig. 83) is a flow of cold, dry, heavy air from the polar regions and a northward and southward flow of warm, moist, lighter weight air from the equatorial regions. The flows are not regular or of the same intensity, thus causing numerous weather phenomena.

The cold polar air will build up in pressure and eventually seek its own level

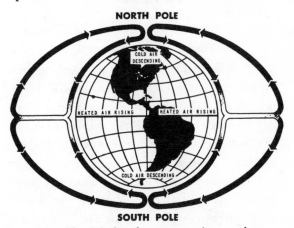

Fig. 80. Winds of a non turning earth.

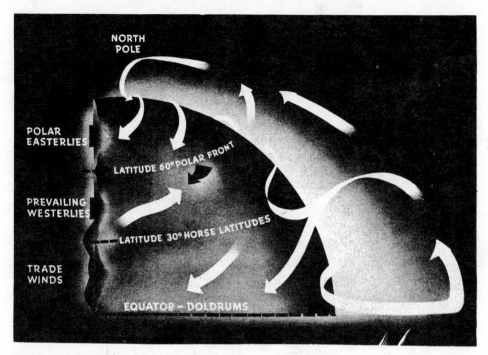

Fig. 81. Winds of a turning earth.

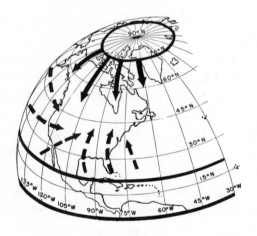

Fig. 82. Air movement.

by flowing southward. The warm moist equatorial air which is rising will flow northwards at various intervals of a few days or weeks. During the winter months the movement of the air masses is faster and more severe.

As stated previously, most of our weather (Fig. 82) occurs along the lines of conflict between cold air and warm air. It is along these lines that the warm moist

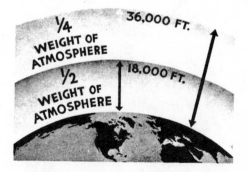

Fig. 83. The atmosphere.

air is condensed to various kinds of precipitation, (rain, snow, etc.) depending on the atmospheric pressure, temperature and moisture at the time.

*Highs and Lows*

High and low pressure (Fig. 82) areas are produced by the two primary kinds of air.

Cold air is (Fig. 84) dryer and heavier; therefore it is settling and produces a high pressure area.

Warm air becomes moist and rises because it weighs less, thus it will produce a low pressure area. (Fig. 85).

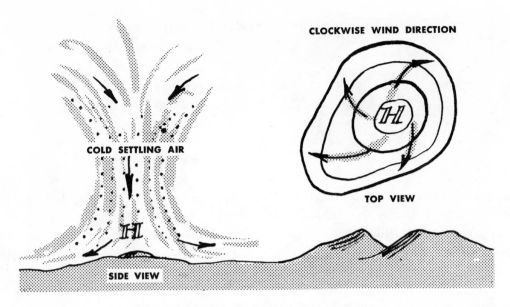

Fig. 84. Formation of a high pressure area.

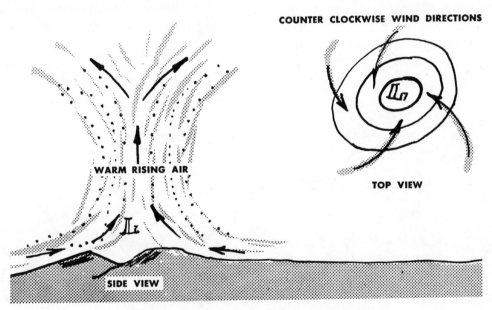

Fig. 85. Formation of a low pressure area.

The entire earth is covered with the two kinds of pressure areas with most of the bad weather occurring when they meet. Cold, high pressure areas tend to travel faster than warm, low pressure areas, but neither moves with the same speed as the earth. If such were the case, a given locality would have the same weather continuously.

## FRONTS AND WEATHER

As the cold air (Fig's. 82 & 83) surges out of the polar region and meets the warm, moist air from the south, (Fig's 82 & 86) there are formed lines of conflict called fronts.

It is here that definite weather patterns are formed which indicate the kind of weather to be expected.

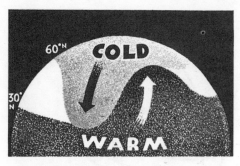

Fig. 86. Fronts and how they form.

At the beginning, the line of conflict is straight but because the cold air is moving faster, a spiralling of air begins. As this continues the counter clock-wise low pressure area with fronts is formed.

The locating of the fronts (Fig. 87) by the Weather Bureau is very important in order to forecast the kind of flying weather the pilot will encounter. The existence of about 750 (and more to come) weather stations, weather ships, and reports from steamships, airlines, etc. greatly assist in determining the nature of the fronts,

their paths, the intensity of the storms, and the kinds of weather that are to follow.

Pilots should take a practical viewpoint of the weather associated with the passing of the weather fronts.

Warm fronts in general move slowly with stratus clouds, poor visibility, drizzle, and rather smooth air. Hidden thunderstorms may be a hazard.

Cold fronts may follow warm fronts. They move rather rapidly and are composed of cumulus clouds. The visibility is usually good, with rather bumpy air that is often accompanied by cold rain or snow.

To study the kinds of weather (Fig's. 88, 89 & 90) with the passing of a front, the following illustrations will point out the sequence of the weather that occurs during the passing of a warm and cold front.

Frequently cold and warm fronts get mixed up, and produce an occluded front

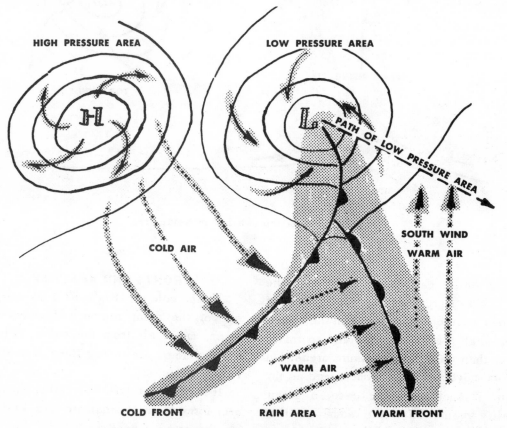

Fig. 87. Frontal formation.

which is a mixture of the two kinds of weather.

The previous discussion has been an airman's view looking down on the weather that is associated with the passing of a front. Another valuable picture is the cross section view that can be seen by the person on the ground. Note the sketch accompanying each frontal diagram.

The time required for the passing of the fronts varies with their intensity and the time of year. Some storms have passed across the entire United States in a few hours, while others may take several

days or even weeks.

The size of the storm area may be from a hundred or so miles, such as illustrated hear, to a thousand miles or more. It will be noted that the kind of weather an observer is experiencing depends on the location of the front. If the front is approaching, some idea of what to expect can be obtained. As the front passes eastward a distinct weather change occurs. Occasionally another front will be right behind the first, therefore some alteration of what is expected may occur.

The important thing about a front is to locate it, study the nature of the particular front, (Figs. 91, 92, 93, 94, 95 & 96) note its path, its expected time of arrival, and

### WEATHER CONDITION – 1st DAY

1. South to southeast wind, moderate velocities.
2. Moderate temperature, barometric pressure unsteady.
3. High thin cirrus clouds becoming cirro stratus.
4. Visibility good.
5. Lower clouds to the west.
6. Air not too bumpy.
7. Flying conditions good, but weather probably will close in later.

### WEATHER CONDITION – 2nd DAY

1. Southeast to southwest winds, increasing, gusty.
2. Temperature has dropped, barometric pressure a few millibars lower.
3. Overcast with nimbo stratus clouds, rain and snow in mountains.
4. Low visibility due to rain.
5. Low clouds in all directions.
6. Flying conditions – bumpy air; icing; instrument flight probably necessary.

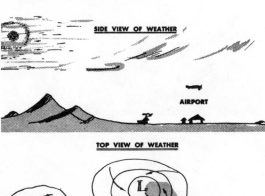

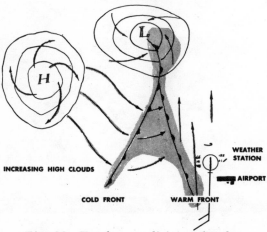

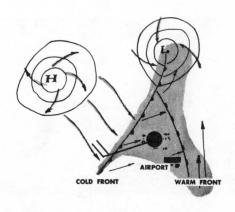

Fig. 88. Weather condition – 1st day.

Fig. 89. Weather condition – 2nd day.

WEATHER CONDITION — 3rd DAY

1. West to northwest wind, increasing possibly to 30 mph or more. Caution for landings.
2. Temperature has dropped. Dew point lowering (dryer air). Barometric pressure rising.
3. Scattered cumulus clouds (fair weather).
4. Visibility excellent.
5. Flying conditions improving; possible strong surface winds.

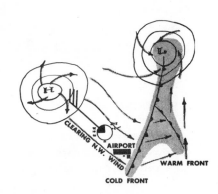

Fig. 90. Weather condition — 3rd day.

fly accordingly. Good weather sense always leads to safety in flight.

It must be remembered, however, that some storms do not have fronts and much bad flying weather can be experienced without the usual frontal forms.

## KINDS OF FRONTS

### Stationary Fronts

Sometimes the opposing forces exerted by adjacent air masses of different densities are such that the frontal surface between them shows little or no movement. In such cases it is usually found that the surface winds tend to blow parallel to the front rather than against or away from it, as is the case with the cold and warm fronts. Since neither air mass is replacing the other, the front is referred to as a "stationary front."

The weather conditions occurring with a stationary front are similar to those found with a warm front but are usually less intense. An annoying feature of the stationary front and its weather pattern is that it persists in one area for several days, and, in some cases, hampers flights in the area for extended periods at a time.

Fig. 91. A fast moving cold front, with unstable warm air.

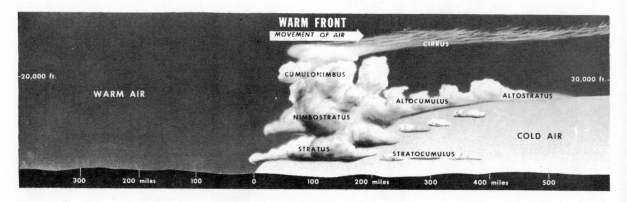

Fig. 92. Example of warm front, with rain areas not shown.

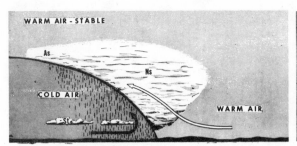

Fig. 93. A slow moving cold front, with stable warm air.

Fig. 95. A warm front, with stable warm air.

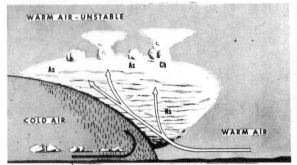

Fig. 94. A slow moving cold front, with unstable warm air.

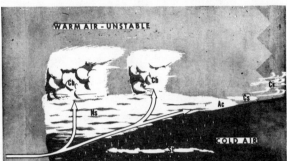

Fig. 96. A warm front, with unstable warm air.

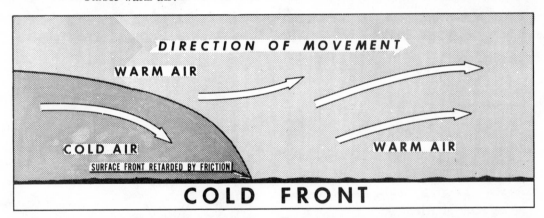

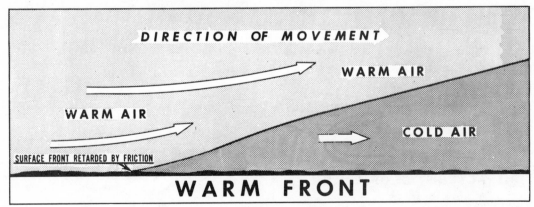

Fig. 97. The slope of a cold front is steeper than the slope of a warm front. (Vertical dimensions are exaggerated in the drawing.)

## FLYING THROUGH A FRONT

Following are some of the weather conditions the pilot may expect to encounter when flying through a front from the warm air to the cold air.

1. Wind will shift in a distance of 25 to 50 miles.
2. In a cold front, turbulence will be encountered in the frontal zone.
3. Temperature will fall.
4. Clouds will lower, and a lower altitude will probably have to be flown to maintain visual reference.
5. Precipitation, and possibly thunderstorms, will be encountered.
6. Icing may occur in clouds or precipitation if the temperature is below freezing.

From a study of the cross sections presented it will be noted that the nature of the weather encountered aloft will depend upon the altitude of the airplane and the character of the front.

## CHARACTERISTICS OF A COLD AIR MASS

Types of clouds — cumulus and cumulonimbus

Ceilings — generally unlimited (except during precipitation)

Visibilities — excellent (except during precipitation)

Unstable air — pronounced trubulence in lower levels (because of convection currents)

Type of precipitation — occasional local thunderstorms or showers-hail, sleet, snow flurries

## CHARACTERISTICS OF A WARM AIR MASS

Type of clouds — stratus stratocumulus (fog, haze)

Ceilings — generally low

Visibilities — poor (smoke and dust held in lower levels)

Stable air — smooth, with little or no turbulence

Type of precipitation — drizzle

## THUNDERSTORMS

When an unstable condition is formed in the atmosphere, such as may occur if the air is heated from below or forced to ascend the side of a mountain or frontal surface, the resulting bouyancy forces will tend to cause the air which is warmer than its surroundings to rise as convection currents. The thunderstorm (Fig. 98 & 100) represents a severe and, for the aircraft operator, dangerous form of atmospheric convection. Here, the upward motions of air are accompanied by downdrafts both within and outside of the thunderstorm.

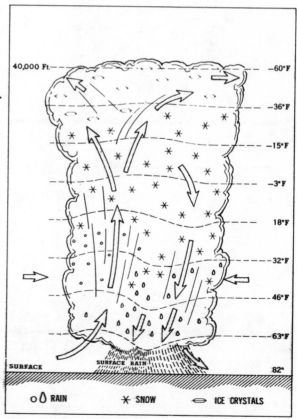

Fig. 98. Idealized cross section of a thunderstorm cell in the mature stage.

## THUNDERSTORMS AND AIRPLANES IN FLIGHT

### Drafts

During the period of activity, virtually the entire region occupied by the thunderstorm is composed of drafts. (Fig. 100) The direction of the draft is largely dependent upon the stage of development of the cloud. In the early stages of development, the motion is mainly upward; throughout later stages it is mainly downward, particularly where rain develops.

Studies of the structure of the thunderstorm (Figs. 98 & 100) indicate that during the cumulus stage of development the updrafts may cover a horizontal area as large as 4 miles in diameter. In the cumulus stage the updraft in many cells extends from below the cloud base to the cloud top, a height greater than 25,000 feet. During the mature stage the updraft disappears from the lowest levels of the cloud, although it continues in upper levels where it may reach a height of 60,000 feet.

Thunderstorm downdrafts are slower and have smaller horizontal and vertical extents than updrafts. The downdraft, however, continues below the base of the cloud and may constitute a serious flying hazard, since significant downward speeds may exist at levels as low as 300 to 400 feet above the terrain. Considering the width and speed of such downdrafts, an airplane flying at 180 miles per hour may be carried downward about 2,000 feet by action of the draft alone.

### Gusts.

Superimposed upon the large-scale continuous flow of the drafts are many irregular, local gusts. They are small eddies or whirling masses of air. The eddies, which are typical of thunderstorm gustiness, vary in size from only a few inches to whirling air masses several hundred feet in diameter. The characteristic response of an airplane intercepting a series of gusts is a number of sharp accelerations or "bumps" without systematic change in altitude. These accel-

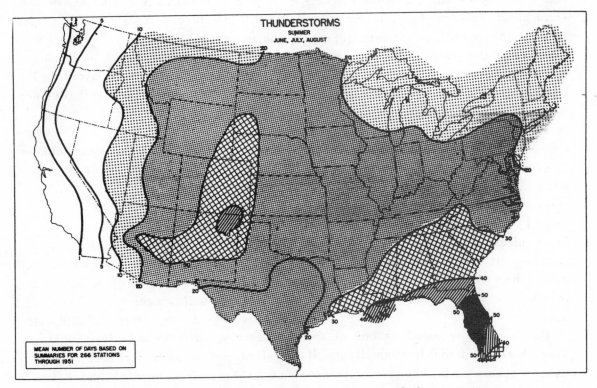

Fig. 99. Average number of days with thunderstorms during summer season.

erations may be accompanied by pitch, yaw, or roll movements and are caused by abrupt changes in the wind field encountered by the airplane. The degree of "bumpiness" experienced in flight is related to both the number of such abrupt changes encountered in a given distance and the strength of the individual changes.

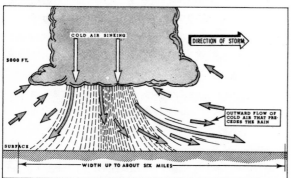

Fig. 100. Cold air dome beneath a thunderstorm cell in the mature stage. Arrows represent deviation of wind flow. Dashed lines indicate rainfall.

In general, (Fig. 101) it has been found that the maximum number of high velocity gusts are found at altitudes of 5,000 to 10,000 feet below the top of the thunderstorm cloud, while the least severe turbulence is encountered, on the average, near the base of the storm. It is important to point out, however, that even though the turbulence at these low levels is at a minimum, it is frequently strong enough to be classified as "heavy to severe".

*Lightning*

Since considerable damage can result when an airplane is struck by lightning, particularly to radio equipment and exposed control surfaces, it is advisable to avoid those areas in the thunderstorm where lightning is most frequent. Lightning strikes less frequently in the lowest flight levels.

*Hail*

Hail may be regarded as one of the worst hazards of thunderstorm flying. It usually occurs during the mature stages having an updraft of more than average

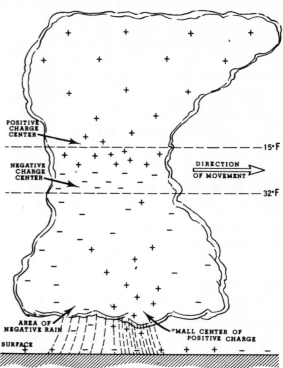

Fig. 101. Location of electric charges inside a typical thunderstorm cell.

intensity, and is found with the greatest frequency between the 10,000-foot and 15,000-foot levels. As a rule, the larger the storm the more likely it is that hail will be encountered. If the active areas of strong updrafts can be avoided, the chances of encountering large hailstones will be reduced.

From the foregoing discussion of thunderstorms there is but one conclusion for the light plane pilot—stay well away from thunderstorms.

## CEILING AND CLOUDS

Ceiling (Fig. 102) is the distance from the ground to the base or bottom of the clouds of a half or more covered sky.

The F.A.A. has very definite rules concerning altitudes to be flown over city and country areas and require flights to be at least five hundred feet below a cloud base.

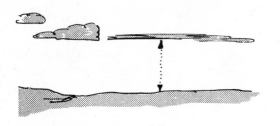

Fig. 103   Ceiling

Fig. 102.  Ceiling.

Pilots are very much interested in clouds, their kinds, and weather associated with them.

Clouds are of two general kinds: Cumulus, (cottony, puffy, billowy); Stratus, (layered, horizontal, sheets).

Clouds are classified as to position above the earth, namely high, middle, and low. Cumulus and stratus (Fig. 105) occur at all three levels.

Combinations of cumulus and stratus may occur such as stratocumulus, (puffy and layered). Fracto, (fractured or broken), clouds combined with cumulus are indicated as Fractomumulus, (broken cumulus), Nimbus, (producing rain), clouds, group with either kind to produce Nimbostratus, (raining stratus), or cumulonimbus, (raining cumulus).

Clouds are indicators of the kind of weather to expect; however, other factors such as pressure, temperature, winds and frontal movements contribute to the general weather picture. In some areas all signs may fail.

For a general classification, clouds are divided into the following ten groups. The U.S. Weather Bureau has subdivided the basic ten into many more types, but all the variations are chiefly to be used by the meteorologist.

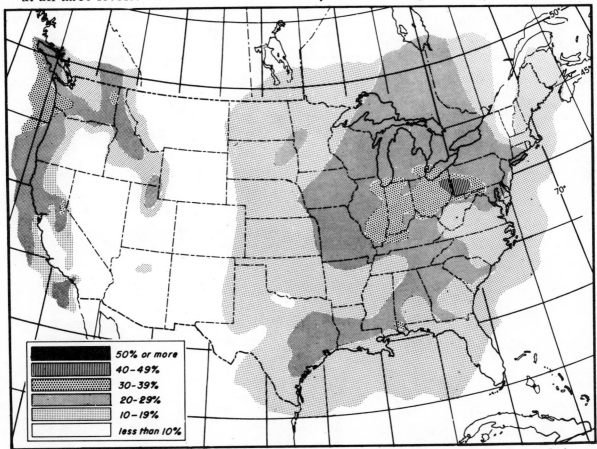

Fig. 103.  Percentage of hours in the winter when the ceiling is below 1,000 feet and the visibility is less than 3 miles.

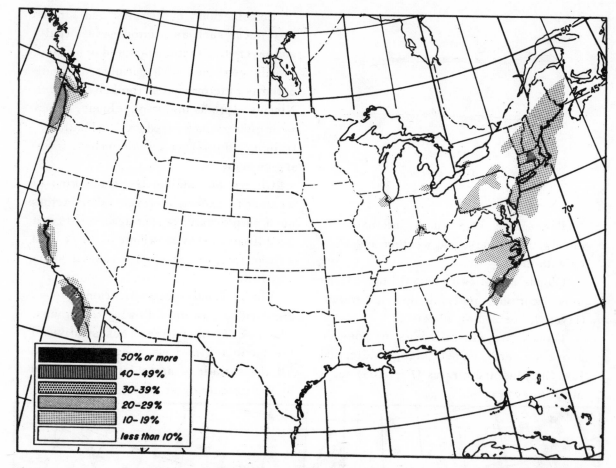

| | |
|---|---|
| ■ | 50% or more |
| ▦ | 40–49% |
| ▨ | 30–39% |
| ▦ | 20–29% |
| ░ | 10–19% |
| ☐ | less than 10% |

Fig. 104. Percentage of hours in the summer when the ceiling is below 1,000 feet and the visibility is less than 3 miles.

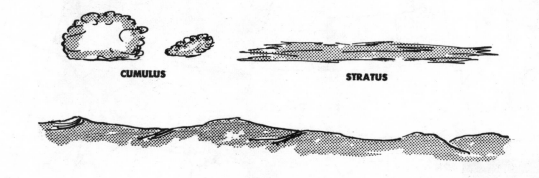

CUMULUS                          STRATUS

Fig. 105. Types of clouds.

| ALTITUDE IN FEET | | NAME and ABBREV. | COMPO-SITION | APPEARANCE (See cloud photos) | SYMBOL | IDENTIFICATION and WEATHER CHANGES THAT MAY OCCUR |
|---|---|---|---|---|---|---|
| HIGH CLOUDS | 20,000' TO 40,000' | CIRRUS Ci | ICE CRYSTALS | Fig. 107 | | **MARES TAILS** May indicate the approach of a storm. |
| | | CIRRO STRATUS Cs | ICE CRYSTALS | Fig. 108 | | **HALO CLOUD** Ring around the sun or moon, storm approaching. |
| | | CIRRO CUMULUS Cc | ICE CRYSTALS | Fig. 109 | | **MACKEREL SKY** Storm approaching. Pilots should check weather frequently. |
| MIDDLE | 6,500' TO 20,000' | ALTO CUMULUS Ac | ICE and WATER | Fig. 110 | | **COLD FRONT** May be near or possibly thunder storms. |
| | | ALTO STRATUS As | WATER | Fig. 111 | | **WARM FRONT** Near which may change to nimbostratus with rain. |
| LOW CLOUDS | SEA LEVEL TO 6,500' | STRATO CUMULUS Sc | WATER | Fig. 112 | | **HEAVY ROLLS** Usually no rain icing possible. Watch the temperature. |
| | | STRATUS St | WATER | Fig. 113 | | **HAZY** Low cloud but not on the ground. Poor visibility. When on the ground its fog. |
| | | NIMBO STRATUS Ns | WATER | Fig. 114 | | **RAIN CLOUD** Very dark, rain, poor visibility. |
| VERTICLE CLOUDS | 1,500' TO 30,000' | CUMULUS Cu | WATER | Fig. 115 | | **FAIR WEATHER** Clearing |
| | | CUMULO NIMBUS Cb | ICE at TOP WATER | Fig. 116 | | **THUNDER HEAD** Violent winds, rain, hail, avoid. |

Fig. 106.  Classification of clouds.

Fig. 107.  Cirrus clouds.

Fig. 110.  Altocumulus clouds.

Fig. 108.  Cirrostratus clouds.

Fig. 111.  Altostratus clouds.

Fig. 112.  Stratocumulus clouds.

Fig. 109.  Cirrocumulus clouds.

Fig. 113.  Stratus clouds.

Fig. 114. Nimbostratus clouds.

Fig. 115. Cumulus clouds.

Fig. 116. Cumulonimbus clouds.

## VISIBILITY

Poor visibility, (Fig. 117) (how far the pilot can see toward the horizon), probably causes more serious accidents than any other factor due to weather.

Fast moving airplanes require quick and accurate control and this demands visible room if safety is to be had. Things can happen very quickly at 150 mph.

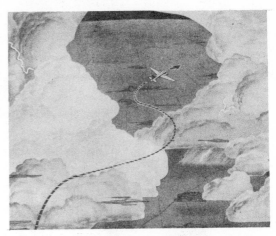

Fig. 117. Visibility

When visibility becomes very poor or ceases altogether, it is difficult to tell if the plane is turning, rising, or gliding. A plane in proper bank gives little or no sensation of turning, consequently the pilot may be in great danger with no visibility.

An examination of visibility shows there are several kinds of poor visibility, namely fog, cloud, dust, smoke, haze, smog as well as combinations.

Fog—(a dense layered cloud located on or near the ground). It is as if a darkened white sheet has been hung before our eyes. It may be very dark in a thick fog, because the sun's light is unable to penetrate the cloud. Fog should ground the aircraft until visibility improves.

Cloud—Flying through a cloud would be like flying through fog; that is, visibility is extremely bad. Normally, aircraft should not be flown through clouds unless equipped for such flight.

Dust—consists of small particles of soil that have been picked up by high winds. Dust may occur over a region some distance from its origin by being carried aloft from place to place. Frequently dust storms indicate high speed surface winds, and thus landing or takeoff may be hazardous.

Smoke and Smog—Centers of industrial activity are bad sources of smoke and fumes. Frequently, fumes from a factory will be clear at the source but on combination with other fumes, they will produce eye-irritating compounds. The result is a lead colored haze which may cut visibility down to less than one mile with flight at the lower levels very dangerous. When the air is moist and hazy, the fumes produce a still denser mass of air.

In certain areas, occasionally the air literally gets upside down. The warm rising air is on top and the cooler denser air is on the bottom. This is known as a temperature inversion. The air becomes stagnant with the smog building up over a few days until the wind stirs and moves the smog away. From an airplane, smog looks like molten lead and it fills the valleys just like fog. Very bad smog has closed airports.

Snow, sleet, hail or rain can all contribute to poor visibility, depending on the intensity of the storm. Hazardous flying may occur.

## FOG

Fog is a definite hazard to flying because airports and obstructions are invisible from the air. Landing with ordinary instruments is not advisable. If the airport is "fogged in", the pilot should turn back or fly to an alternate airport which is clear.

Fog is a low stratus cloud that differs from the ordinary stratus in that the droplets are smaller and more diffused, (spread in all directions).

Fog formation will occur in the same manner as cloud formation- that is, whenever the temperature and dew point are near the same.

Three conditions are necessary for the formation of fogs; first, the air must be moist, second, the temperature must drop and third, there must be some air movement. Most fogs are associated with the movement of air masses from place to place.

Cooling for the formation of fog is done in two ways: advection, (horizontal transfer of heat by the flow of air), and radiation, (transfer of heat by wave motion).

### Advection Fogs

Advection fogs (Fig. 118) are common wherever warm moist air flows over colder land or water. Most of the fog will occur during the night while the earth is losing much heat by radiation. The next day, if the air flow is not too strong, the sun will literally "burn off" the advection fog by returning the moisture to the invisible vapor form.

Fig. 118. Advection fog.

### Radiation Fogs

Radiation fogs, (Fig's. 119 & 120) (ground fogs), are formed by the cooling of the land surfaces by radiation, (loss of heat by wave motion) to the sky. As the land gets colder the dew point and temperature become the same, and fog can form. If a cloud ceiling is above the area it will slow down radiation and usually prevent a radiation fog.

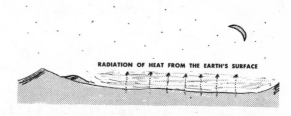

Fig. 119. Radiation fog.

Fig. 120. Land suitable for ground fog formation.

Radiation fogs or ground fogs, as they are usually called, will form under any of the following conditions:—

(a) When there is a surface temperature inversion.

(b) If winds blow lightly, not a dead calm.

(c) If there is enough saturated air present. That is, if the air has all the moisture it can hold at any given temperature.

(d) The surface of the land must be such that fog can accumulate.

Forecasting fogs can be done if the following facts are thoroughly understood.

(1) There is enough moisture in the air at low levels.

(2) Light winds are blowing.

(3) The land surface is suitable for ground fog formation.

(4) There is no cloud ceiling. The night is clear and cool.

(5) If the ground is already cold- other things being equal- fog will form sooner.

(6) The temperature and dew point are close together, such as, temperature 46° F., dew point 44° F.

## DUST

In some sections of the country dust becomes a major weather hazard. Usually there are strong surface winds at the time of dust storms; therefore, most smaller aircraft are on the ground and firmly tied down.

## ICING

Icing is another major hazard to flying, because it not only collects on the aircraft structure, but may form in the carburetor of the motor, thereby disturbing the engine operation— see the chapter on engines. (Fig. 121) Ice will form on the surface of the aircraft when the temperature and the dew point are at or near freezing (32° F. or 0° C.).

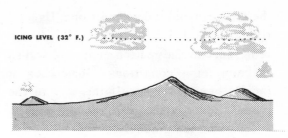

Fig. 121. Icing level.

Pilots flying at or near freezing conditions will be well aware of the freezing or icing level. Information about this condition can be obtained from the Weather Bureau before or during flight by telephone or radio.

Ice formation consists of two kinds:- hard ice, (Fig. 122) which is like any cake of ice; and grainy ice (rime), (Fig. 123) which is like shaved ice. Both formations become serious when large amounts of ice accumulate on the aircraft. The ice increases the weight that the plane must carry, and also it spoils the smooth lifting qualities of the airfoil-lift is reduced.

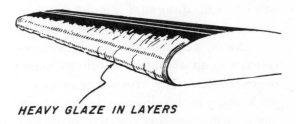

**HEAVY GLAZE IN LAYERS**

Fig. 122. Hard icing.

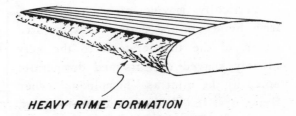

**HEAVY RIME FORMATION**

Fig. 123. Grainy icing.

Most small aircraft do not have ice destroying devices; therefore, it is up to the pilot to avoid icing conditions. Usually flying at a lower altitude will prevent icing, but extreme caution must be observed for any icing conditions. Sometimes it rapidly becomes cold all the way to the ground. Under such conditions, be a doubter and stay on the ground.

## STABILITY OF THE AIR

To a pilot, the stability of his airplane is of vital concern. A stable aircraft if placed in an abnormal attitude, will return to normal flight when the controls are placed in neutral. On the other hand, an unstable aircraft will continue to move away from the normal flight attitude.

So it is with the atmosphere. The normal flow of the wind tends to be horizontal. If the winds are disturbed by obstacles (Fig. 124) or by intense heating from below, a stable atmosphere will resist any upward or downward displacement and will tend to quickly return to normal horizontal flow. On the other hand, an unstable atmosphere will allow these upward and downward disturbances to grow. Thus, updrafts and compensating downdrafts develop which, when flown through in an aircraft, are felt as bumps or turbulence. The clearest example of such unstable development in the atmosphere is the towering thunderstorm which develops as a result of a large intensive vertical movement of air, culminating in condensation, precipitation, lightning, and thunder.

Vertically moving air currents vary from the severe and more or less isolated cases of the thunderstorm to the very closely spaced updrafts and downdrafts noted by the pilot as "bumpiness" when flying over flat land areas on warm days.

*Lapse Rates*

The tendency of the atmosphere to resist vertical motion is called "stability" To get some measure of this resistance it

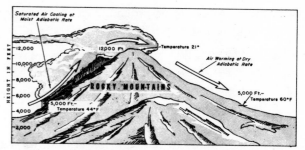

Fig. 124. Satuated air flowing up mountain slope cools at moist rate. Flowing down the opposite slope, it warms at dry rate. Thus it is warmer on ice side of mountain than on windward side.

is necessary to observe the temperature distribution with height. The rate of change of temperature with height (Fig's. 125 & 126) is called the "lapse rate". Normally, the temperature decreases with increasing altitude. However, it is sometimes found that the temperature increases with altitude, and when this occurs, the zone of increasing temperature is said to have a "temperature inversion".

When unsaturated (Fig. 125) air is forced to ascend, such as when heated from below or when lifted up the slope of a mountain, the temperature of the air within this rising current will decrease at the rate of $5\frac{1}{2}°$ F. per 1,000 feet. This cooling rate of unsaturated air is known as the "dry adiabatic lapse rate," and the decrease in temperature is caused by

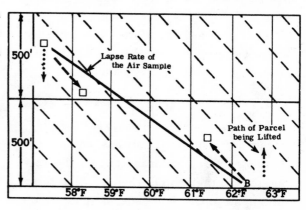

Fig. 125. The broken lines show rates at which dry air cools as it ascends. The solid line shows greater cooling rate encountered in an actual flight, indicating that the air is unstable.

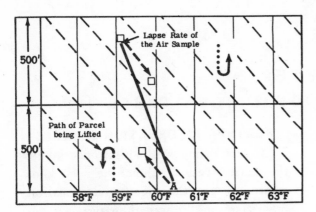

Fig. 126. Solid line indicates cooling rate of air encountered in actual flight, with cooling at less than dry-air rate (broken lines), showing that air is stable.

the expansion of the air as it rises. The temperature of the air must decrease as it expands, because the energy used by the air in the expansion process must come from the air itself.

When saturated air is lifted, condensation occurs, the heat released as the result of condensation or absorbed by the air, and, as a result, the adiabatic cooling rate is decreased. The resulting rate of cooling, called the "moist adiabatic lapse rate," varies from about 2° F. to 5° F. per 1,000 feet as the temperature changes.

In Summary:

(1) Normal lapse rate ($3\frac{1}{2}$°F./1,000 feet)– The average rate of temperature decrease in the atmosphere.

(2) Dry adiabatic lapse rate ($5\frac{1}{2}$°F./1,000 feet)– Produced by a mixing process such as convection in dry air. Clouds may form at the top of a layer of air with a dry adiabatic lapse rate.

(3) Moist adiabatic lapse rate (varies from 2° to 5° per 1,000 feet)– Produced by a mixing process such as convection in saturated air, as within a cumulus cloud. The lapse rate varies with temperature, being small (2° or 3° per 1,000 feet) at high temperatures, and large (4° or 5° per 1,000 feet) at low temperatures.

(4) Inversion lapse rate (temperature increases with height)– Produced by contact cooling near the ground or by advection of warm air over a cold land or water surface.

## LAPSE RATES AND PROBABLE TURBULENCE

| LAPSE RATE | °F. PER 1,000 FT. DEGREES | STABILITY | PROBABLE TURBULENCE |
|---|---|---|---|
| No clouds; dry air: | | | |
| Inversion | +10[1] | Very stable | Smooth |
| Isothermal | 0 | Very stable | Smooth |
| Normal | 3-1/2 | Stable | Smooth |
| Dry adiabatic | 5-1/2 | Neutral | Light to moderate turbulence |
| Superadiabatic | 7[2] | Unstable | Heavy turbulence |
| In clouds; saturated air: | | | |
| Inversion | +10[1] | Stable | Smooth |
| Isothermal | 0 | Stable | Smooth |
| Normal | 3-1/2 | Unstable at high temperature | Light to moderate turbulence |
| Dry adiabatic | 5-1/2 | Very unstable | Heavy turbulence |

(1) Any temperature increase with height. +10° used for this example.

(2) Any temperature decrease greater than 5-1/2°F. per 1,000 feet, 7° used for this example.

Note: As the lapse rate increases, the probable turbulence normally also increases. However, turbulence can be caused by factors other than unstable air. This is discussed in greater detail in chapter XI.

Table 4.

# CHAPTER 8
## WEATHER INFORMATION & HOW TO USE IT

### WEATHER SENSE

There are no substitutes for weather knowledge and the realization of the limitations of weather forecasting.

Weather is always on the move from place to place. Todays weather was somewhere else yesterday, generally to the north, south and west of us. There are no accurate weather devices to tell the pilot exactly what the weather will be two hours from now.

Many pilots develop "weather sense" which is a combination of knowledge and judgement. The dumb and happy pilot never develops this thing called "weather sense". He doesn't live long enough.

Not only does the weather move, but it changes as it moves. Weather patterns are very complex and change rapidly when pressure, temperature, winds etc. changes occur.

Pilots should not blame the weather bureau for inaccurate weather forecasts. Such a thing cannot be accurate where complex phenomena are involved.

The Weather Bureau is very extensive in operation with thousands of stations and observers. The weather data is collected and sent by teletype to eleven central stations. It is there, that weather maps are drawn, published, posted and made available. Even so, the weather information is two or more hours old.

Each year, there are a number of air accidents caused by weather, usually because of a lack of "weather sense" or just plain boldness. Frequently during a discussion is heard. "He should have stayed on the ground." "Why did he do it?", "He was a fine pilot, but never learned much about weather", and so on.

### WEATHER INFORMATION SOURCES

No matter how well a pilot understands the basic weather science he must know where to get the weather information, otherwise the practical nature of the knowledge will be of little value.

There are several sources of weather information such as newspapers, weather maps, observation, television, telephone, radio broadcasting stations, and radio range weather reports. The latter are issued by the F.A.A. in conjunction with the U.S. Weather Bureau.

*Newspapers*

Most newspapers (Fig's. 127 & 128) print daily weather summaries and forecasts. A one-thirty A.M. weather indication may be of little value a few hours later; therefore, newspaper weather reports are useful for general information, but are not recent and extensive enough for flyers.

*Television*

Television weather forecasts have the advantage of showing the apparent weather pattern. However, they will have a limited value. TV weather information does have the great advantage of showing many people how weather changes occur.

*Telephone*

Weather bureau stations welcome telephone calls for weather information. The U.S. Weather Bureau is a government agency and is owned by the people. Pilots frequently call in for the latest weather information before planning a flight; however, mass telephone calls would disrupt the fine work being done. Pilots, identify themselves and receive prompt weather information

## WEATHER REPORT
### OFFICIAL

#### FORECASTS

**Los Angeles and Vicinity:** Mostly clear today and tomorrow but early morning fog patches near coast tomorrow. Warmer today, with high near 80.

**Southern California:** Mostly clear today and tomorrow but patches early morning fog along coast today, increasing tonight and tomorrow morning. Dry easterly winds over mountains and locally below coastal passes. High fire hazard mountain areas. Warmer west portion today and slightly warmer interior sections tomorrow afternoon.

**Southern California Coastal and Intermediate Valleys:** Mostly clear today and tomorrow. Local dry easterly winds below coastal passes today. Warmer today.

**Southern California Mountain Areas:** Generally clear today and tomorrow. Dry easterly winds with high fire hazard. Slightly warmer tomorrow.

**Southern California Interior and Desert Regions:** Mostly clear today and tomorrow. Slightly warmer tomorrow afternoon. High temperatures today. 64 to 70 deg. upper valleys and 70 to 80 lower valleys.

**Arizona:** Mostly clear today and tomorrow but scattered high cloudiness southeast portion today. Slightly cooler north portion today and tonight but a little warmer tomorrow afternoon.

#### WIND AND WEATHER

**Point Conception to San Diego:** Light variable winds mornings and at night, becoming westerly 8 to 16 m.p.h. in afternoons today and tomorrow. But local northwesterly winds 20 to 30 m.p.h. at times off Point Conception today. Fog patches early today with increasing fog tonight and tomorrow morning, otherwise clear. Slightly warmer today.

#### WESTERN WEATHER SUMMARY

Barometers have risen considerably during the last 24 hours and are now relatively high over the Pacific Northwest and Plateau States. A weak low pressure trough lies along the coast of Southern California. As a result drier air is flowing from the interior over the coastal areas. It is not cool enough, however, to reach the surface along the coast and patches of heavy fog may form along and just off-shore. Barometers are also high over Western Canada and Eastern Alaska with highest pressure centered in the Yukon. The Pacific high cell is centered near 36 N, 134 W. Deep Pacific storm is centered near 50 N, 147 W. moving northeastward.

#### NATIONAL WEATHER SUMMARY

In the Atlantic States and the South it was unseasonably warm yesterday and across the Southwest through Southern California it was mild but in all other sections of the country it was quite cool and the temperature continued its downward trend. New York had 68; Nashville 71; Shreveport, 83, and New Orleans tied the previous record with 86. On the other hand, the highest temperature yesterday at Denver was 32 with Casper recording 30 and Cheyenne 24. In the Texas Panhandle, a norther set in and temperatures were now falling rapidly. Rain turning to snow in the Ozark country was heavy in the afternoon with Springfield, Mo., reporting 1.32. Moderate to heavy showers fell in the Southeast and a little snow in Minnesota and Wisconsin. Elsewhere in the country, precipitation was only light and spotty.

Fig. 127. Newspaper weather report.

### Radio Broadcasting Stations

Radio broadcasting stations give a number of weather forecasts during the day, but with few exceptions, the information is very general and not recent enough for aviation purposes.

## WEATHER BUREAU INFORMATION

### Weather Maps

The weather bureau prints excellent weather maps, either daily or at six-hour intervals. If a person lives near a central weather station and has quick access to the maps, there is nothing better. All weather maps are very useful to show the weather patterns as an aid to predicting what weather may come.

### Observation

Personal observation is an exceedingly important part of understanding the weather, and after a time, many persons acquire Weather Sense. The difficulty is that observation is entirely local and gives no indication of fast moving weather changes about to occur. We need to extend our weather analysis for a distance of a hundred or so miles.

### Radio Range Weather Reports

The radio range system which is set up and maintained by the F.A.A. is primarily a navigational aid; but it also gives out weather and other useful information to pilots, and others.

The weather reports and forecasts come out over the Radio Range Frequencies at thirty minute intervals from each radio range station.

## FACTORS AFFECTING THE WEATHER

When apprising and forecasting the weather, there are several factors that must be considered to properly get the weather picture.

### Latitude

(Fig. 129) Latitude, (position north or south of the equator), of the locality affects weather. In which of the great weather belts is the local airport located?

A quick look at the diagram will give an over-all picture; however, it must be remembered that it is not as simple as it appears. Variations occur all over the world due to mountains, ocean currents, etc.

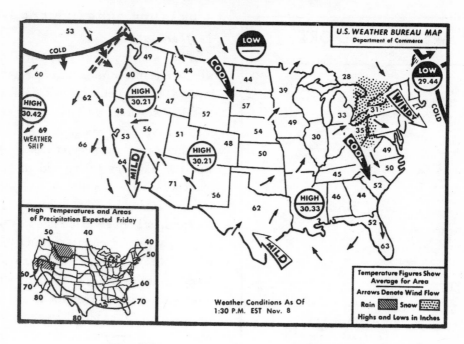

Fig. 128.  Daily weather map (newspaper).

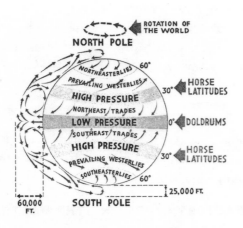

Fig. 129.  Weather belts.

*Local Topography*

(Fig. 130) Local topography (nature of the ground surface, mountains, valleys, etc.), also affects weather. A locality near a wet weather belt may be very dry due to mountains, valleys, air currents, or ocean currents. For instance, moist air, when lifted, will be cooled and condensed in the form of rain, snow, or mist. Much of the moisture will then have left the air, but when it descends, it will warm up and be ready to pick up more moisture. If there are no bodies of water in the area, the air will remain warm and dry with a desert condition resulting. As a mass of air

Fig. 130.  Local topography

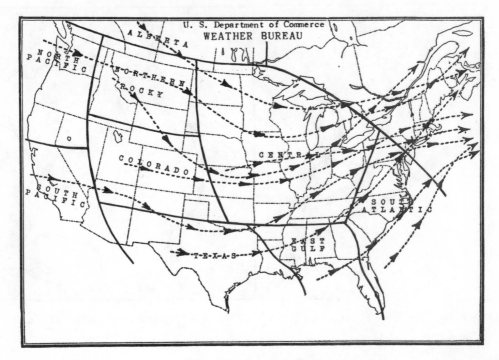

Fig. 131. Storm paths.

trayels from west to east across the U.S.A. it may change its nature, from wet to dry, several times depending on its temperature and the land over wnich it passes.

*Seasonal Weather Pattern*

In general, winter storms follow more or less definite paths from year to year. (Fig's. 131 through 136.)

Occasionally, for reasons unknown at present, these storm tracks change either to the north or south or to the east or west. Examples of this phenomenon are an unusually warm winter along the east coast or very cold freezing weather in Southern California. During these changes which may last for several months, the usual weather pattern is altered, sometimes to a great degree. Therefore, the pilot will find it necessary to change his usual thinking concerning winter flights. An interesting fact is that once the storms start a path, the condition may continue for some time, but again, may break up and form a new pattern at any time.

Ot utmost importance is, what kind of cross-country flying weather can be ex-

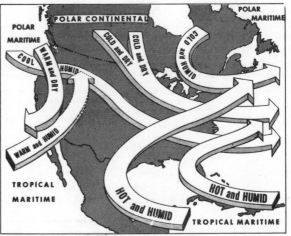

Fig. 132. Typical paths taken by air masses entering the United States.

pected during summer and winter?

Extreme weather changes can be expected for different localities and if flying from one condition to another, the pilot must have a knowledge of what to expect.

During winter (Fig. 135) temperature is a major condition and this varies from place to place.

During the summer season (Fig. 136) flying conditions are very different with much maritime tropical air pushing up from the gulf of Mexico.

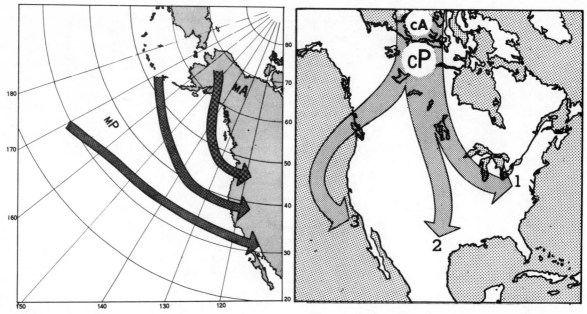

Fig. 133.  Paths of maritime polar and artic.          Fig. 134.  Continental polar and artic air.

| AIR MASS | CLOUDS | CEILINGS | VISIBILITIES | TURBULENCE | SURFACE TEMPERA- TURE F. |
|---|---|---|---|---|---|
| cP (near source region) | None | Unlimited | Excellent (except near indus- trial areas, then 1 - 4 miles). | Smooth except with high wind velocities. | -10 to -60. |
| cP (southeast of Great Lakes) | Stratocumulus and cumulus tops 7,000 - 10,000 feet. | 500 - 1,000 feet, 0 over mountains. | 1 - 5 miles, 0 in snow flurries. | Moderate turbulence up to 10,000 feet. | 0 to 20. |
| mP (on Pacific coast) | Cumulus tops above 20,000 feet. | 1,000 - 3,000 ft., 0 over mountains. | Good except 0 over mountains and in showers. | Moderate to strong turbulence. | 45 to 55. |
| mP (east of Rockies) | None | Unlimited | Excellent except near indus- trial areas, then 1 - 4 miles. | Smooth except in lower levels with high winds. | 30 to 40. |
| mP (east coast) | Stratocumulus and stratus tops, 6,000 - 8,000 feet. | 0 - 1,000 feet | Fair except 0 in precipi- tation area. | Rough in lower levels. | 30 to 40. |
| mT (Pacific coast) | Stratus or stratocumulus. | 500 - 1,500 feet | Good | Smooth | 55 to 60. |
| mT (east of Rockies) | Stratus or stratocumulus. | 100 - 1,500 feet | Good | Smooth | 60 to 70. |

Fig. 135.  Properties of air masses from the standpoint of flying during the winter season.

| AIR MASS | CLOUDS | CEILINGS | VISIBILITIES | TURBULENCE | SURFACE TEMPERA- TURE °F. |
|---|---|---|---|---|---|
| cP (near source region) | Scattered cumulus | Unlimited | Good | Moderate turbulence up to 10,000 feet. | 55-60 |
| mP (Pacific coast) | Stratus tops, 2,000 - 5,000 feet | 100 feet-2,500 feet, un- limited during day over | 1/2 - 10 miles | Slightly rough in clouds. Smooth above. | 50-60 |
| mP (east of Pacific) | None except scattered cumu- lus near mountains | Unlimited | Excellent | Generally smooth except over desert regions in afternoon. | 60-70 |
| S (Mississippi Valley) | None | Unlimited | Excellent | Slightly rough up to 15,000 feet. | 75-85 |
| mT (east of Rockies) | Stratocumulus early morning; cumulonimbus afternoon. | 500 - 1,500 feet a.m.; 3,000 - 4,000 feet p.m. | Excellent | Smooth except in thunderstorms, then strong turbulence | 75-85 |

Fig. 136.  Properties of air masses from the standpoint of flying during the summer season.

The radio range reports are very recent and occur fifteen minutes before the hour and fifteen minutes after the hour. These facts are very important to the pilot planning a flight. Weather information must be recent to be useful.

*Receiving the information*

It will be noted that several kinds of data are received from the radio range system. They concern airways weather, and are:—

Ceiling—clouds

Visibility—how far can the pilot see

Temperature—ground level and higher up

Wind-direction and velocity

Dew point—moisture in the air

Altimeter setting—pressure of the air

Miscellaneous—sand storms etc.

Forecast—weather to come

## PRE-FLIGHT WEATHER PLANNING

There are no substitutes for careful weather checks before planning a flight. No amount of flying skill plus a lot of luck will take the place of a knowledge of the present weather plus an estimation of the weather to come.

There are several sources of weather information available and all are very useful.

## WEATHER MAP

Cloud symbols show the weather map reader the possible cloud ceilings, and also indicate the kind of weather to expect. It should be recalled that clouds are classified as high, middle, low, as well as those with vertical development. Therefore, it is possible to make some forecast of the ceiling to be expected.

*Station Model*

The station model (Fig. 137) shows the state of the weather for a local weather station. Observations are made every thirty minutes or oftener, and the information is relayed immediately to the district weather

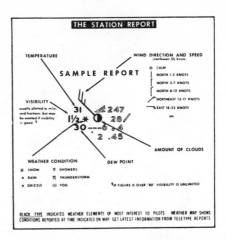

Fig. 137. Station model.

bureau, where the maps are printed. The above diagram is a complete station, while a simplified (Fig. 131) weather map shows only part of the weather information. The station model shows mainly local flying conditions.

Visibility (Fig. 138) information is shown by the symbols, all of which show distinct flying hazard.

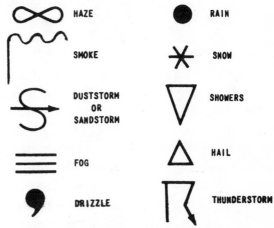

Fig. 138. Visibilities.

Sky cover symbols (Fig. 139) indicate the amount of overcast which is to be expected for a local area.

Wind direction and velocity (Fig. 140) information helps show weather patterns and takeoff or landing problems.

*Weather Symbols*

Isobars (Fig. 141) are lines of equal atmospheric pressure and are expressed as millibars or inches of mercury.

| SKY COVER | NO CLOUDS | 1/10 | 2/10 3/10 | 4/10 5/10 6/10 | 7/10 8/10 | 9/10 | COMPLETELY COVERED | SKY OBSCURED |
|---|---|---|---|---|---|---|---|---|
| SYMBOL | ○ | ◑ | ◔ | ◓ | ◕ | ● | ● | ⊗ |
| TERM | CLEAR | SCATTERED | | BROKEN | | | OVERCAST | DUSTSTORM, HAZE, SMOKE ETC. |

Fig. 139. Sky covers

Frontal areas, (Fig. 141) as previously studied, show the areas where the warm and cold air are in conflict, thus producing clouds, winds, and precipitation. The determination of the location of the fronts by the Weather Bureau provides very useful information for the pilot.

As previously stated, the weather areas generally move from west to east, some rapidly and others slowly. The speed of the approaching weather front should be noted so as to time the weather change.

Some years show considerable change in the normal paths of the storm areas; therefore this fact must be taken into consideration when studying weather.

*Daily Weather Maps*

The daily weather map shows (Fig. 141) the weather picture of the kinds of weather occuring. This is very important to the pilot because it gives him an idea of the local as well as nationwide weather to be expected. The weather information must be recent to be useful, and the pilot should use his radio for up-to-date conditions. If a pilot is on a long cross-country flight, he will need to check frequently for weather conditions ahead, so as to plan a safe flight.

One feature of the map (Fig. 141) is the very large high pressure area that is over the western part of the nation. The weather there is clear with cool temperatures and low dew point (dry air).

Another feature of this particular map is the large intensive low pressure area located south of the Great Lakes. The

| Plotted | Miles (Statute) Per Hour | Knots |
|---|---|---|
| ◎ | Calm | Calm |
| — | 1 - 4 | 1 - 2 |
| ⌐ | 5 - 8 | 3 - 7 |
| ⌐ | 9 - 14 | 8 - 12 |
| ⌐ | 15 - 20 | 13 - 17 |
| ⌐ | 21 - 25 | 18 - 22 |

Fig. 140. Wind directions and velocities.

central pressure is 990 millibars with 25 mile an hour winds in some regions. There is considerable rain and snow in the east along the warm front part of the system. The air temperatures are in the low 40°F west of the cold front with partly cloudy to clearing in the westward.

The third feature of the map is a long cold front between the high and low areas. Considerable precipitation in the form of thunderstorms offer a distinct hazard to flying in that region.

From the foregoing discussion, it will be noted that considerable weather information can be obtained by the pilot. The problem is to apprise the weather correctly and try to figure out what is to come.

Meteorologists can predict weather information fairly well, and on an average, their predictions are 80% correct.

The average pilot will not analyse weather that well, however, he must constantly try to improve his ability, for his own safety as well as for his passengers.

No foolproof system exists for weather forecasting, because the movement of the high and low areas from west to east is very complex and uncertain.

Several devices that help to forecast weather are available, and one of the best is the chart that follows. (Fig. 142).

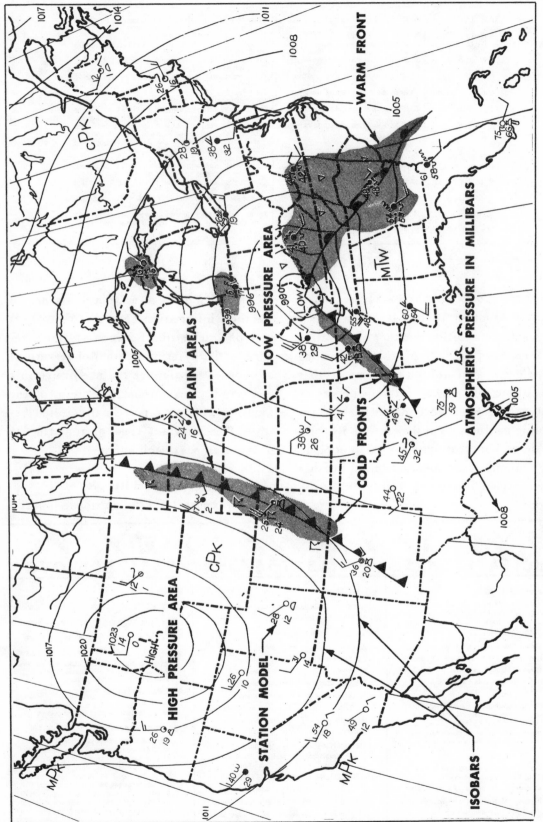

Fig. 141. A simplified weather map.

| Wind direction | Barometer reduced to sea level | Character of weather indicated |
|---|---|---|
| SW. to NW | 30.10 to 30.20 and steady | Fair, with slight temperature changes, for 1 to 2 days. |
| SW. to NW | 30.10 to 30.20 and rising rapidly | Fair, followed within 2 days by rain. |
| SW. to NW | 30.20 and above and stationary | Continued fair, with no decided temperature change. |
| SW. to NW | 30.20 and above and falling slowly | Slowly rising temperature and fair for 2 days. |
| S. to SE | 30.10 to 30.20 and falling slowly | Rain within 24 hours. |
| S. to SE | 30.10 to 30.20 and falling rapidly | Wind increasing in force, with rain within 12 to 24 hours. |
| SE. to NE | 30.10 to 30.20 and falling slowly | Rain in 12 to 18 hours. |
| SE. to NE | 30.10 to 30.20 and falling rapidly | Increasing wind, and rain within 12 hours. |
| E. to NE | 30.10 and above and falling slowly | In summer, with light winds, rain may not fall for several days. In winter, rain within 24 hours. |
| E. to NE | 30.10 and above and falling rapidly | In summer, rain probable within 12 to 24 hours. In winter, rain or snow, with increasing winds, will often set in when the barometer begins to fall and the wind sets in from the NE. |
| SE. to NE | 30.00 or below and falling slowly | Rain will continue 1 to 2 days. |
| SE. to NE | 30.00 or below and falling rapidly | Rain, with high wind, followed, within 36 hours, by clearing, and in winter by colder. |
| S. to SW | 30.00 or below and rising slowly | Clearing within a few hours, and fair for several days. |
| S. to E | 29.80 or below and falling rapidly | Severe storm imminent, followed, within 24 hours, by clearing, and in winter by colder. |
| E. to N | 29.80 or below and falling rapidly | Severe northeast gale and heavy precipitation: in winter, heavy snow, followed by a cold wave. |
| Going to W | 29.80 or below and rising rapidly | Clearing and colder. |

Fig. 142. Weather forecasting.

*Weather Reports Sent by Teletype*

### Aviation Weather Reports

A surface aviation weather observation is comprised of individual observations of selected meteorological elements that are within the sight of the observer or that can be read from indicating and recording instruments at the station. Reports of these observations may also include any available radar observations or weather observations made by pilots while in flight.

In order that a maximum amount of weather information (Fig's. 143 & 144) may be transmitted between stations, reports of the aviation weather observations are condensed through the use of symbols and word contractions. The form of the aviation weather report is illustrated below. The standard time of reporting is 30 minutes past each hour.

### Upper Wind Reports

Approximately 125 stations, spaced

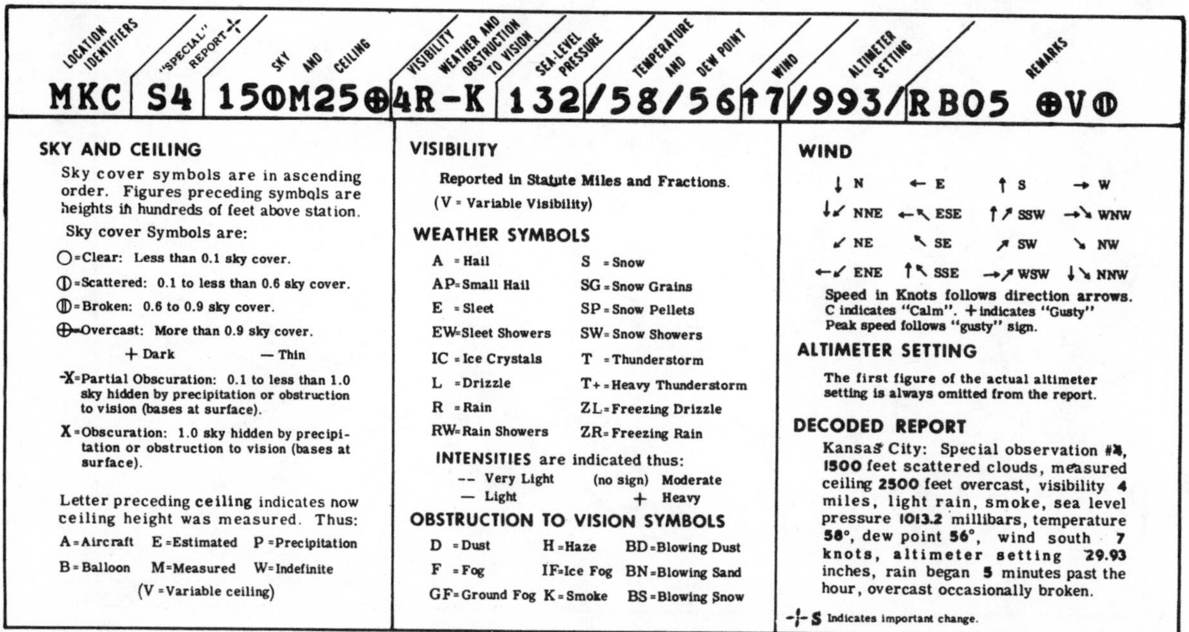

Fig. 143. Key to aviation weather report.

| REMARKS | EXPLANATION |
|---|---|
| CIG 15V18 | Ceiling variable from 1500 feet to 1800 feet. |
| 18●V⊙ | Layer of broken sky cover at 1800 feet is occasionally scattered. |
| T OVHD MOVG EWD | Thunderstorm overhead moving eastward. |
| FQT LTGIC NW | Frequent lightning in clouds northwest. |
| OCNL RW | Occasional rainshowers. (No report of rain in the weather position in the report indicates that rain was not occurring at the time of observation in which case the remark is added when showers are considered probable within 15 minutes.) |
| RU OVR RDG N | Rain, intensity unknown, over ridge to north. |

**Examples of typical remarks in Aviation Weather Reports**

Fig. 144. Typical "remarks" which may be added to aviation weather observation.

throughout the United States, report four times each day the wind speed and direction at designated altitudes. The wind speed and direction are obtained by several methods, by following meteorological balloons with optical theodolites and by tracking balloons with radio direction finding equipment or radar (radio direction finding and ranging) equipment. In all of these methods, the elevation angle (angle above the horizon) and the azimuth angle of the ascending balloon are recorded at one-minute intervals. The wind speed and direction data are computed from the azi-

muth- and elevation-angle data, and the height data. The wind speed is reported in knots, and the direction in ten degree intervals measured clockwise from true north. (Refer to Fig. 145).

Winds are computed for 1,000-feet intervals from the surface to 10,000 feet.

### IN-THE-AIR

The important facts of being relaxed and alert apply to weather as well as flying the airplane. The pilot often makes quick decisions because of weather changes.

There are aids to help the pilot in making his decisions. He may call the airport control tower, and listen to Radio Range information and forecasts.

If the pilot has carefully planned before takeoff, he will know beforehand of possible weather changes. When the in-the-air forecasts show changes one way or the other, he can make the correct weather appraisal.

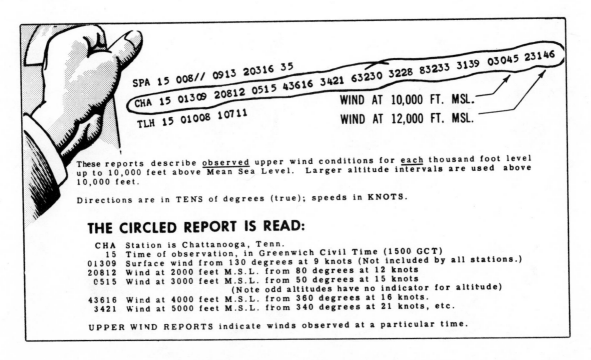

Fig. 145. Key to report of winds aloft.

# PART THREE
# ON COURSE

Aero Commander

# CHAPTER 9

# WHERE AM I?

Possibly the most important thought or spoken word of the pilot is "Where am I? How far have I flown? What locality should I be over? Where will the next check point be?" and so on.

Some student pilots and private pilots think the word navigation means difficult mathematics. Of course, advanced navigation becomes somewhat complex, but for the private pilot the mathematics is not at all difficult. If a pilot can fly the airplane, he can navigate it sucessfully. This volume is concerned with the smaller aircraft and will not discuss the more complicated navigation problems.

Flying from here to there involves simple and basic facts that must be mastered because:

First— The airplane is traveling at a great speed and navigation cannot be done in a very leisurely manner.

Second— There are no sign posts to direct the pilot, although he will constantly fly by the aid of prominent landmarks, if any are visible.

Third— The aircraft, because it flies through the air, is subject to all kinds of weather and particularly wind currents which can upset all previous plans.

Fourth— An airplane can only land on suitable runways; therefore landing problems and available fuel supplies are important considerations.

Fifth— Other basic facts concern the earth itself and how position, direction, distance and time are determined.

## POSITION ON THE EARTH

The determination of position, Fig. 146) (location on the earth), is important to a pilot or navigator, especially if he is flying a long distance. For local flights the pilot usually is flying by visual reference to well known land marks; therefore, he is not concerned with longitude, (east or west), and latitude, (north or south).

The grid system of longitude (Fig. 147 and 148) and latitude was devised long ago and is a very easy way to determine the location of a city or town on the earth.

A starting point for north or south position (Fig. 147) was necessary, so the equator was selected for N-S position.

Locating position on the earth is very much like finding a location in a town or city. For instance, a store is located so many blocks east and so many blocks north of a given point— one block east and two blocks north of the railroad station.

Similarily, the location of places anywhere on the earth can easily be obtained by knowing the longitude and latitude. For example, Denver, Colorado has a latitude of 39°45' and a longitude of 105°. For latitude, read degrees north of the equator. For longitude, read degrees west of the Prime Meridian.

The problem of a starting line for east-west position determination was solved by using the town of Greenwich, England which is near London as a base point. (Fig. 148).

Combining the previous diagrams produces a completed grid system (Fig. 149).

Fig. 146. Longitude, Latitude, Magnetic North, and True North.

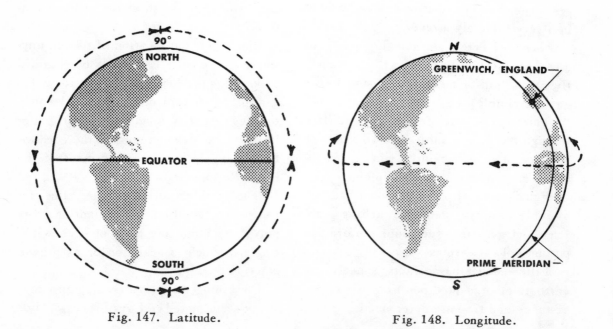

Fig. 147. Latitude.                         Fig. 148. Longitude.

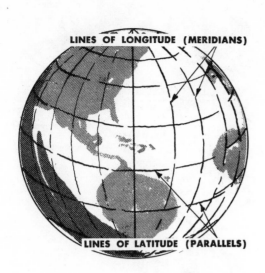

Fig. 149. Grid system.

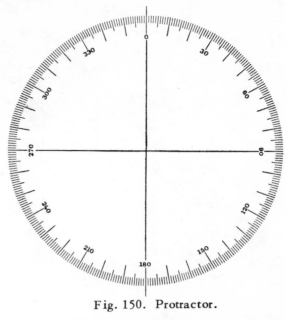

Fig. 150. Protractor.

## DIRECTION ON THE EARTH

When flying from place to place over the earth, a pilot is constantly faced with the need for a knowledge of direction, (the path of flight with reference to true north), and how to fly a course, (the path to be flown or the direction to be taken.)

The aeronautical charts that are published by the U.S. Coast and Geodetic Survey are based on the Lambert projection because they reproduce the earth's surface almost as it exists, thereby having definite advantages.

Direction is measured on the chart by an instrument called a protractor (Fig. 150), which is a circle or part of a circle that is marked off in degrees. Each of the 360° in a circle are divided into 60 minutes and each minute into 60 seconds.

By drawing a line from the start of a flight (Fig. 151) to the end of a flight, a course is established. By placing the protractor on the point where the flight starts- with the protractor heading toward true north- a measurement in degrees can be obtained for the direction of the flight.

The magnetic compass (Fig's. 152 & 153) is the basic instrument used in flying a course. There are mechanical and electronic devices now available which also

aid a pilot in flying a given direction, but they are expensive and take up space, so they are not usually found in smaller aircraft.

The operation of the magnetic compass (Fig. 153) is quite simple. A magnetized needle is suspended on a delicate bearing similar to a jewel bearing in a watch. The needle has previously been magnetized during which time it took on a north pole and, at the opposite end, a south pole.

*Variation*

Our earth acts very much like a giant magnet and long, long ago developed its north and south magnetic poles.

A simple experiment (Fig. 154) shows that similar poles of two magnets will repel each other while the unlike poles will attract or pull toward each other. It is this fact that causes one end of the magnetic needle of a compass to point toward an area near the north pole.

The unfortunate (Fig. 146) fact is that the true geographic north pole- as established by the grid system of longitude and latitude- and the magnetic north pole are not in the same place. The magnetic field is located in the vicinity of Hudson Bay in northern Canada some 1300 miles from the true north pole. With this fact in

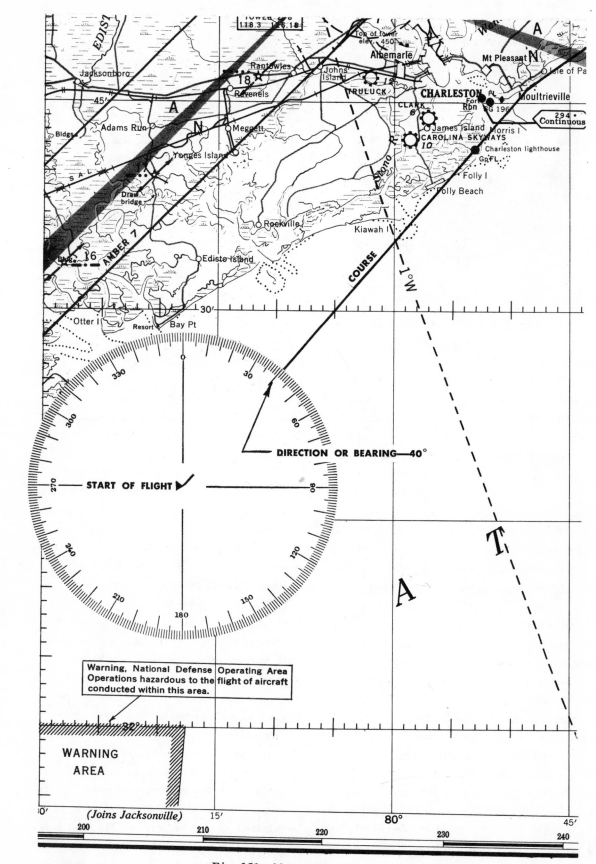

Fig. 151. Measuring a direction.

mind, it can be realized that if the pilot is to depend on the magnetic compass for flying a course, some correction for the magnetic north error must be made.

Fig. 152. Magnetic compass.

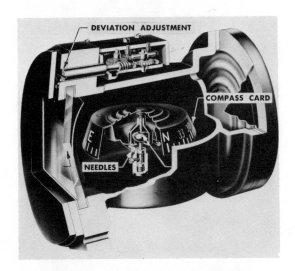

Fig. 153. Construction of a compass.

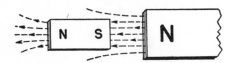

Fig. 154. Magnetic attraction.

The U.S. Coast and Geodetic survey is constantly determining the amount of the error with very delicate instruments.

Their results are published from time to time as isogonic maps. (Refer to Fig. 155).

Aeronautical charts are also useful for showing the amount of the error which is called variation for a given area. It does not make any difference which way the plane is headed, the error is the same.

*Deviation*

Remembering the fact that the compass needle is affected by the magnetic pull of the north magnetic pole, it will be clear that any other magnetized object will cause another error.

All aircraft require considerable iron and steel in the engines and frame. Iron and its alloys are magnetic metals; that is, they take on magnetic properties and will affect the magnetic compass. This error is called deviation.

The deviation error (Fig. 156) is found by swinging the plane as follows. At a chosen place on the runway, painted lines or stakes are accurately marked according to magnetic north.

When the plane is headed toward magnetic north, the magnetic needle or compass card should point to magnetic north. If so, there is no deviation. However, there may be a difference of one degree or so between the compass reading and the marks on the runway. This difference is the deviation of that plane's compass; and when flying this particular plane, the pilot must always remember that his compass does not show exact magnetic north.

As the ship is swung completely around the swinging circle on the runway, errors are noted and tabulated on a deviation card which is placed on the instrument panel near the magnetic compass. Some compasses have small magnets in the instrument case which, when adjusted, will eliminate all or most of the deviation error. The two errors, variation, (difference between true north and magnetic north), and deviation, (error caused by iron in the plane), require correction before a satisfactory navigation flight can be accomplished. Fortunately, this can be done by the use of a simple compass work form. (Fig. 157.)

The arithmetic of this compass work form (Fig. 157) is very simple. The form depends on either of these two quotations: "add west down" or "subtract east down". This sounds strange, but it simply means

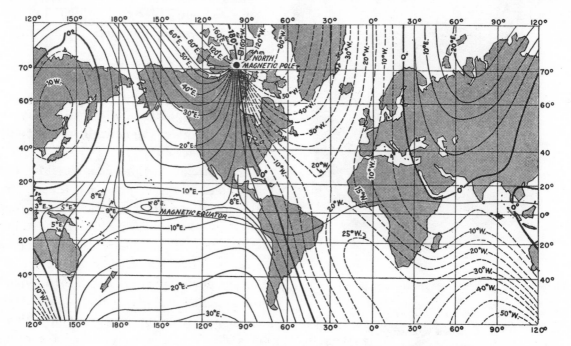

Fig. 155. The Earth's magnetic equator and isogonic lines.

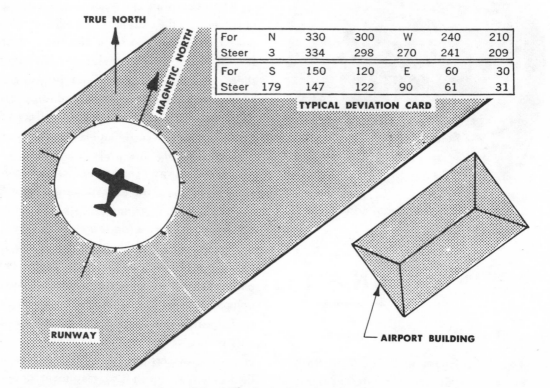

| For | N | 330 | 300 | W | 240 | 210 |
|-----|-----|-----|-----|-----|-----|-----|
| Steer | 3 | 334 | 298 | 270 | 241 | 209 |
| For | S | 150 | 120 | E | 60 | 30 |
| Steer | 179 | 147 | 122 | 90 | 61 | 31 |

TYPICAL DEVIATION CARD

Fig. 156. Swinging the plane.

## COMPASS WORK FORM

| Work Form | Abbrev. | Reference |
|---|---|---|
| True Course | TC | Direction or course of flight with reference to TRUE NORTH in degrees. |
| Variation | V | From isogonic chart or aeronautical chart. Difference between TRUE NORTH and MAGNETIC NORTH. |
| Magnetic Course | MC | Direction in degrees of planned flight with reference to MAGNETIC NORTH. |
| Deviation | D | Error in degrees caused by magnetic metal in the plane. The deviation card is on the instrument panel of the plane. |
| Compass Course | CC | The result of using this form. The pilot will see this in the window of the compass. |

Fig. 157. Compass work form.

that when our form reads "add west down", we work from the top of the form to the bottom, and merely add any deviation or variation that is noted as west. (Or subtract any value that is east).

In this particular flight, we want to fly a true course of 75°, but we must actually see 60° in the compass window. (Fig. 158.)

A great circle (Fig. 159) is the shortest distance between two points on a sphere, and is formed when the sphere is divided into two equal parts. A rhumb line is a line that crosses all meridians of longitude at the same angle.

When flying on local flights, a pilot will always fly a rhumb line which is in a constant direction. However, when flights are about two thousand miles or more in length, it is customary to fly a great circle route. Thus, the pilot is able to save the extra flying miles that would be involved if he flew the rhumb line.

### DISTANCE ON THE EARTH

The earth's surface is measured for distance by two systems: (Fig. 160)

(a) The metric system, which is based on decimals and used by many countries throughout the world.

(b) The traditional system, which is used in the United States, England, and Canada.

The statute mile is used for land measurement, for automobile travel, and other distances.

The nautical mile has long been used for sea navigation and starting in 1952 it was used for air navigation over all land areas as well as sea areas. The nautical mile is based on the division of the distance around the earth by the number of degrees in a circle (360°). One degree on the earth's surface equals 60 nautical miles; and each nautical mile is 6082 feet long. There are 60 minutes in a degree; therefore, one minute will equal one nautical mile.

The most common instruments used for measuring distance are the plotter (Fig. 161), and the ruler, (or a folded piece of paper).

To use the instruments, the course line is first drawn between the ends of the flight. The proper scale (refer to Fig's

## COMPASS WORK FORM PROBLEM
### (ADD WEST DOWN)

| TC | 75° | Proposed **DIRECTION** of flight. |
|----|-----|-----------------------------------|
| V  | 16°E | **VARIATION** for the locality. |
| MC | 59° | Subtraction of 16°E from 75°. |
| D  | 1°W | **DEVIATION** from deviation card. Add 1° to 59° |
| CC | 60° | The pilot steers 60° (see photo). |

Fig. 158.  Compass course.

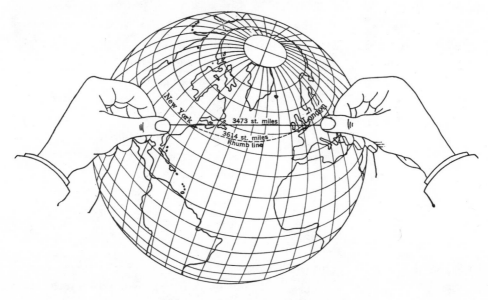

Fig. 159.  Great circles and the rhumb line.

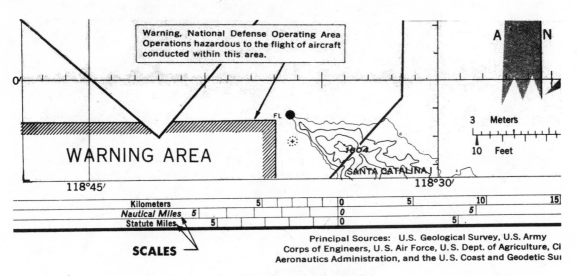

Fig. 160. Conversion scales.

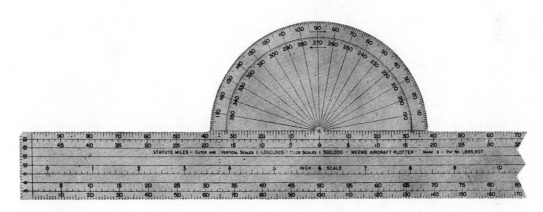

Fig. 161. The Weems plotter.

160 & 162) is selected according to the map being used, and then the distance can be determined.

There is no instrument in an aircraft that measures distance flown over the ground. However, by calculation (to solve by mathematics) it is possible to obtain such information.

## TIME ON THE EARTH

As the earth turns on its axis once every 24 hours, the sun's light creeps toward the west.

This fact establishes the need for time belts (Fig. 163) so as to have a sunrise in each area at about the same time each morning. When flying east the time is set ahead one hour and when going west the watch is set back an hour as each time belt is crossed.

The problem of where to start a new day was solved by international agreement; and the International Date Line was positioned approximately along the 180° meridian.

Long ago, the 12 hour clock (Fig. 164) was invented with the hour hand going around twice in each 24 hours. This made necessary an A.M. (morning) and P.M. (afternoon) time. For some purposes this can be very confusing, especially if for some reason the A.M. or P.M. designations are left off.

The 24 hour clock, which has the hour

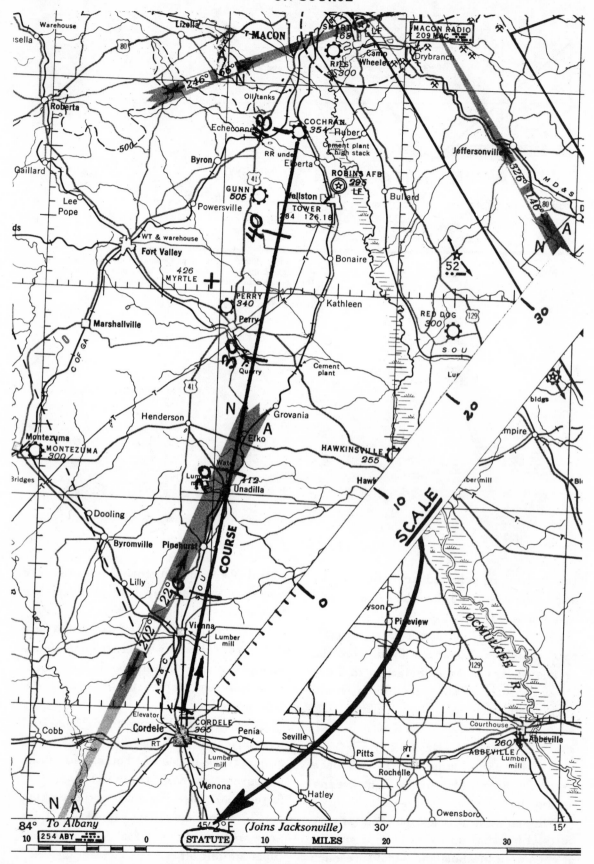

Fig. 162.  Measuring distance with paper scale.

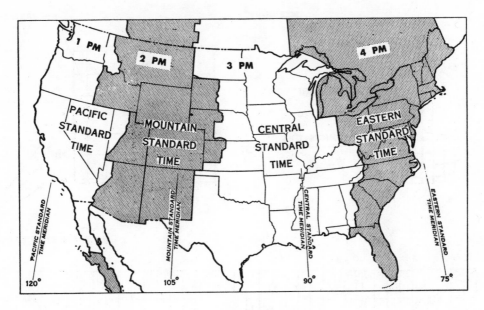

Fig. 163. Time belts.

Fig. 164. Aircraft clock

hand going around only once in 24 hours, eliminates the A.M. and P.M. error and is therefore an improvement. Twenty four hour time is used by the military and some airlines and may come into wide spread use.

## MAPPING THE EARTH

Probably the greatest problem confronting the map maker is that of producing an accurate map. Many attempts have been made to flatten out the earth in the form of a useable flat-surface map. But so far,

no perfect flat map of the earth has been made. All attempts result in stretching and splitting to such an extent that there is a great deal of distortion. For example, continents and bodies of water are not shown in their correct proportions and positions. Numerous types of projections have been devised, but all of them have good and bad features. Some are suitable for one locality and unusable elsewhere.

The Mercator projection is used for all types of navigation including dead reckoning and celestial navigation, as well as being used by ships at sea.

The U.S. Coast and Geodetic Survey, which produces airway maps, selected the Lambert Chart for aviation use, because it is very suitable for pilotage and radio navigation.

Polar flights, which are very important routes of travel, require another type of map projection known as the polar projection.

The following discussions of these three important projections will give an idea of their good and bad points.

*The Mercator Projection*

*(Cylinder around the earth) (Fig. 165)*

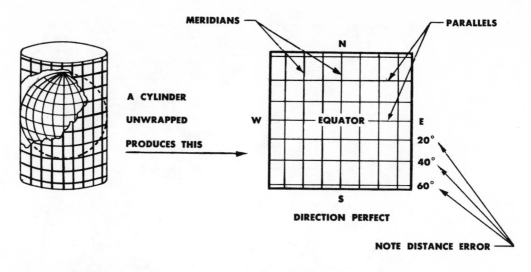

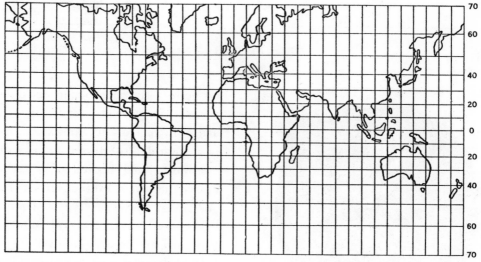

Fig. 165.  Mercator development

Good Features:— All parallels and meridians cross at right angles (90°); therefore direction on this map is perfect. All lines of flight will cross the meridians at the same angle, thereby making a straight line.

Poor Features:— Distance is satisfactorily measured near the equator, but the distortion increases toward the poles until a great error exists in Alaska and Greenland. The Great Circle Route which is the shortest distance on a sphere is curved and therefore more difficult to plan.

*The Lambert Projection*

*(Cone around the earth) (Fig. 166)*

Good Features:— This projection closely resembles the earth as it exists, therefore distance is satisfactory. Great Circle Routes are nearly straight lines, which greatly assist in planning such flights.

Poor Features:— Some correction is needed for direction, but this can easily be done and is discussed in the section on direction which is later in this chapter.

*The Polar Gnomonic Projection*

*(Flat Plate Tangent) (Fig. 167)*

Good Features:— Great Circles are straight lines which assist in planning flights over the pole. The map is very accurate at the point of tangency.

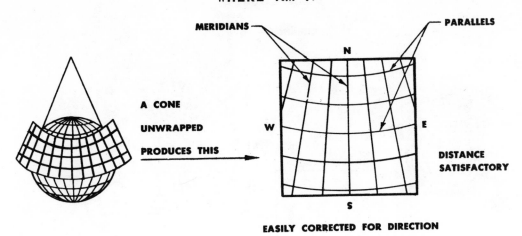

Fig. 166. Lambert Conical development.

Poor Features:— Distance varies on this type of map. This produces greatly distorted land areas away from the center of the projection.

## AERONAUTICAL CHARTS

The local aeronautical chart, (Fig. 168 is a portion of one of the most widely used maps that are printed by the U.S. Coast and Geodetic Survey for aerial navigation. This reprint is given to show the scale of the map and indicate the types of information. Much more detail is given on the maps with the largest scales. Note that some runways are even shown on the Local Chart.

Given below is a brief description of the three types of charts. The actual maps themselves are printed in several colors, with the different altitudes-from valleys to mountains— shown in various colors. A color chart is printed on the side of each map to show what color represents what altitude.

*Local Aeronautical Charts: (Fig. 168)*

Scale 1: 250,000 (1 inch = 4 statute miles- approx.) These charts are designed primarily for visual flying in the vicinity of prominent airports of large cities. They are intended to be used as supplementary charts to the smaller ones, such as the Sectionals, etc. Topographic and aero-

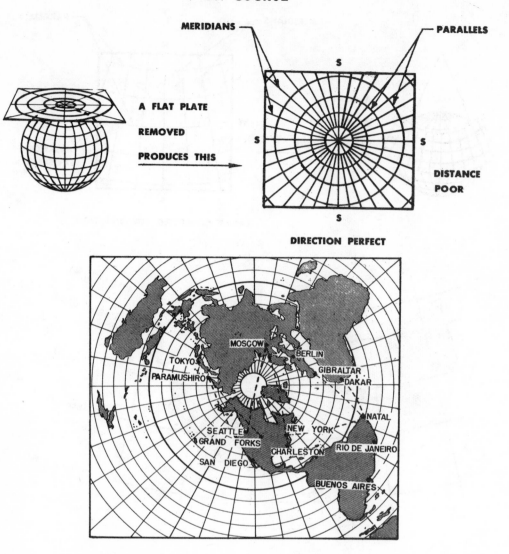

Fig. 167. Polar Gnomic development

nautical information is similar to that given on the smaller scale charts, but is in great detail.

*Sectional Aeronautical Charts: (Fig. 169)*

Scale 1 : 500,000 (1 inch = 8 statute miles— approx.) These charts are designed for contact flying. They show detailed topography including landmarks. The aeronautical information that is shown includes airways, radio and aircraft facilities as well as visual aids and isogonic lines.

*World Aeronautical Charts: (Fig. 169)*

Scale 1 : 1,000,000 (1 inch = 16 statute miles— approx.) These charts are designed for long flights and for flights made at high speed. The aeronautical information

that is shown includes airways, radio and visual aids, aircraft facilities, isogonic lines and compass roses.

Many symbols (Fig's 170, 171 & 172) are required to show features the pilot can recognize on the ground, therefore, considerable study is required to acquaint the airman with the symbols. This knowledge will pay big dividends in safe, pleasant flight.

## THE WIND TRIANGLE

Aircraft are usually flying through masses of air that are moving from place to place. Meterologists call these moving air masses, winds.

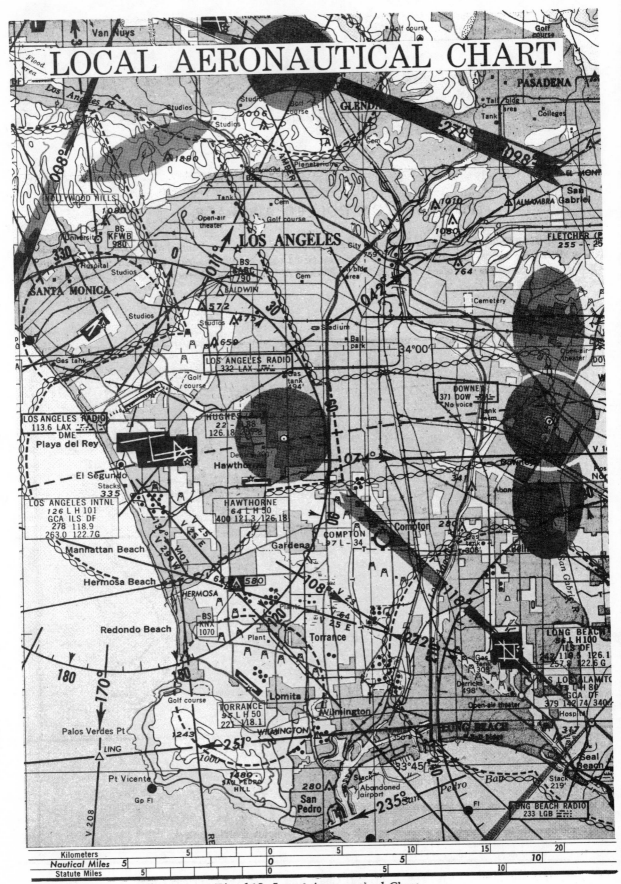

Fig. 168. Local Aeronautical Chart

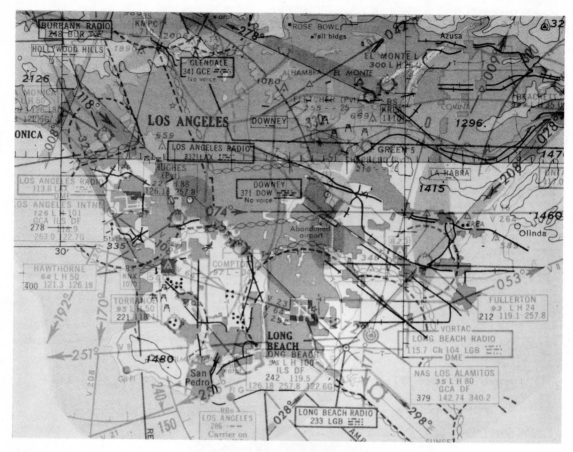

## LOS ANGELES
### SECTIONAL AERONAUTICAL CHART

| Kilometers | | 10 | | 0 | | 10 | | 20 | | 30 | | 40 |
| Nautical Miles | 10 | | | 0 | | | 10 | | | 20 | | |
| Statute Miles | | 10 | | 0 | | | 10 | | | 20 | | |

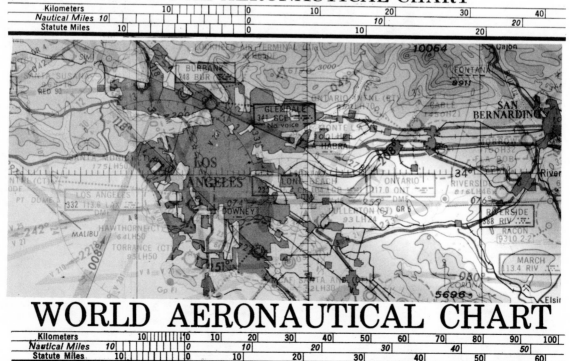

# WORLD AERONAUTICAL CHART

| Kilometers | | 10 | | 0 | 10 | 20 | 30 | 40 | 50 | 60 | 70 | 80 | 90 | 100 |
| Nautical Miles | 10 | | | 0 | | 10 | | 20 | | 30 | | 40 | | 50 | |
| Statute Miles | | 10 | | 0 | 10 | 20 | 30 | 40 | 50 | 60 |

Fig. 169. Sectional Chart and World Aeronautical Chart.

# AERONAUTICAL SYMBOLS

## AERODROMES

LANDPLANE  SEAPLANE

| | | |
|---|---|---|
| ⊙ | (anchor) | Military base |
| ☼ | (anchor) | Civil | Of major aeronautical importance |
| ☼ | (anchor) | Joint civil and military base |
| ○ | (anchor) | Military |
| ◇ | (anchor) | Civil | Offering services that include repairs for normal traffic and/or refueling |
| ◇ | (anchor) | Joint civil and military |
| ○ | ⚓ | Landing area or anchorage | No public services available |

## AERODROME DATA

LANDPLANE

HARMON FIELD
18 L H 46
Airport of entry
GCA SYSTEM
278  126.18

18  Elevation in feet
L  Minimum lighting
H  Hard surfaced runway
46  Length of longest runway
to nearest hundred feet

SEAPLANE

00  Elevation in feet
L  Minimum lighting
S  Normally sheltered
Take-off area
62  Length of longest runway
to nearest hundred feet

NAS ANACOSTIA
00 L S 62
2870

278  126.18  2870  Control tower transmitting frequencies

When information is lacking, the respective character will be replaced by a dash — { VALLEY
750 L — 32

## AIR NAVIGATION LIGHTS

Rotating light — — — — — — — — — — ☆
Rotating light (With flashing code) — — — — —·· ☀
Rotating light (With course lights) — — — 17 —☆—
Flashing light — — — — — — — — — — ★

Flashing light (With code) — — — — — —·—·· ☀
Marine light — — — — — — — — — — — ●
Lightship — — — — — — — — — — — ⚓

F-fixed  FL-flashing  Occ-occulting  Alt-alternating  Gp-group  R-red  W-white  G-green  B-blue  (U)-unwatched  SEC-sector  sec-second
Marine alternating lights are red and white unless otherwise indicated. Marine lights are white unless colors are stated.

## RADIO FACILITIES

**Use of the word "Radio" within the box indicates voice facilities**

Radio range
(Without voice)  ⊙ —— WOODY RANGE
251 FWA ·—·

Marine radiobeacon
(Without voice)  ⊙ —— RBn
EVERETT
224  ·—·
10m-20m & 30m-40m

Radio broadcasting station  ⊙ —— BS
WOL
1260

Radiobeacon, nondirectional
(homing)  ⊙ BEDFORD RADIO
522 DBH ···

## MISCELLANEOUS

Isogonic line or isogonal  — — 8°E — —
(Values for 1950)

Mooring mast  — — — — — — — ⌐

Obstruction  — — — — — — — — 1180
—∧
(Numerals indicate elevation above sea level of top.)

Prohibited area (hatched box)
Danger area (hatched box)
Caution area (hatched box)

Civil airway        Control zone

**Blue tint indicates extent of all controlled areas**

NEWTON
(Reporting point)

A
N  090°

AURAL RANGE
(bearings are magnetic at the station)

5 watts

AVON

100 watts

FORNEY

Fan Marker Beacons
(75 meg)

EASTON

N
270°
A

# VERY HIGH FREQUENCIES (VHF) PRINTED IN BLUE

## VHF FOUR-COURSE VISUAL-AURAL RADIO RANGE

VAR
MATAWAN RADIO
W 109.1 MWA ·—·

The Blue and Yellow Visual Sectors are indicated by a B and Y; the Aural Sectors by A and N
Letter preceding frequency in box indicates channel

Fig. 170. Aeronautical symbols.

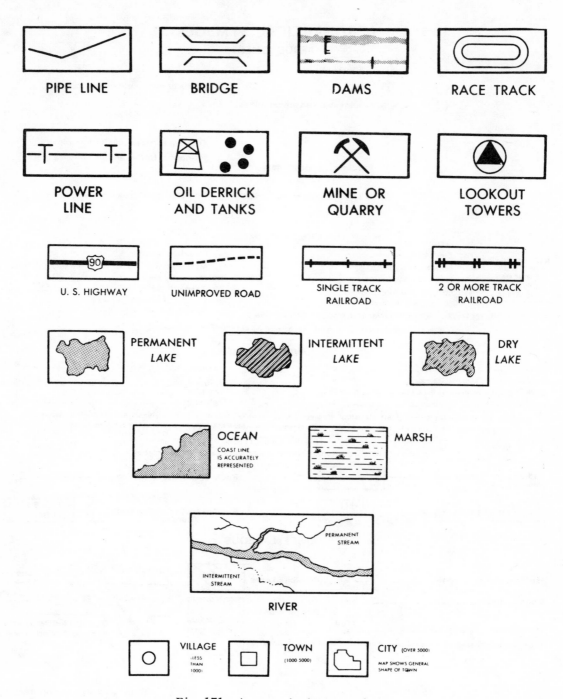

Fig. 171. Aeronautical map symbols.

The path of a plane over the ground depends on the motion of the air through which the plane is flying. Thus, the wind may cause the plane to drift to the side unless a correction is made by the pilot.

The pilot can determine before flight, the wind direction and velocity by listening to the radio, or reading weather reports of surface and upper air. Every good pilot soon learns to estimate wind velocities and usually starts by studying the Beaufort Scale. (Refer to Part II).

The problem before the pilot is: How many degrees should the nose of the plane be turned to the right or left to prevent drifting from the selected course? The

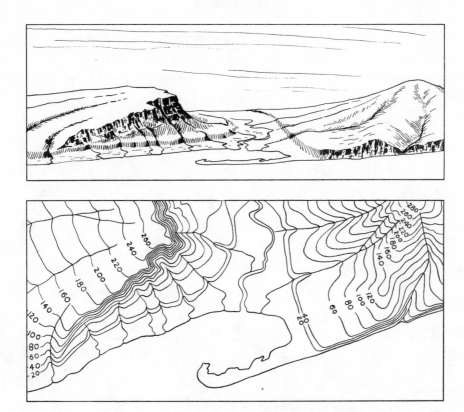

Fig. 172. Altitude, form, and slope of terrain are indicated by contour
lines and numerals. (U.S. Geological Survey.)

solving of the problem is quite simple, and is done here by drawing or graphic method.

*Sample problem:—(Prob. 1A, Fig. 173)*
*Wind Drift Correction for Flight Out.*
Given— True course, 250°
     True airspeed, 100 Knots.
     Wind, from north, 30 Knots.
     Variation, 16° E.
     Deviation, 6° W.
Determine— Wind correction and
      ground speed.

The following step-by-step discussion will show how to solve a wind drift problem. (Also see Fig. 191.)

It should be remembered that the airspeed indicator (Fig. 175) shows the approximate airspeed and therefore will require correcting. The airspeed indicator is operated by air pressure from outside the cockpit, through the pitot static tube, (Fig. 174) and any change in altitude will produce an error in airspeed. This is because the air is thinner and less air goes into the pitot tube to operate the instrument. The instruments read accurately at sea level. A general rule for obtaining true air speed (T.A.S.) is:— Add 2% of the indicated airspeed for every 1000 feet of altitude. (To be more accurate, a computer should be used).

*The Compass Work Form For Wind Drift Correction.*

It will be noted (Fig. 176) that courses except for the true course have disappeared from the form. Headings, (direction of the nose of the aircraft), become important because wind drift is now being considered.

The all important points of heading the aircraft in the correct direction and knowing the speed over the ground, (ground speed), make it possible for the pilot to know the following:

(1)— Course- He will be on the course because of allowing for wind drift. The path of flight of the plane should be the

## Problem 1-A. Wind Drift Correction for Flight Out

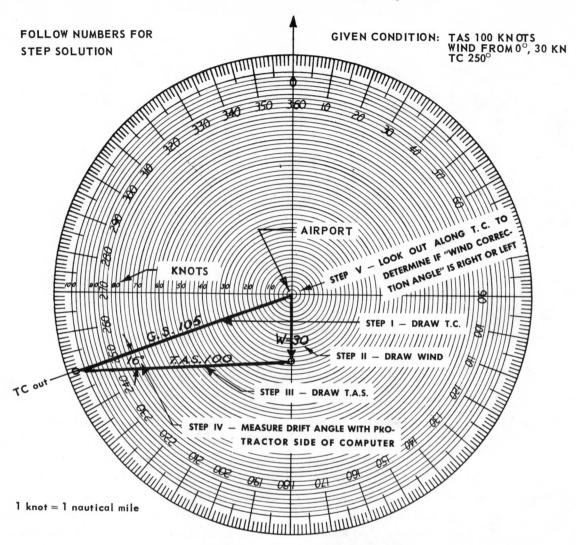

FOLLOW NUMBERS FOR
STEP SOLUTION

GIVEN CONDITION: TAS 100 KNOTS
WIND FROM 0°, 30 KN
TC 250°

AIRPORT

KNOTS

STEP V – LOOK OUT ALONG T.C. TO DETERMINE IF "WIND CORRECTION ANGLE" IS RIGHT OR LEFT

G.S. 105

W 30

STEP I – DRAW T.C.

STEP II – DRAW WIND

T.A.S. 100

16°

STEP III – DRAW T.A.S.

TC out

STEP IV – MEASURE DRIFT ANGLE WITH PROTRACTOR SIDE OF COMPUTER

1 knot = 1 nautical mile

Fig. 173. Steps in solving for wind drift.

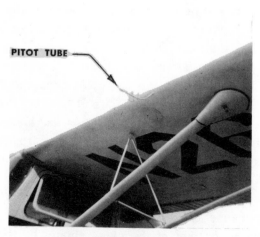

PITOT TUBE

Fig. 174. Pitot tube.

Fig. 175. Airspeed indicator.

## COMPASS WORK FORM

|  | Abbrev. | Sample Problem | Information Source |
|---|---|---|---|
| True course | TC | 250° | Aeronautical chart |
| Wind correction angle | WCA | 16°R | Wind triangle problem "add right wind down" |
| True heading | TH | 266° |  |
| Variation | V | 16°E | Aeronautical chart "add west down" |
| Magnetic heading | MH | 250° |  |
| Deviation | D | 6°W | Deviation card in plane "add west down" |
| Compass heading | CH | 256° | What is seen in the compass window to fly a TC |
| Ground speed | GS | 105° |  |

Fig. 176. Work form.

same as the course.

(2)— Distance- He will know the ground speed and can tell how far along the course the aircraft has flown.

(3)— Time- He can figure the time in flight by knowing the distance flown at the ground speed.

(4)— Position- By putting all these facts together he can mark his actual positions on the map.

Flight over land makes it possible for the pilot to occasionally see a prominent land mark, called a check point. When planning a flight, the pilot or navigator will pick out check points at suitable intervals and use them during flight for checking his progress.

During bad weather or over-water flights, the pilot may be flying only by what he sees on the instrument faces and by the radio aids to navigation. This kind of flying is called instrument flight and requires many many hours of flying experience and practice. Airline pilots become experts at instrument flight after long periods of study, practice and ex-

perience. The F.A.A. rule for this kind of flying should be studied further by those desiring more information.

There are other kinds of wind triangle problems that more experienced pilots or navigators need to know.

Pilots will nearly always want to know the Ground Speed (G.S.) and the wind correction angle on the flight back to the airport.

Conversion Table: Knots to statute miles.

| knots | 0 | 1 | 2 | 3 | 4 | 5 | 6 | 7 | 8 | 9 |
|---|---|---|---|---|---|---|---|---|---|---|
|  | mph | mph | mph | mph | mph | mph | mph | mph | mph | mph |
| 0 | 0.0 | 1.2 | 2.3 | 3.5 | 4.6 | 5.8 | 6.9 | 8.1 | 9.2 | 10.4 |
| 10 | 11.5 | 12.7 | 13.8 | 15.0 | 16.1 | 17.3 | 18.4 | 19.6 | 20.7 | 21.9 |
| 20 | 23.0 | 24.2 | 25.3 | 26.5 | 27.6 | 28.8 | 29.9 | 31.1 | 32.2 | 33.4 |
| 30 | 34.5 | 35.7 | 36.8 | 38.0 | 39.2 | 40.3 | 41.5 | 42.6 | 43.8 | 44.9 |
| 40 | 46.1 | 47.2 | 48.4 | 49.5 | 50.7 | 51.8 | 53.0 | 54.1 | 55.3 | 56.4 |
| 50 | 57.6 | 58.7 | 59.9 | 61.0 | 62.2 | 63.3 | 64.5 | 65.6 | 66.8 | 67.9 |
| 60 | 69.1 | 70.2 | 71.4 | 72.5 | 73.7 | 74.9 | 76.0 | 77.2 | 78.3 | 79.5 |
| 70 | 80.6 | 81.8 | 82.9 | 84.1 | 85.2 | 86.4 | 87.5 | 88.7 | 89.8 | 91.0 |
| 80 | 92.1 | 93.3 | 94.4 | 95.6 | 96.7 | 97.9 | 99.0 | 100.2 | 101.3 | 102.5 |
| 90 | 103.6 | 104.8 | 105.9 | 107.1 | 108.2 | 109.4 | 110.5 | 111.7 | 112.9 | 114.0 |
| 100 | 115.2 | 116.3 | 117.5 | 118.6 | 119.8 | 120.9 | 122.1 | 123.2 | 124.4 | 125.5 |
| 110 | 126.7 | 127.8 | 129.0 | 130.1 | 131.3 | 132.4 | 133.6 | 134.7 | 135.9 | 137.0 |
| 120 | 138.2 | 139.3 | 140.5 | 141.6 | 142.8 | 143.9 | 145.1 | 146.2 | 147.4 | 148.6 |
| 130 | 149.7 | 150.9 | 152.0 | 153.2 | 154.3 | 155.5 | 156.6 | 157.8 | 158.9 | 160.1 |
| 140 | 161.2 | 162.4 | 163.5 | 164.7 | 165.8 | 167.0 | 168.1 | 169.3 | 170.4 | 171.6 |
| 150 | 172.7 | 173.9 | 175.0 | 176.2 | 177.3 | 178.5 | 179.6 | 180.8 | 181.9 | 183.1 |
| 160 | 184.2 | 185.4 | 186.6 | 187.7 | 188.9 | 190.0 | 191.2 | 192.3 | 193.5 | 194.6 |
| 170 | 195.8 | 196.9 | 198.1 | 199.2 | 200.4 | 201.5 | 202.7 | 203.8 | 205.0 | 206.1 |
| 180 | 207.3 | 208.4 | 209.6 | 210.7 | 211.9 | 213.0 | 214.2 | 215.3 | 216.5 | 217.6 |
| 190 | 218.8 | 219.9 | 221.1 | 222.2 | 223.4 | 224.6 | 225.7 | 226.9 | 228.0 | 229.2 |

(1 Knot=1.15078 MPH)

Fig. 177. Conversion Table

*Problem 1-B. Wind Drift Correction for flight back to the airport.*

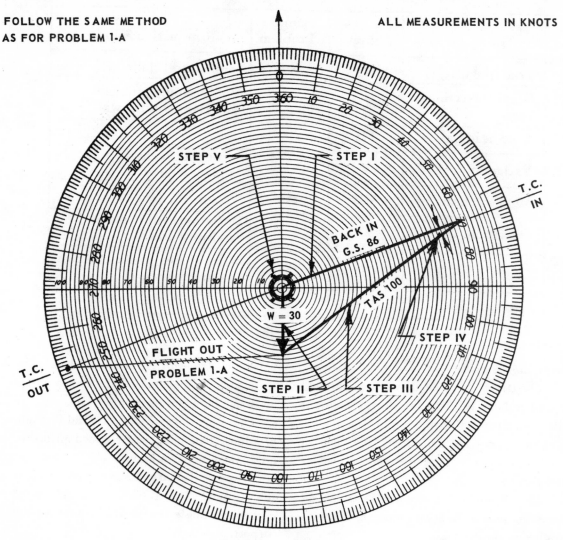

Fig. 178.  Flight back.

*Sample problem:—(Prob. 1B, Fig. 178) Wind Drift Correction for Flight Back to the Airport.*

The graphic solution (Fig. 178) of the problem gives some idea of the flight back. By checking with visual land marks, further correcting can be made as the flight progresses.

Frequently while flying on a known heading (true heading) and knowing true air speed and a knowledge of the wind (radio or visual estimation), a pilot wants his track and ground speed.

*Sample problem:—(Prob. 2, Fig. 179) To Find Tracks and Ground Speed*

This graphic solution (Fig. 179) easily produces the track and ground speed.

Wind is the deciding factor of navigation accuracy and all the information known is most important.

*Sample problem:—(Prob. 3, Fig. 180) To Find Direction and Velocity of the Wind During Flight.*

This graphic solution (Fig. 180) shows a step by step method of obtaining wind information

## THE MATHEMATICS OF NAVIGATION

For private pilots, only a working knowledge of addition, subtraction, multi-

## Problem 2. To find Track and Ground Speed.

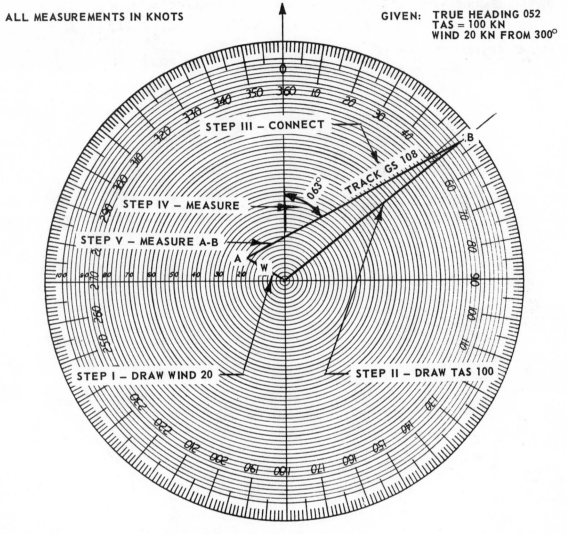

Fig. 179. Track and speed.

plication, and division is required. Contrary to general belief, the average person can thoroughly understand the basic principles of navigation. It is true, however that long range flights, as well as those flown at night or over water, will require much mathematics. Such flights are the responsibility of the few navigators that do that type of work. Get your computer and try the following computer problems. (Fig. 181).

The ratio (mathematical relationship) is 1.15 to 1. To change nautical to statute, multiply the number of nautical miles you have by 1.15. To change statute to nauti-

cal, divide the number of statute miles you have by 1.15. Check with Fig. 177. (There will always be more statute miles because they are shorter). (Fig's 182 & 183).

Pilots are very much interested in their fuel supply (Fig. 185) and how fast it is being used. Aircraft engines are rated at using so many gallons of fuel per hour.

From the foregoing statements it can be seen the amount of fuel used is based on flying time (minutes of flight).

A typical problem is as follows: A small plane using 5 G.P.H. (gallons per hour), has been flying 30 minutes. How

## Problem 3. To find Direction and Velocity of the wind during flight.

GIVEN:  HEADING – 255
            TAS – 100

ALL MEASUREMENTS IN KNOTS

CONDITION:
TWO CHECK POINTS
HAVE BEEN FLOWN
OVER IN 5 MIN. THEY
WERE 5 MILES APART.
TC OR PATH OBSERVED = 248°

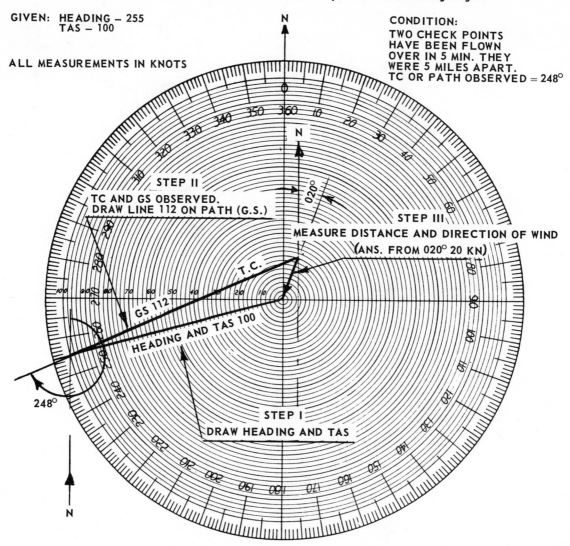

Fig. 180. Wind direction and velocity.

much fuel has been used?

Computers (Fig's. 184 & 185) are modified circular slide rules which will multiply, divide, and do proportion. These devices are very valuable to the airman because calculating can be done quickly and accurately enough for most flight problems. Computers are easy to manipulate and most persons soon become proficient with them.

There are several other types of computers, but all are based on the same principle.

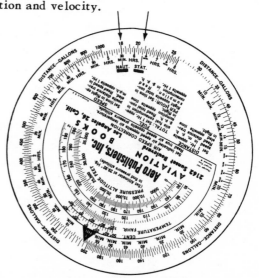

Fig. 181. Solving by computer.

The RATIO of the KILOMETER (1000 meters) to the STATUTE MILE is 0.62 to 1.0 or $\frac{62}{100}$. This equals about $\frac{3}{5}$; therefore, to change statute miles to kilometers, multiply the number of statute miles you have by 5 and divide by 3.

EXAMPLE:—

$$\frac{5 \text{ (statute miles)}}{1} \times \frac{5}{3} = \frac{25}{3} = 8\frac{1}{3} \text{ kilometers}$$

$$\frac{10 \text{ (kilometers)}}{1} \times \frac{3}{5} = \frac{30}{5} = 6 \text{ statute miles.}$$

Airmen are very much interested in TIME, DISTANCE, and SPEED. Typical questions they must answer are—"How much time will it take to go a certain number of MILES at a given SPEED?", etc.

FOR TIME:—

$$\text{time (minutes)} = \frac{\text{distance (miles) x 60 (minutes in an hour)}}{\text{speed (mph over the ground)}}$$

FOR DISTANCE:—

$$\text{distance (miles)} = \frac{\text{speed (mph over the ground) x time (in minutes)}}{60 \text{ (minutes in an hour)}}$$

FOR SPEED:—

$$\text{speed (mph over the ground)} = \frac{\text{distance (miles) x 60 minutes in an hour)}}{\text{time (in minutes)}}$$

Fig. 182. Conversion

$$\text{FUEL USED} = \frac{\text{flying time (in minutes) x g.p.h. (gallons used per hour)}}{60 \text{ (minutes in an hour)}}$$

$$\text{or} = \frac{30 \times 5}{60} = \frac{15}{6} = 2\frac{1}{2} \text{ gallons used}$$

Fig. 183. Fuel used.

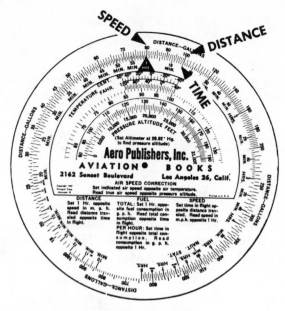

Computer settings for T-D-S problems.

PROBLEM:     SPEED ................................................ 80 M. P. H.
             DISTANCE ......................................... 100 Miles
             FLYING TIME ................................. 75 Minutes

Fig. 184. Solving for time, distance and speed.

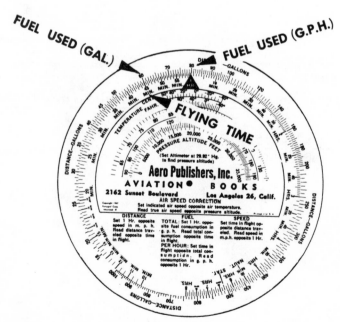

Computer settings for FUEL problems.

PROBLEM:     FLYING TIME ............................ 45 Minutes
             FUEL CONSUMPTION ............... 8 Gal. per hr.
             FUEL USED ............................... 6 Gal.

Fig. 185. Solving for fuel.

# CHAPTER 10

## KIND OF NAVIGATION

There are four kinds of navigation.

1. Dead reckoning, which is the basis for all navigation.
2. Pilotage, also called contact flying.
3. Radio navigation, and radar navigation.
4. Celestial navigation, which is flying by the aid of the sun and other stars.

This volume will cover the simpler forms of pilotage and dead reckoning.

One very important point to remember is that a good pilot will use all the forms of navigation to make a successful flight.

Celestial navigation is not the concern of the private pilot. Its an expert navigator's job.

### PILOTAGE

The basic form of navigation for the inexperienced pilot is pilotage, and it should be mastered first. An understanding of the principles of dead reckoning, however, will enable him to make necessary calculations of flight time and fuel consumption. The ever increasing use of radio equipment in private planes makes it highly desirable that the pilot have a thorough knowledge of the use of radio for navigation and communications purposes.

Pilotage is a form of dead reckoning navigation with visual reference, or view, kept at all times with prominent land marks on the ground. This being the case, the flight will be made at lower altitudes (3500 feet or under) and with good visibilities. The F.A.A. has very definite rules about pilotage, therefore the latest edition of Civil Air Regulations For Pilots, Aero Publishers, concerning visual flight rules should be studied by the prospective pilot.

The selection of the landmarks is very important because, from the air, in a plane moving 100 miles per hour or more, there is not much time to find hard-to-see ground objects.

The procedures for pilotage navigation are similar to other types, in that some kind of a record plan is necessary. The course should be layed out and dead reckoning considerations of time, distance and speed should be made. (See Fig. 186)

*Laying Out The Course:— (Fig. 187)*

Step 1— The pilot should decide if a direct route is the best and safest; because, in many cases, a longer route will be safer. His next consideration will be the position of the suitable landmarks in relation to the proposed course of flight. Landmarks can be on the course, to the left or to the right. From the practical standpoint it is sometimes easier to see the contact points if they are on the pilots left or right rather than directly underneath him.

Step II— After selecting the course, mark at 10 or 20 mile intervals, a line at right angles to the course line. These distance markers are valuable in locating landmarks and for indicating the progress of the flight.

Step III— The true course (direction) of the proposed flight is measured with the protractor. In review it will be remembered that the magnetic compass is the basic instrument for direction and has two serious errors— Variation and Deviation. During any kind of cross country

**CONTACT FLIGHT LOG**

PILOTAGE

PILOT: J. D. Roe
PLANE: Cessna 170 N 73491

SPEED: 120 M. P. H.
FUEL: 8 G. P. H.
WEATHER: Calm and clear

| FROM | TO | DIST. | TIME OF DEPART. | FLYING TIME (Min.) | FUEL (Gal.) | EST. TIME OF ARRIVAL | CONTACTS | CONTACTS Check Positions | | | |
|---|---|---|---|---|---|---|---|---|---|---|---|
| | | | | | | | | Dist. From | Left | On Course | Right |
| Vail Field | Monrovia | 12 | 1000 | 6 | 0.8 | 1006 | Rosemead Airport<br>Monrovia Airport | 6<br>6 | | ✓<br>✓ | |
| Monrovia | Claremont | 18 | 1006 | 9 | 1.2 | 1015 | R. R. & Cross Road<br>Claremont Field | 9<br>9 | ⅜ mile | <br>✓ | |
| | | | | | — REFERENCES — | | | | | | |
| MAP | MAP | MAP | TIME | COMPUTER | COMPUTER | TIME | MAP | MAP | MAP | MAP | MAP |

Fig. 186. Flight planning.

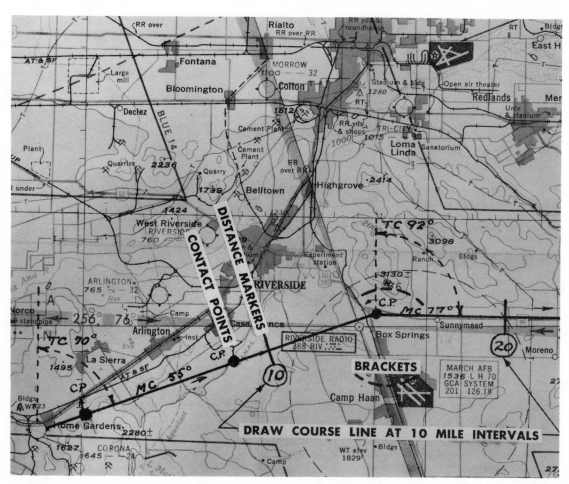

Fig. 187. Laying out the course.

pilotage, the compass becomes a valuable aid if it is thoroughly understood by the pilot.

Step IV-- Contact points are selected along the route at intervals, depending on their size and position. It is desirable to have the first landmark not too far from the airport, but after the plane has been headed along the course. It will be noted the course on this map avoids a busy airforce base and uses a very prominent highway intersection as a turning point.

Step V— Bracketing, such as noted between the A.F.B. and the prominent mountain to the north assists the pilot in case he is off course due to inattention or wind drift. He can head between the brackets and again be on course.

Step VI— Wind drift is usually present and the pilot can, by observation, correct for it by heading the nose of the plane toward the wind direction. A look at the compass to determine the number of degrees corrected for wind will show the approximate wind correction angle.

Step VII— Progress along the route is very important to the pilot. In other words is the aircraft on the course and how far has it progressed? Occasionally a landmark doesn't show up where the pilot expected to find it. In such cases, prob-

ably clear thinking and planning is better than circling, because a little time will usually solve the difficulty. Another recognizable landmark will usually come into view.

Step VIII— Ground speed determination will indicate to the pilot the estimated time of arrival (E.T.A.) and progress of the flight. The handy computer will quickly give the ground speed information as will be seen in Fig. 188.

Step IX— Fuel used- Every good pilot is very conscious of the amount of fuel being used and is aware of the fact that the F.A.A. requires an extra fuel supply in the tanks for safety. The useful computer will quickly solve the fuel problem and indicate if a landing and refueling is necessary. (Fig. 189).

*Procedure When Lost*

Owing to inattention, poor visibility, or unusual wind conditions, the pilot may miss his checkpoint and, as a result, he

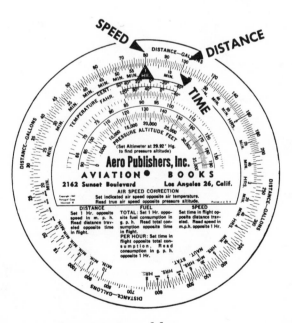

Computer settings for T-D-S problems.

PROBLEM:      SPEED ............................................. 80 M. P. H.
              DISTANCE ...................................... 100 Miles
              FLYING TIME ........................... 75 Minutes

Fig. 188. Computer settings for T-D-S problems.

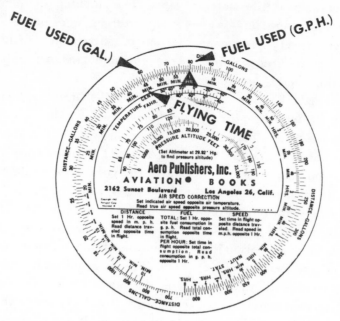

Computer settings for FUEL problems.

PROBLEM:        FLYING TIME ............................ 45 Minutes
                FUEL CONSUMPTION................ 8 Gal. per hr.
                FUEL USED ................................ 6 Gal.

Fig. 189.  Computer settings for fuel problems.

may become confused and reach that state of mind in which he thinks he is lost.

Assuming that he has no radio, he should simply follow a logical procedure to determine his position, locate satisfactory landmarks, and change his course if necessary. In no case should the pilot alter his course radically without first determining his position. Circling aimlessly, doubling back on course, flying on hunches, etc., will only create confusion and will make it impossible for him to follow any definite plan.

A recommended procedure is to continue on the established heading, watching for prominent landmarks which can be identified on the chart. The pilot sometimes discovers that he has prematurely identified a checkpoint, or has failed to observe one.

He should carefully check the visible landmarks available with his calculated position on the chart. The downwind side of the course is the area which should be checked first. If he fails to identify his position within 10 or 15 minutes, he should alter course slightly toward a conspicuous bracket. He should then follow this bracket in the direction most likely to give him a definite fix.

When a landmark is finally recognized, the pilot should accept it with caution and confirm his position by identifying other landmarks before proceeding with assurance. He would then determine the reason for error, and correct his heading to prevent flying off course again.

Beacuse a majority of small airplanes are now equipped with radio, these procedures are normally combined with the use of radio aids in determining position. *Air Markers*

Air markers of the type shown in Fig. 190, often prove a boon to pilots. In many instances, pilots who were lost, low in gas, and with radios inoperative have

Fig. 190. Air markers.

located their positions by means of air markers, and have made emergency landings at nearby airports. Each air marker consists of the name of the town painted in large chrome yellow letters on a dark background; an arrow shows the direction and distance to the nearest airport. These markers usually are painted on rooftops of large buildings which are conspicuous from the air.

Several thousand communities in the United States have been airmarked through the efforts of the FAA, State and local agencies, and private organizations. However, the number of markers is far too small to be relied upon by pilots for navigation purposes.

## DEAD RECKONING

In the section on pilotage the discussion went beyond elementary pilotage and included some dead reckoning with the use of the computer.

Far more accurate navigation can be done by carefully planning the flight before take-off. Then while in the air, it can be only a matter of checking. However, weather conditions can change, but even so the pilot is far better informed.

The basis for all kinds of navigation from pilotage to celestial is known as dead reckoning. The term dead comes from the word deduce which means to arrive at a conclusion, whereas reckoning means keeping account of.

Therefore, it follows that a definition of dead reckoning navigation is, *(to know the position of the aircraft by keeping account of the distance, the course direction, the time in the air, and the actual speed over the ground.) Fig. 191.*

The simplest kind of dead reckoning assumes that the air is calm. Thus, the pilot or navigator should know about where the aircraft is at all times. If the speed remains the same, the plane's track (path) over the ground will be the same as the course, (direction of proposed flight).

In actual flight, winds may cause considerable error unless some sort of correction is made, either before or during flight. (Refer to Fig. 191).

It is important to have a log (Fig's. 192 & 193) or plan of dead reckoning flight so that the pilot or navigator can tell at a glance how the flight is proceeding. Several forms are available for the "plan" or "log"; however, some pilots prefer to work out their own forms. The important thing is to have some kind of workable plan, and then to use it during the progress of the flight. Thus, the basic idea of the dead reckoning is to know, by planning before-hand, and checking during flight, the position of the plane over the surface of the earth.

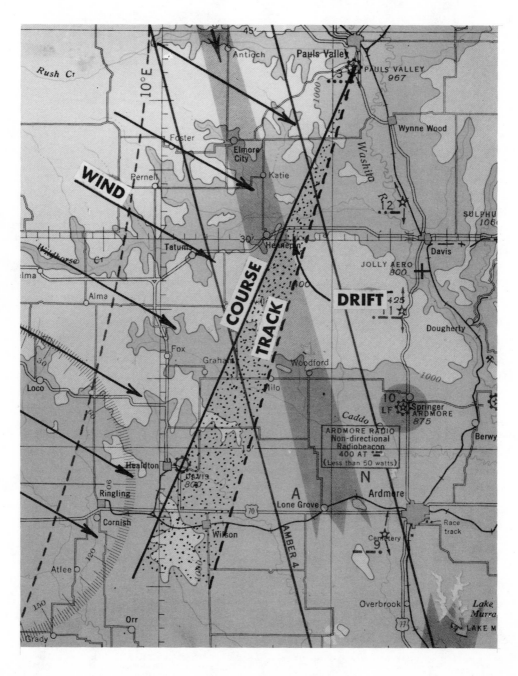

Fig. 191. Wind drift.

## PILOT'S PLANNING SHEET

Plane Identification                                      Date

| | | | WIND | | VAR | | | | | | TOTAL | | TOTAL | FUEL | TOTAL |
| | TC | | MPH FROM | WCA R+ L− | TH | W+ E− | MH | DEV | CH | | MILES | CH | GS | TIME | RATE | FUEL |
|---|---|---|---|---|---|---|---|---|---|---|---|---|---|---|---|---|
| CRUISING AIRSPEED | | | | | | | | | | | | | | | | |
| From: | | | | | | | | | | | | | | | | |
| To: | | | | | | | | | | | | | | | | |
| From: | | | | | | | | | | | | | | | | |
| To: | | | | | | | | | | | | | | | | |

Fig. 192. Pilot's planning sheet and visual flight log.

## VISUAL FLIGHT LOG

| | RADIO FREQUENCIES | DISTANCE | ELAPSED TIME | CLOCK TIME | GS | CH | REMARKS |
| | TOWER RANGE | POINT TO POINT CUMULATIVE | ESTIMATED ACTUAL | ESTIMATED ACTUAL | ESTIMATED ACTUAL | ESTIMATED ACTUAL | BRACKETS, WEATHER, ETC. |
|---|---|---|---|---|---|---|---|
| TIME OF DEPARTURE | | | | | | | |
| POINT OF DEPARTURE | | | | | | | |
| CHECKPOINTS | | | | | | | |
| 1. | | | | | | | |
| 2. | | | | | | | |
| 3. | | | | | | | |
| 4. | | | | | | | |
| 5. | | | | | | | |
| DESTINATION | | | | | | | |
| 6. | | | | | | | |

The Pilot's Planning Sheet provides space for entering dead-reckoning data.

The Visual Flight Log may be prepared in advance by entering the selected checkpoints, together with the following data: Distance between checkpoints, and cumulative distance; estimated time between checkpoints; clock or cumulative time; groundspeed and Compass Heading.

As the flight progresses, the actual time, groundspeed and Compass Heading should be filled in, thus completing the log.

Fig. 193. Pilot's planning sheet.

# CHAPTER 11

## PLANNING THE FLIGHT

### PRE-FLIGHT PLANNING

Correct selection of the type of chart to be used for the flight is essential for flight planning. Study the chart carefully from point of departure to the destination. Look for check points and possible landing areas.

Fig. 194 shows two flight paths under consideration by a pilot. He first planned a direct flight down the coast with a return inland.

This part of California has a very rugged, often clouded and fogged-in coast. Inland it is usually clear with good visibilities. This is a summer time flight.

After laying out the two courses and being aware of the rough terrain and possible bad weather along the coast, there is only one good choice, and that is course B, inland.

For distance there is only a matter of about thirteen miles or about eleven or twelve minutes flying time, with no wind. The winds are mostly westerly so no great difference in time would occur.

### STEPS IN PLANNING THE FLIGHT

The pre-flight ground inspection of the airplane will be before takeoff.

1. Carefully study the map for the best path. (Fig. 194)

2. Draw the true course lines. (Note the R.R. will be on the left side from Soledad to Spreckels.) (Fig. 194)

3. With a protractor measure the true course. (Fig. 151)

4. Determine the variation for the area. (Fig. 155)

5. Mark off courses at ten mile inter-vals. Select an alternate airport. (Fig. 194).

6. Mark check points with a large dot showing on which side you will see them. (Fig. 194)

7. Obtain weather data. Winds lower and upper, sky condition and forecast. (Part II)

8. Determine wind correction for each leg of the flight by solving wind triangles. (Fig. 173)

9. Use the compass work form to secure headings. (refer to compass section). (Fig. 176)

10. Estimate the true altitude.

11. Estimate the time of arrival at each check point and ten mile marker. — Use computer.

12. Calculate fuel requirements. — Use computer. (Fig. 185)

13. File a flight plan. (Fig. 195)

14. Enter the pre-flight planning data in the visual flight log. (Fig's 192 & 193).

### THE FLIGHT PLAN

File a flight plan. (Fig. 195)

Choose a cruising altitude, using weather information and winds aloft forecast.

Determine estimated ground speed, compass heading, estimated time of arrival (ETA), based on forecasted wind at cruising altitude. (See method described.)

File flight plan with FAA Communications Station. (Although a flight plan is not required on a VFR flight, it is good insurance in case you should have difficulty and a search should become necessary. VFR flight plans are handled by FAA soley for search and rescue purposes.)

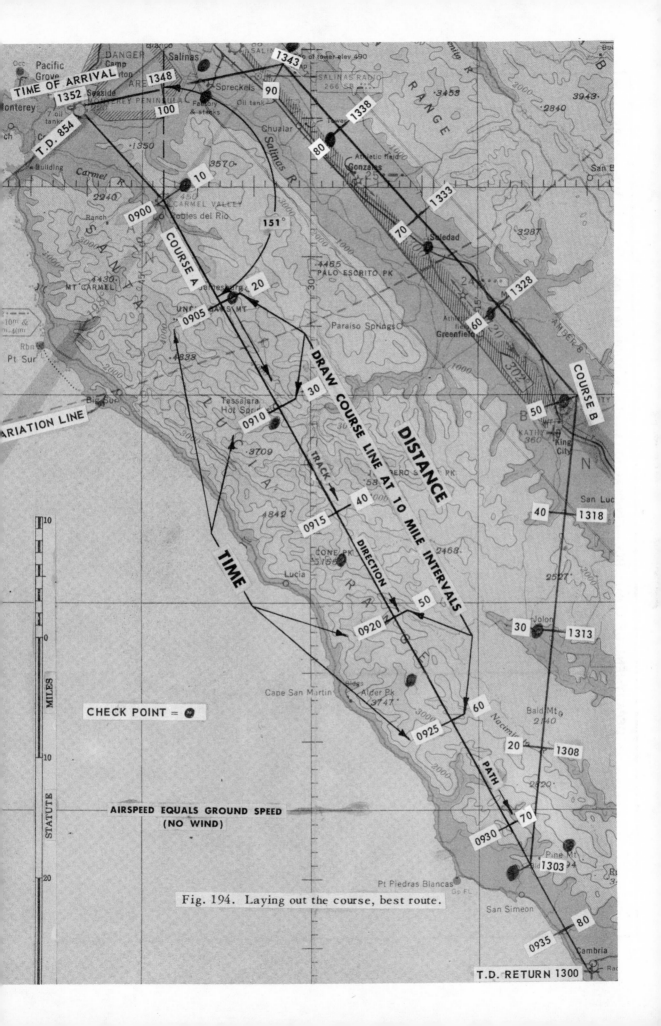

Fig. 194. Laying out the course, best route.

## DEPARTMENT OF COMMERCE—CIVIL AERONAUTICS ADMINISTRATION

Form approved.
Budget Bureau No. 41-R073.4.

# FLIGHT PLAN

**FOR VFR—Complete all except shaded items.   FOR IFR—Complete all items.**
**FOR DVFR—Complete all items except "Alternate Airport."**

| AIRCRAFT IDENTIFICATION NO. | COLOR OF AIRCRAFT | TYPE OF AIRCRAFT (If formation flight, types and number of aircraft) | |
|---|---|---|---|
| NAME OF PILOT OR FLIGHT COMMANDER | PILOT'S OR FLIGHT COMMANDER'S ADDRESS | | CERTIFICATE NO. OF PILOT OR FLIGHT COMMANDER |
| POINT OF DEPARTURE | CRUISING ALTITUDE(S) AND ROUTE TO BE FOLLOWED | | |

POINT OF FIRST INTENDED LANDING (IFR); OR INTERMEDIATE STOPS AND DESTINATION (VFR)

| | PROPOSED TRUE AIR SPEED AT CRUISING ALT. | PROPOSED TIME OF DEPARTURE | ACTUAL TIME OF DEPARTURE |
|---|---|---|---|
| ALTERNATE AIRPORT | | P | D |

FUEL ON BOARD — HOURS | MINUTES

FREQUENCY OF RADIO EQUIPMENT — RECEIVER | TRANSMITTER

ESTIMATED ELAPSED TIME UNTIL ARRIVAL OVER POINT OF FIRST INTENDED LANDING — HOURS | MINUTES

ANY OTHER INFORMATION PERTINENT TO AIR TRAFFIC CONTROL, SEARCH AND RESCUE, OR SECURITY CONTROL

## CLOSE FLIGHT PLAN UPON ARRIVAL

Fig. 195.   Flight plan form which the pilot files with the Federal Aviation Agency.

by radio, telephone, or in person at FAA Communications Stations and Towers. They are not closed by towers automatically as a result of landing. A specific request must be made to the tower controller.

The topics found in this section deal principally with the preflight preparations important to navigation. Other preparations such as pre-flight inspection, servicing, and loading of the airplane are equally important and are discussed in other publications.

Flight plans may be filed with FAA Communications Stations in person and by telephone. Under certain conditions they may be filed by radio while in the air. This latter procedure is least desirable, since it is time consuming and will interfere with communications of other aircraft.

Arrange to close Flight Plan. It is imperative that pilots close their flight plans. Failure to do so means that a search will be initiated which may result in the dispatching of search planes and rescue parties.

# CHAPTER 12
## IN-FLIGHT NAVIGATION

### IN-FLIGHT CHECKING

The pilot has left Cambria, made his turn at Pine Mountain (buildings) and is proceeding towards King City. (Refer to Fig. 192).

The airplane arrives at Jolon at 1313 on course.

The visibility being excellent, he arrives at King City on time and on course.

The turn is made with the railroad on the right hand side making a fine bracket.

Noting the painted roof airways marking at Soledad the pilot now keeps the R.R. on the left side. However he has noted a considerable change in wind direction and velocity. He can quickly draw wind triangle problem no. 3 (Wind Triangles) or make visual corrections for the different wind drift.

He also noted his 70 mile mark time to 2 minutes off. It was 1335.

The airplane's ground speed was somewhat less so the time of arrival at the 490 tower was 4 minutes more (1347).

The final leg of the flight required new calculations of drift and ground speed. Safe landing at Monterey with a dense fog bank two miles off shore. His alternate airport was Salinas.

### FLIGHT ASSISTANCE SERVICE

In making preflight preparations as described in previous paragraphs, pilots should take advantage of the flight assistance service provided by FAA Air Traffic Control Facilities (communications stations, towers, and centers). Other agencies cooperating in this service are the U.S. Weather Bureau and the U.S. Air Force.

Flight assistance service includes five principal categories of aid, all of which are of interest to private pilots.

*Pre-Flight Assistance*

When preparing for cross-country flights, pilots should contact the nearest Weather Bureau Airport Station or FAA Communications Station. Services provided include supplying latest weather reports and forecasts, and assistance in completing flight plans. Other available information includes; notices to airmen, availability of fuel and services en route, and time of sundown at the destination.

At airports which have Weather Bureau offices, preflight weather briefing is done by Weather Bureau personnel; FAA stations provide this information at other locations. The weather data available includes hourly and special aviation weather reports, pilot weather reports, radar weather reports, winds aloft reports and forecasts, and terminal and area forecasts.

*In-Flight Radio Assistance*

A few of the services provided the pilot in flight are: Broadcasting aviation weather reports twice each hour, furnishing weather information when requested by radio, advising of any hazards along the route of flight, and complying with any reasonable request for aid or information.

*Emergency Flight Assistance*

This service provides every possible assistance in cases of aircraft emergencies. For example, air traffic personnel are trained to assist pilots in establishing position by visual reference to terrain features, VHF omnirange indications, and low-frequency radio range orientation.

A pilot who is lost or otherwise in difficulty should give the nearest FAA facility an immediate call by radio. Trained personnel will then make every effort to lend assistance.

### Search and Rescue Action

When an airplane is overdue or is known to have made an emergency landing, FAA conducts a communications search, and if this proved negative, the appropriate Rescue Coordination Center is alerted so that physical search and rescue operations can be conducted. Here again, the importance of a flight plan is obvious. If the pilot has filed a flight plan and has not deviated from the proposed route to be flown, search and rescue operations will be greatly facilitated.

It is equally obvious that pilots who successfully complete their flights should file an Arrival Report, to prevent costly and useless search operations.

### Airport Information Service

Although FAA communications stations may not exercise control of airport traffic, station personnel will supply advisory information to arriving and departing aircraft at points where no air traffic control tower is located. This advisory information may include wind direction and speed, altimeter setting, field conditions, and traffic known to be in the area of the airport.

Many additional procedures and refinements are useful in connection with flight planning and VFR, cross-country flying. It is strongly recommended that a thorough study be made of the Pilots' Radio Handbook (FAA Technical Manual No. 102), which discusses many aspects of radio communications and radio aids to navigation. The Flight Information Manual, published annually, and the Airman's Guide, a biweekly publication, contain a wealth of information important in cross-country flying. Both of these publications are prepared by the Federal Aviation Agency.

# CHAPTER 13

## RADIO NAVIGATION

In addition to the communications services discussed in the preceding section, the Federal Airways System of the Federal Aviation Agency provides several radio aids to air navigation. For example, the VHF omnirange (VOR) and the four-course low-frequency range are particularly useful to VFR pilots, both for navigational guidance and for purposes of en route communications. For assistance, mainly to instrument pilots, are such aids as radar and Instrument Landing Systems (ILS).

New and improved types of electronic equipment are constantly being developed to make flying safer and easier. One such system is VOR-TAC, which seems destined to solve many of the navigational problems of pilots. This system provides, in addition to the bearing information obtained from the omnirange, the distance of an airplane from the station. (Distance-from station information may also be supplied by Distance Measuring Equipment (DME). With bearing and distance known, the pilot can determine his position; therefore, the need for bearings on two or more stations is eliminated. Completion of all ground installations and widespread availability of low-cost equipment for use in personal-type planes will bring fullest utilization of this simplified means of determining position. (Fig. 196).

### THE VHF OMNIRANGE

In recent years, the VHF omnirange (VOR) has replaced the low-frequency range as the basic radio aid to navigation. Frequencies of standard omnirange stations are in the VHF band, between 112

Fig. 196. A typical VORTAC Station.

and 118 megacycles, while TVOR's and LVOR's, both low-powered stations, operate in the 108-112 mc. band. The word "omni" means all, and an omnirange is a VHF radio range which projects courses in all directions from the station, like spokes from the hub of a wheel. In contrast to low-frequency ranges, which have only four range legs, flights to and from omniranges are possible from all directions.

The following are a few of the advantages of flying omniranges:

1. An approach may be made to a VOR from any direction, by flying the bearing (or course) to the station.

2. An approach may be made to any destination from the station by selecting the proper radial. It is important to remember that VOR radials, as shown on charts, are always from the station, never toward.

3. When within range of two or more VOR's, a fix may be determined quickly and easily by taking bearings on the stations and determining position on a chart.

4. Other advantages include static-free reception and the elimination of complex orientation procedures which are often used by instrument pilots flying low-frequency ranges.

An important fact is that VOR signals, like other VHF transmissions, follow an approximate line-of-sight course. Therefore, reception distance increases with an increase in the flight altitude of an aircraft. A means is usually provided with omnireceivers to indicate to the pilot when the signal is too weak for satisfactory reception.

In addition to their use for navigational guidance, omnirange frequencies are used by station personnel for weather broadcasts and communications purposes. Stations are assigned three-letter identifications. At some stations these identification letters are broadcast continuously in code. Other stations are identified by a voice recording (example: Baltimore Omni), alternating with the usual Morse Code identification.

## VOR Receivers

VOR receivers are very simple to operate. Selection of the desired frequency is accomplished in the same manner as with other radio receivers. Three basic instruments are normally provided with receivers used in omnirange flying. (Fig. 197) One instrument in the cockpit is the omnibearing (course) selector, which enables the pilot to select the course he desires to fly. A second instrument is the "TO-FROM" indicator (also known as the ambiguity meter or sense indicator), provided to show him whether the bearing is TO or FROM the station. The third is a deviation indicator (often referred to as the "LEFT-RIGHT" indicator or vertical needle), which tells him when he is on course, or left or right of course. Using these three instruments, the pilot obtains visual indications which provide him with

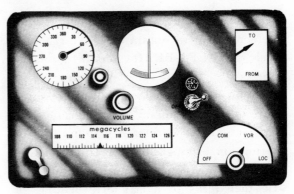

Fig. 197. Composite drawing of omnireceiver.

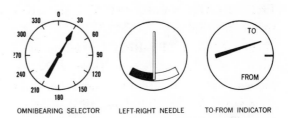

OMNIBEARING SELECTOR    LEFT-RIGHT NEEDLE    TO-FROM INDICATOR

Fig. 198. Omnireceiver indications when an aircraft is ON a selected bearing TO a station.

a variety of information and guidance. (Although the arrangement of instruments varies, most VOR receivers operate on a three-element principle. Sometimes all 3 indications are combined in 1 instrument. There were some early sets, however, which did not use the three-element presentation). (Refer to Fig. 198).

Because accuracy is an important factor in any navigational equipment, pilots should check their omnireceivers periodically to determine whether they are functioning properly. Procedures and locations for checking VOR receivers are published by the FAA in the Flight Information Manual.

When flying directly to a VOR facility, the pilot first tunes his receiver to the frequency of the omnirange, positively identifying the station either by code or voice recording.

Next, he manually rotates the omnibearing selector until the LEFT-RIGHT needle is centered at the bottom of the dial. He then checks to see that the TO-FROM indicator reads "TO." If it should read "FROM," he merely turns the course selector 180° to obtain a "TO" reading, and the LEFT-RIGHT needle is again centered. The reading on the course selector is the magnetic bearing which will take the airplane to the omnirange. In figure 198 the pilot has found (by rotating his omnibearing selector) that his magnetic course TO the station is 030°. He then turns to a magnetic heading of approximately 030°. By making small corrections in heading, he keeps the LEFT-RIGHT needle centered and flies to the station.

In case his LEFT-RIGHT needle moves to the position shown in figure 199, he knows that to return to course he must fly toward the needle, holding this heading until the needle is centered. Whether an airplane is to the right or left of course (assuming that the pointer indicates "TO" and that he has not passed over the station), it is always necessary to fly toward the needle to return to course.

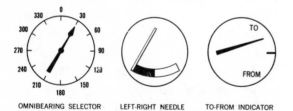

OMNIBEARING SELECTOR  LEFT-RIGHT NEEDLE  TO-FROM INDICATOR

Fig. 199. Omnireceiver indications when an aircraft is OFF the selected bearing TO a station.

If the airplane remains on a magnetic course of 030° after flying over the station, the "TO-FROM" pointer will indicate FROM and the "LEFT-RIGHT" needle will remain centered, as shown in Fig. 200. To continue in the same direction, the pilot merely continues to keep the needle centered in the same manner as described in the previous paragraph.

## THE LOW FREQUENCY RANGE

Until the advent of the omnirange, the

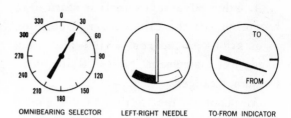

OMNIBEARING SELECTOR  LEFT-RIGHT NEEDLE  TO-FROM INDICATOR

Fig. 200. Omnireceiver indications when an aircraft is ON a selected bearing FROM a station.

low frequency radiorange was the principal air navigational aid in the United States. (Some range stations operate in the medium frequency band; therefore, they are more correctly referred to as low-frequency, medium-frequency (LF/MF stations.) These ranges were placed in use at a time when comparatively few planes were in operation, and four courses were ample for navigational and air traffic control purposes. Besides the limited number of courses, low-frequency ranges have other limitations, such as poor reception due to static, and the necessity for complex orientation procedures (mainly of concern to instrument pilots).

Despite these limitations, low-frequency ranges have certain advantages. They operate in the 200 to 400 kc. band, and a low-frequency receiver is the only equipment needed to receive them. Under normal conditions, the low-frequency range is usable for distances of 50 to 100 miles, and can be received at low altitudes and on the ground. Like omniranges, each low-frequency range station is assigned a three-letter identification known as a call sign. Range signals are interrupted every 30 seconds while the station identification signals are transmitted in code. For example, the low-frequency range station at Dallas, Tex., is identified by DAL (− . . . − . − . .).

Figure 201 represents a typical four-course range. The signals in International Morse Code for A (.−) and N (− .) are

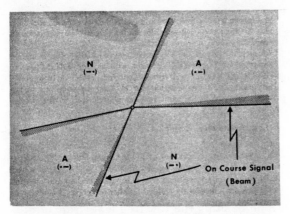

Fig. 201. Quadrants and courses of a LF/MF Radio Range. (Note.—On Sectional Aeronautical charts, the "N" quadrants are outlined by heavy red lines along the range courses.)

broadcast directionally from special antennas into opposite quadrants. Unless a pilot is flying on or near one of the four courses of the range, he will receive either "dit dah" (. —) or "dah dit" (— .) signals, depending upon the quadrant in which the plane is located. When the pilot is flying on a range leg, the A and N signals interlock, giving a monotone or steady oncourse hum, popularly known as the beam. Beams (equisignal zones) are wedge-shaped zones which are approximately 3° wide. On aeronautical charts, the magnetic course to the station is printed on each range leg.

The areas in each quadrant adjacent to range courses are known as bisignal zones. Here, the pilot receives the oncourse hum with an A or N in the background, depending upon the quadrant in which he is located. In those portions of each of the quadrants remote from the range legs, either an A or N will be received.

Pilots making VFR cross-country flights need not be proficient in complex orientation procedures on low frequency ranges. They will, however, find these ranges most helpful when used in connection with pilotage, dead reckoning, and omnirange flying, for directional guidance to determine position.

An example of the use of a low-frequency range on a cross-country flight is given later in this chapter.

## THE AUTOMATIC DIRECTION FINDER

Many personal-type airplanes are equipped with low-cost Automatic Direction Finder (ADF) radio sets which operate in the low and medium frequency bands. By tuning to low frequency radio stations such as four-course ranges, radio beacons, and commercial broadcast stations, a pilot may use ADF for navigational purposes in cross-country flying. Frequencies of radio aids to navigation are readily obtained from aeronautical charts (and the Airman's Guide), while the Flight Information Manual contains a listing of standard broadcasting stations most likely to be used by pilots. Positive identification of the station to which the set is tuned is extremely important.

Probably the most common use of ADF is that of homing by flying the needle to a station. Another useful practice is to first obtain bearings from two or more radio stations, and then plot radio lines of position on an aeronautical chart to establish position. This is knwon as plotting a radio fix. Since ADF does not account for wind drift and is susceptible to difficulties due to thunderstorms and static, it lacks several of the advantages of Omni. Nevertheless, pilots who do extensive cross-country flying will do well to make a thorough study of ADF and its uses.

## AN ILLUSTRATION OF VFR FLIGHT USING RADIO AIDS

To illustrate the use of radio aids in cross-country flying, let us assume that a pilot is making a flight, using the Dallas Sectional Chart. He decides to fly from Graham Airport (33°06' N.; 98° 33' W.),

Graham, Tex., direct to the Fort Worth Omni, and then fly direct to Majors Field (33°04' N.; 96°04' W.), Greenville, Tex. It is suggested that the reader draw these courses on a Dallas Chart.

With his omnireceiver tuned to the frequency of the Fort Worth VOR, he listens carefully for code or voice identification of Fort Worth Radio. Next, he turns his course selector (omnibearing selector) until the LEFT-RIGHT (vertical needle centers at the bottom of the dial and the TO-FROM pointer indicates "TO" the omnirange. His magnetic course to the station is 070°. By keeping the needle centered, making corrections toward the needle to return to course, he flies directly to the station. While passing over the station the LEFT-RIGHT needle swings sharply back and forth, and the TO-FROM needle then settles on "FROM", indicating he is now heading away from the station.

Corrections for wind drift and magnetic variation have not been mentioned, because in flying omni, the pilot automatically compensates for them when making heading corrections to keep the LEFT-RIGHT needle centered. Since all radials from an omnirange are magnetic rather than true bearings, magnetic variation is corrected in the omnirange itself. Wind drift correction is made automatically by the pilot when he crabs the proper amount to keep the needle centered, thus enabling him to fly a straight-line course to the station.

After he has passed over the Fort Worth Omni, the pilot turns his course selector to 087°, which is the outbound bearing from the Fort Worth VOR to Majors Field. After making sure that the TO-FROM indicator shows "FROM", he simply keeps the LEFT-RIGHT needle centered to stay on course.

Between Decatur and Denton, he checks his position by tuning the low frequency receiver to the Fort Worth LF/MF range. East of Decatur, he receives an "A" signal (in code), with a steady oncourse hum in the background. When this signal becomes a steady hum (an oncourse signal with no "A" or "N" in the background), he knows that his exact position is the intersection of his course and the north leg of the Fort Worth low frequency range. Upon passing the low frequency range leg, he first receives an oncourse signal with an "N" in the background. The "N" signal becomes progressively more prominent with the steady hum finally disappearing. Upon reaching the vicinity of the north course of the Dallas LF range, he retunes his low frequency receiver to Dallas, and his progress is again checked in a similar manner.

Before getting out of range of the Fort Worth VOR, he obtains a fix using bearings from the Fort Worth and Dallas VOR's. While tuned to Fort Worth, his LEFT-RIGHT needle is centered, indicating that he is on course. Next he tunes the omnireceiver to the Dallas VOR, and turns the bearing selector until the vertical needle centers, and the TO-FROM indicator reads "FROM." From the course selector, he determines that his bearing from the Dallas VOR is 307°. Upon plotting this bearing, he finds that it intersects the bearing from the Fort Worth VOR (the course which he is flying) at a point over Lake Dallas. Although this type of fix is most accurate when the cross bearings are 90° apart, the fix over Lake Dallas is one of sufficient accuracy. In situations where more than two VOR's are within reception distance, additional radio bearings may be taken to confirm a fix.

During the latter portion of the flight (assuming he is at relatively low altitude), he will be out of range of the Fort Worth VOR. However, he will be able to obtain bearings from the Dallas Omni to check progress along his course. For example, suppose that he plans to start his letdown over the small lake adjacent to Lavon Reservoir, 26 miles west of Majors Field. The bearing from Dallas VOR to this point on his course is 023°. In order to confirm his position, he sets his course selector at 023° with the TO-FROM indicator show-ing "FROM" the station. Before reaching the point for reducing power for letdown, his vertical needle is to the RIGHT. While approaching this bearing, the needle gradually moves to the LEFT. When the needle becomes centered he knows that 023° radial has been reached, and he double checks his position by chart read-ing before beginning the letdown.

# PART FOUR
# ATTITUDE INSTRUMENT FLYING

# INTRODUCTION TO PART IV

The F.A.A. ruled that as of March 16, 1960, all private and commercial pilots being certificated, be required to demonstrate sufficient instrument flying skill for safety of themselves and others. THEY MUST SHOW PROFICIENCY IN GETTING OUT OF AN UNINTENTIONAL ENTRY INTO INSTRUMENT WEATHER.

Attitude Instrument Flight and visual flight are much the same. In the first case a pilots vision is on the basic instruments while observing the readings, the other is with visual references to ground objects and the horizon.

Every pilot, new or old, should be well acquainted with the basic instruments, know the construction, operation, and use of them.

Frequent scanning and study of the instruments involved will, in time, help the pilot to become quite proficient and confident.

Experiments have recently been conducted at the Universities of Illinois and West Virginia showing that Attitude Instrument Flying can be taught along with Contact Flying with little added flying time required. THEREFORE, IT IS NOT DIFFICULT FOR ANY PILOT TO MASTER THE ART.

Previous chapters of this book have discussed the physiological effects of flight. Refer to chapter 4.

Instruments and their uses have previously been discussed briefly where applicable. Chapter 14, The Basic Six Instruments for Attitude Instrument Flying discusses in considerable detail the construction and function of the instruments.

Chapter 15, Attitude Instrument Flying discusses and illustrates with many diagrams and photographs the instrument readings to be expected for most situations.

Exerpts applicable from NAVAER 00-80T-60.

# CHAPTER 14

## THE BASIC SIX INSTRUMENTS

The pitot-static and suction instruments are grouped together here because both types are actuated by air. This chapter thus covers virtually all the non-electric attitude or speed-indicating instruments in common use today.

The pitot-static instruments measure pressure or pressure differentials. They include the airspeed indicator, Machmeter, altimeter, and vertical-speed indicator. The suction instruments depend on gyroscopes which run on suction from the engine-driven vacuum pump. This group includes the air-driven turn-and-

bank indicator, the gyro-driven heading indicator, and the horizon indicator. These instruments are also manufactured in electrically operated versions which are discussed in the following chapter.

### PITOT-STATIC INSTRUMENTS

*Pitot-Static Tube*

The source of the pressures for operating the airspeed indicator, the vertical-speed indicator, and the altimeter is the pitot-static system which provides two kinds of pressures to the instruments it serves. The pitot part of the system pro-

AIR SPEED INDICATOR     COMPASS     HORIZON INDICATOR

ALTIMETER     BANK—TURN INDICATOR     CLIMB INDICATOR

Fig. 202. Pitot-Static and Suction Instruments.

vides the impact air pressure—that is, the pressure of the airstream as the plane flies through the air. The static part of the system provides the still air pressure— that is, the pressure of the undisturbed air at the flight level.

There are three major parts to the pitot-static system: (1) the impact-pressure chamber and line, (2) the static-pressure chamber and lines, and (3) the heating unit to prevent the icing of the pitot tube. Up to a short time ago, all three parts constituted a single unit—the pitot-static tube.

Recently, however, the pitot and static sources were separated in some aircraft in an effort to improve pitot-static performance. Where the sources are separated, the impact pressure is taken from the pitot tube (mounted on the leading edge of the wing, the nose section, or the vertical stabilizer), while the static pressure is taken from the static line attached flush with the side of the fuselage. On most aircraft using a flush-type static source, there are two vents, one on each side of the fuselage or nose. This is to compensate for any possible error in pressure that might occur on one of the vents when there are erratic changes in attitude, as in a steep turn, or roll. The vents are connected by a Y-type fitting. It is important to check the flush-type vents visually to see that they are not clogged.

Sometimes, in certain aircraft, an abrupt movement causes a momentary loss of impact or static pressure, and this causes temporarily wrong indications on the vertical-speed indicator and on the altimeter. Such erratic readings are particularly noticeable on the vertical-speed indicator, where they appear either as brief, excessive vertical motions or as motions in the direction opposite to the actual. If this effect appears to be greater than normal, have the flush-type vents checked for clogging.

*Operation of the Pitot-Static System*

The pitot chamber receives the impact pressure of the air on the open pitot tube as the aircraft moves along. The static chamber, if it is contained in the pitot head, is vented to the free undisturbed air through small holes on the top and bottom of the tube. For most accurate operation, the pitot-static tube should be parallel to the line of the relative wind. To achieve this condition, the tube is mounted parallel to the longitudinal axis of the aircraft.

In most conventional-type aircraft, there is an alternate source for static pressure in case of an emergency. This

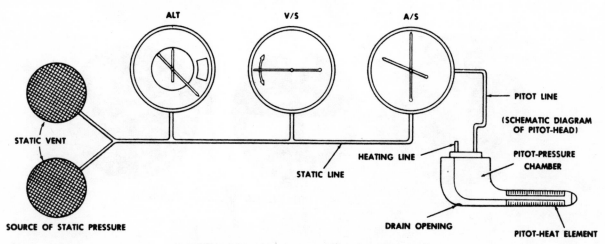

Fig. 203. Flush-type static source

source usually taps its pressure from within the cockpit. Because of the venturi effect from the flow of air over openings in the aircraft, this alternate static pressure is usually lower than the pressure provided by the pitot-static tube. Therefore, when the static source switch is placed in the alternate position, the altimeter usually reads higher, the indicated airspeed is greater, and the vertical-speed indicator momentarily indicates a climb. When possible, check the alternate source in flight before going into instrument flight conditions.

Jet aircraft and aircraft with pressurized cockpits are usually equipped with the flush-type vent and no alternate source. On such aircraft, if the pitot-static system fails, first dump cabin pressure; *then* break the glass of either the airspeed indicator or the altimeter with a sharp instrument which will fracture the glass without damaging the instrument or bending the needle. The instruments will then read with approximate accuracy. If you must use a blunt object (such as your heel) to break the glass, smash the glass in the vertical-speed indicator because it is the least essential to safe flight. With this procedure, however, the instrument readings will not be correct. If the vertical-speed glass is broken, it will read in reverse, and the other pitot-static instruments will have a pronounced lag in their readings.

## AIRSPEED INDICATOR

The airspeed indicator is a differential pressure instrument. It measures the difference between the impact pressure and static pressure, and converts it into an indication of speed. The case of the airspeed indicator (which is air-tight) is connected to the static line from the pitot-static tube. Inside the case is a small diaphragm made of phosphor bronze or beryllium copper. The diaphragm, which is very sensitive to changes in pressure, is connected to the impact pressure line. The needle or pointer is connected through a series of levers and gears with the free side of the diaphragm.

When the aircraft is stationary, there is no difference between the pitot and static pressures, and the pointer is at 0. When the aircraft moves through the air, however, the pressure in the impact line becomes greater than the pressure in the static line. The faster the aircraft moves, the greater the pressure differential becomes. Since the diaphragm is connected directly to the impact pressure line, it is expanded by this increase in impact pressure. (See Fig. 204.) The expansion or contraction of the diaphragm, in turn, controls the position of the needle by a series of levers and gears to the face of the instrument. The dial is so scaled that the needle indicates the pressure differential in knots.

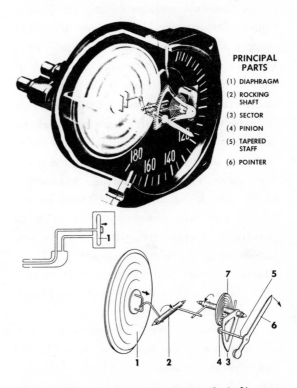

PRINCIPAL PARTS

(1) DIAPHRAGM
(2) ROCKING SHAFT
(3) SECTOR
(4) PINION
(5) TAPERED STAFF
(6) POINTER

Fig. 204. Diagram of airspeed indicator operation.

## Corrections to Indicated Airspeed

There are four kinds of airspeed figures: indicated, calibrated, equivalent, and true. Indicated airspeed is the airspeed read directly from the instrument. Calibrated airspeed is the indicated airspeed corrected for instrument installation error. Equivalent airspeed is calibrated airspeed corrected for compressibility error, and true airspeed is calibrated airspeed corrected for altitude and temperature.

The indicated airspeed has to be corrected for installation error because no pitot tube installation can be perfect. As a result, the differential actually established by the pitot tube is slightly different from the differential pressure it should establish theoretically. You can derive the calibrated airspeed (CAS) from the indicated airspeed (IAS) by using the calibration card in the aircraft. If there is no card, consider the calibrated airspeed to be the same as the indicated airspeed.

To convert calibrated airspeed into equivalent airspeed, you must take the compressibility error into account. This error is due to the fact that the angle of airflow across the head of the pitot tube decreases as the speed of the aircraft increases. As a result, the air molecules are compressed before entering the tube and they increase the pressure in the pitot line above what it should be. At speeds below 250 knots and at altitudes below 10,000 feet, the compressibility error is practically negligible; that's why it has not been considered important until recently. You can find a table of corrections for compressibility in the Operating Handbook for your aircraft.

The final correction—correcting for air-density error to get true airspeed (TAS) —is the most important of all. Usually the TAS exceeds the CAS by a considerable amount. The difference between TAS and CAS increases with altitude because the airspeed indicator is calibrated for an atmospheric pressure of 29.92 in. Hg. and a temperature of 15°C. and it cannot adjust for changes in density. You make the correction for altitude and temperature (air density) on the navigational computer. The importance of this correction is shown by the fact that, at very high altitudes, the true airspeed may be double the indicated airspeed.

## Use of the Airspeed Indicator

In climbs and descents, the airspeed indicator serves as a guide for controlling the attitude of the aircraft. Although in climbs and descents, the horizon indicator is the primary instrument, the airspeed indicator is important as a basic cross-check instrument in controlling the attitude of the aircraft. Predetermined power settings are used and aircraft attitude is controlled so as to obtain a predetermined airspeed.

The indicated airspeed at which an aircraft will stall is the same at any altitude or temperature. The airspeed indicator therefore provides a correct indication at all altitudes of safe flying speed. It indicates immediately, with very little lag, any change in aircraft speed. At times, there appears to be a lag in the airspeed indicator, after the aircraft has changed attitude. But that is not a lag in the indicator. It is the aircraft itself that is not changing airspeed as rapidly as expected because time is required to change the momentum of the aircraft.

The airspeed indicator is also a most useful instrument when flying through turbulent air. Reference to it permits the pilot to hold his airspeed within safe limits and, by varying the power setting, to maintain altitude.

## Airspeed and Mach Number Indicators

There are two types of instruments in

naval aircraft which indicate both airspeed and Mach number. The first of these uses a needle to indicate the *limiting airspeed* for the operating altitude, while the other uses a movable scale to allow the airspeed needle to show the *actual Mach number.* You must distinguish clearly between these two types, as their use is different.

The first type properly described is a Maximum Allowable Type Airspeed Indicator. The needle which shows the maximum allowable airspeed is adjusted to a specific maximum allowable airspeed at sea level on a standard day. Then, after proper adjustment, it indicates the maximum allowable airspeed for any altitude. As the aircraft climbs, the indication of the needle goes lower. This needle is moved by an aneroid diaphragm, which operates on atmospheric pressure; so in effect it is an altimeter scaled to show maximum allowable airspeed for the pressure altitude encountered. *It does not show actual Mach number at all.* Like the "red line" on conventional aircraft airspeed indicators, it shows just the maximum allowable airspeed.

The other type of airspeed Mach combination (Fig. 205) is mechanically similar. In this instrument, however, the aneroid unit rotates a movable dial so that at airspeeds in excess of 150 knots the single needle indicates both the airspeed on the fixed inner scale and the actual Mach number on the movable outer scale. As the altitude increases, the Mach scale moves so that the Mach indication reduces properly for the pressure altitude involved. The diaphragm which drives the needle and the aneroid diaphragm which drives the Mach scale are not connected to each other in any way. At low altitudes, the movable dial is masked by the stationary dial, which is graduated in knots.

The range of the instrument is 80 to 650 knots IAS and 0.5 to 2.0 Mach number,

Fig. 205. Airspeed and Mach-number indicator.

with a maximum operating limit of 50,000 feet. The instrument also incorporates a landing speed index and a Mach number setting index. You can set both indices manually through a knob at the lower left hand corner of the bezel. You can set the landing speed index from 80 to 145 knots by turning the knob in its normal out position. You can set the Mach limit anywhere in the entire Mach range by depressing the knob and turning it.

## VERTICAL-SPEED INDICATOR

The vertical-speed indicator, often called the rate-of-climb indicator, is of extreme value during smooth, precision instrument flying, as it provides the pilot with the first indication that a change of altitude is taking place. This is the secondary pitch-control instrument, the primary instrument being the horizon indicator. The vertical-speed indicator indicates the rate of climb or descent by measuring the rate of change in the atmospheric pressure.

In effect, the vertical-speed indicator consists of one air chamber inside another. The inside chamber is a diaphragm similar to the one used in the airspeed indicator. It expands when the inside air pressure becomes greater than the outside air pressure, and it contracts when the inside air pressure becomes less than the outside air pressure. The outer air chamber (the one around the diaphragm) is the airtight case of the instrument itself. The diaphragm is connected directly to the static line of the pitot-static system; therefore the air inside the diaphragm is at atmospheric pressure. The case is also connected to the static line but by a very small opening called a capillary tube.

When the atmospheric pressure is constant, the air pressure in the diaphragm and in the instrument case are equal. At this time the needle, which is connected to the flexible diaphragm, reads zero. As the atmospheric pressure changes, the pressure of the air in the diaphragm keeps up with the change, but the air in the case lags behind because it has to leak through the capillary tube to change toward the new pressure level. Thus, a differential pressure is established between the instantaneous static pressure in the diaphragm and the trapped static pressure in the case, and the diaphragm expands or contracts accordingly. A system of levers and gears transmits this expansion or contraction to the pointer to indicate the rate of pressure change as a descent or climb.

As you know, atmospheric pressure decreases at higher altitude. During a climb, therefore, the trapped pressure inside the case is higher than that of the atmosphere and higher than that in the diaphragm. Thus during a climb, the diaphragm contracts; during a descent, it expands. If the climb or descent is more rapid, the degree of contraction or expansion is greater and the pointer shows comparably greater rate of climb or descent. As the diaphragm approaches the limits of its ability to contract or expand, each thousand feet of additional vertical speed causes a smaller amount of con-

traction or expansion. That's why the face of the instrument (see Fig. 206) is calibrated to show each additional thousand feet of vertical speed as an ever-smaller unit on the dial.

The flow of air through the capillary tube is automatically controlled so that variations in air density due to changes in temperature and atmospheric pressure do not materially affect the indications of the instrument. (Note the interior view of a vertical speed indicator shown in Fig. 207.

Fig. 206. Virtical-speed indicator.

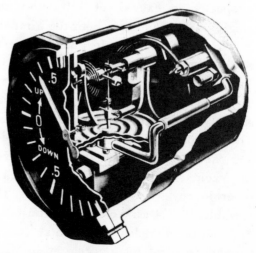

Fig. 207. Cutaway view of vertical-speed indicator.

The vertical-speed indicator is reliable whenever the rate of climb or descent is fairly constant. It usually reads correctly also when you have been flying level and begin a climb or descent; in these cases, though, there is a small lag before it indicates the full rate. However, when you have been climbing or descending and then level off or change the rate of vertical speed, there is a noticeable time lag before the instrument reads correctly.

The leak in the case is so calibrated that it maintains a definite ratio between the pressure in the diaphragm and the pressure in the case so long as a constant rate of climb (or descent) is maintained. When the aircraft levels off, though, it takes the calibrated leak from 6 to 9 seconds to equalize the pressure in the case with the pressure in the diaphragm. This causes a lag of from 6 to 9 seconds in the indications of the instrument. When the aircraft is descending, the pressure inside the diaphragm is increasing. Again, the calibrated leak maintains a constant relation between the pressure in the diaphragm and the pressure in the case.

The indications of the vertical-speed indicator are not reliable in extremely rough air or when the attitude of the aircraft is constantly changing. This is due in part to the lag in the instrument. Still, you can use the instrument to an advantage for indications of nose attitude if you have a thorough understanding of the instrument's lag and consider this lag in interpreting the indications.

Remember, though, that in a few aircraft equipped with the flush-type static air source, an abrupt movement of the aircraft or a change of power setting may cause momentary pressure changes at the point on the aircraft where the flush sources are located and momentary wrong indications on the vertical speed indicator and the altimeter. These erroneous readings are very brief. Do not "chase the needle." Wait for it to stabilize.

If the pointer does not read zero when the aircraft is on the ground, turn the zero adjustment screw or knob to correct the discrepancy.

## THE ALTIMETER

The importance of the altimeter cannot be overrated. Particularly important is the proper setting and reading of this instrument. Many aircraft accidents have been caused by faulty settings of the altimeter by the pilot. Some midair collisions, for example, can be attributed to failure to maintain the proper assigned altitude, because of improper settings. More recently there have been an increasing number of accidents caused by improper reading of the instrument—often 10,000-foot errors.

This chapter discusses only the barometric type of altimeter—one which measures altitude on the basis of the relationship between pressure and height in a standard atmosphere. The type of altimeter discussed here is like a barometer because it measures the weight of the air above it and calibrates this data in terms of feet of altitude.

The altimeter case is airtight except for one opening which is connected to the outside air through the static side of the pitot-static tube. The pressure in the static tube and in the case is always the atmospheric pressure just outside the aircraft. Inside the case is the diaphragm— the part of the instrument which is affected by changes of atmospheric pressure. It consists of one or more aneroids, or airtight cells, from which 99 percent of the air has been evacuated. The more airtight the cells involved, the more sensitivity is obtainable. As the pressure around the diaphragm (the atmospheric pressure) decreases, the diaphragm expands. As the pressure around the diaphragm (the at-

mospheric pressure), increases, the diaphragm contracts. The contraction or expansion of the diaphragm is transmitted
by a system of levers and gears to three
indicating hands on the face of the instrument.

*Reading the Altimeter*

There are many types of altimeter
dials in use. The same basic dial is
found on all of them, but some recent
changes may cause slight confusion at
first.

The old type, which is shown in Fig.
208, may still be found in a few aircraft.
The largest pointer shows the hundreds
of feet, each numeral indicating 100 feet;
the broad short pointer shows the thousands of feet, each numeral indicating
1,000 feet; and the little, slender pointer
shows the tens of thousands of feet, each
numeral indicating 10,000 feet. Thus, the
instrument dial shown in Fig. 208 reads
13,455 feet altitude. The altimeter setting
(30.3 in Hg.) shows in the small window.
This type of altimeter dial has been
abandoned because it is too hard to determine rapidly the thousands and tens of
thousands of feet, particularly the ten
thousands.

Fig. 208. Old-type altimeter dial.

This problem has been attacked by
two new altimeter dials. One uses a
larger 10,000-foot pointer which reaches

Fig. 209. MC-1 altimeter.

the edge of the dial, and it also has a
cross-hatched "flag" which shows when
the altitude is below 10,000 feet. The
other has no pointers except the hundred-
foot pointer and shows thousands of feet
as numerals.

The MB-2 (see Fig. 210) was developed
both as a new altimeter and as a conversion for older models. It has a cross-
hatched "flag" on the lower part of the
dial and, instead of a 10,000-foot needle,
it has a disk with a pointer extending out
to the edge of the dial. There is a hole
in the disk so located that at about 15,000
feet the edge of the flag just barely shows.
At altitudes below 10,000 feet the whole
flag shows.

The MC-1 (see Fig. 209) is probably
the easiest altimeter to read, though it
looks rather different when you first see
it. The single long pointer indicates

Fig. 210. MB-2 altimeter.

hundreds of feet only. Thousands of feet show as numerals in the window on the left side of the dial. Below 10,000 feet, the first numeral box shows a cross-hatched area, thus warning the pilot that he is below 10,000 feet.

*Determining Altitude*

An altimeter reading of 9,000 feet does not necessarily mean that you are at 9,000 feet. You are merely at an indicated altitude of 9,000 feet above mean sea level if your altimeter is set to the local pressure corrected to sea level. This is not necessarily your true altitude, nor is it your altitude above the terrain.

By definition, altitude is the vertical distance from some reference point. The following types of altitudes and reference points are important to you.

TRUE ALTITUDE is the height above sea level.

ABSOLUTE ALTITUDE is the height above terrain.

PRESSURE ALTITUDE is the height, or vertical distance, from the standard datum plane. This is a theoretical plane where the air pressure (corrected to plus 15° C.) is equal to 29.92 inches of mercury.

DENSITY ALTITUDE is pressure altitude corrected for temperature When conditions are standard, the pressure altitude and the density altitude are the same; if the temperature is *above* standard, the density altitude is *higher* than the pressure altitude; if the temperature is *below* standard, the density altitude is *lower* than the pressure altitude.

The first step in determining your actual altitude, whether true, absolute, or pressure, is to determine your *calibrated altitude*. All pressure altimeters are subject to small errors due to the effect of the temperature on the various metals of the instrument. The corrections to be applied to the dial reading to compensate for these effects are shown on a calibra-

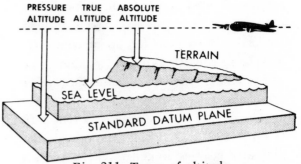

Fig. 211. Types of altitude.

tion card which should be posted near the altimeter. By applying the appropriate correction to the indicated altitude you get the calibrated altitude. However, unless extreme accuracy is required, or if there is no calibration card, you may substitute indicated altitude for calibrated altitude when you correct for free-air temperature in determining the actual altitude by use of the E-6D computer.

*Setting the Altimeter*

The various factors of sea-level pressures and temperatures require frequent calculation to determine true altitude. If the pilots of two approaching aircraft had computed their true altitude on different pressure-temperature data because of the different areas through which they had flown, it would be very hazardous for them to attempt to pass. To achieve vertical clearance, therefore, all aircraft in an area are given an arbitrary pressure level known as an altimeter setting. The weather officer computes the altimeter setting by use of the barographs and scale, every 30 minutes for sequence reports and on request. The altimeter setting may be generally defined as the pressure in inches of mercury of the reporting station corrected to sea-level pressure.

Setting the pressure scale to the altimeter setting causes the altimeter to read indicated altitude. Flying indicated altitude ensures traffic separation, since in passing, the different altimeters are equally affected by whatever pressure and temperature conditions may exist. You need not make allowance for nonstandard atmospheric conditions but must keep your altimeter adjusted to the latest altimeter setting

The danger of this system is that safe terrain clearance is not guaranteed; the indicated reading is generally the correct altitude only when the aircraft is about to land at the airport from which the setting was furnished. To determine adequate terrain clearance, you must allow for possible errors in your indicated altitude, such as mechanical errors, temperature errors, change of pressure from the time the altimeter setting was computed to the time it is used, and the difference in pressure between the position of the aircraft and the station which reports the altimeter setting. During instrument flight and under conditions of poor visibility, it is very important that you frequently reset your altimeter to the latest altimeter setting which you can obtain from a range station or control tower. Look at Fig. 212 and you can see the need for doing this, particularly when flying from a high-pressure area into an area of lower pressure.

In flying between shore stations, using the corrected local pressure as the altimeter setting provides the greatest accuracy and safety. The altitude always represents an indicated altitude value for the approximate local pressure, provided you obtain current settings as you travel. Over oceans, however, a different system is used because there are no terrain obstructions and it is not important to maintain the indicated altitude as near to actual altitude. Prevention of mid-air collisions is the only serious problem. Therefore, trans-oceanic flights are conducted on pressure altitude. As soon as the plane is clear of land, the altimeter is set to 29.92. By proper assignment of pressure altitude flight levels, collisions are avoided.

Sometimes local instructions direct use of field pressure instead of the altimeter setting for local training or tactical flights. The altimeter is adjusted to read zero before take-off, regardless of field elevation. The setting window will then show uncorrected local pressure (uncorrected for field elevation.) Do not use such settings in flight from one field to another.

*Temperature Correction*

Since pressure altimeters are pressure gages calibrated in feet on the basis of a standard pressure-altitude relationship, nonstandard atmospheric conditions will make their readings inherently wrong. On a warm day, the air expands and weighs less per unit volume than on a standard or colder day; so it is necessary to climb an additional 550 feet to reach the pressure level that will indicate 10,000 feet on a standard day. Much more dangerous to the pilot is the cold day. On a cold day, when you reach a pressure level that

LOW PRESSURE AREA

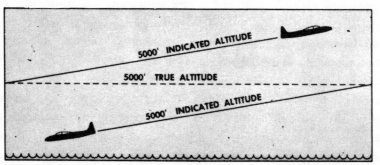

5000' INDICATED ALTITUDE

5000' TRUE ALTITUDE

5000' INDICATED ALTITUDE

HIGH PRESSURE AREA

Fig. 212. The effect of pressure on altitude.

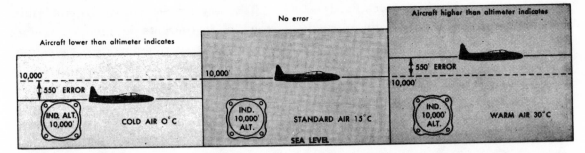

Fig. 213. Inherent altimeter error due to temperature changes.

indicates 10,000 feet, you are actually flying several hundred feet lower.

### Altimeter Errors

A particularly important source of error may be the altimeter itself. The scale may not be correctly oriented to standard pressure conditions. Altimeters should be checked periodically for scale errors in altitude test chambers where standard conditions exist. Large errors should be removed mechanically; small errors should be recorded on the calibration card.

Another type of error is due to lag. The altimeter may tend to lag, particularly when large changes of altitude are made. This type of error, which is called "hysteresis" or "after effect," varies with the climb and descent. When an altimeter is taken aloft, to 19,000 feet for example, the indicated reading will be slightly low, gradually increasing as time passes. This increase, called "drift," is due to the elastic characteristics of the diaphragm. On the ground, it is loaded in a state of equilibrium by the heavier pressures of ground level, and it requires time to reach a state of equilibrium under the lighter pressures at 19,000 feet. Likewise, if it remains at altitude for several hours, the instrument reads slightly high on descending and gradually decreases, or "recovers" over a period of time.

Friction is also a possible source of error. Regardless of construction, all mechanical devices are subject to friction error, and the altimeter is no exception.

Still another cause of error is the effect of varying temperatures on different metals of the altimeter, mentioned before in connection with calibrated altitude. The calibration card should provide for these errors. It cannot provide, however, for errors due to improper installation, damage, icing, or clogging of the pitot-static tube. The different positions, or attitudes, that the altimeter assumes in flight may also be a possible cause for error; however, the use of counterweights in construction has largely eliminated incorrect readings due to the position of the instrument or any of its parts.

### Using the Altimeter

During instrument flight along airways, you maintain flight altitude by flying indicated altitude. To be sure of terrain clearance, though, you must correct the indicated altitude for instrument and temperature errors. When you fly from an area of high pressure to an area of low pressure, the actual altitude becomes lower than the indicated altitude, creating a dangerous situation; so keep the barometric scale of the altimeter set to the latest altimeter setting. When you fly through air colder than standard, the actual altitude becomes lower than the indicated altitude; calculate your true altitude by using the E-6D computer.

At higher altitudes, different altimeters do not read alike because of differences in construction and scale errors. Different aircraft models show variations caused by different static air sources, and individual altimeters may vary by as much as 800 feet. Pilots flying formation, therefore, should cross check between themselves and adjust their altimeters to an average of the various instruments. For the same reason, ATC assigns flight altitudes over 29,000 feet at 2,000-foot intervals instead of 1,000-foot intervals.

DON'T IGNORE DENSITY ALTITUDE. It determines the power output of your engine and becomes especially important in take-off. The Operating Handbook tells you how many feet of runway are needed for take-off at different altitudes, but these are density altitudes. Density altitude is the altitude for which a given air density exists in the standard atmosphere. If the barometric pressure is lower or the temperature is higher than standard, then the density altitude of the field is higher than its actual elevation. Every pilot knows this through observation of its effect; on hot days your plane requires more take-off runway and doesn't climb so well as usual. The effect is greater, however, than you may realize.

## GYRO-SUCTION INSTRUMENTS

The gyroscope of a gyro-suction instrument is driven by air sucked in by an engine-driven vacuum pump. Multi-engine aircraft usually have more than one pump. In any event, operation of this set of instruments depends on the proper operation of the vacuum system. Pump failure shows in the form of reduced pressure on the vacuum gage, usually regulated to 4 in. Hg. Since the air must be filtered before entering the delicate gyro mechanism, a clogged filter also shows as a pressure drop on the vacuum gage if there is a master filter. If the aircraft has individual filters on each instrument, as in older aircraft, the individual instrument with a clogged filter will operate improperly but the vacuum gage will provide no clue.

The key to the construction of this group of instruments is the gyro motor, which may be suction-operated or electrically operated. Therefore each of these instruments is also made in an electrically operated version, which is discussed in the next chapter.

Although the electric-type gyros are more likely to fail, they do operate under conditions which the suction-type cannot master. Aircraft vacuum pumps cannot maintain an adequate pressure differential between the atmospheric pressure and the vacuum line at altitudes above about 30,000 feet; the temperatures below -35° F. also make vacuum-driven gyroscopes unreliable. Therefore, jet and other high-altitude aircraft are usually equipped with electric gyro-instruments. To understand either type of gyro instruments, you must first understand the principle of the gyroscope.

## THE GYROSCOPE

Any spinning object exhibits gyroscopic properties, but only a wheel designed and mounted to utilize these properties is called a gyroscope. A gyroscope is a spinning wheel, or rotor, which is universally mounted—that is, mounted so that the spin axis can assume any direction in space. The mountings of the gyro wheels, called "gimbals," may be circular rings, rectangular frames, or, in flight instruments, a part of the instrument case itself. Note, in Fig. 216, that the rotor is free to spin about axis x-x on bearings in the inner ring or gimbal; the inner gimbal is free to turn about axis y-y on pivots in the outer gimbal; and the outer gimbal is free to turn about axis z-z on pivots in the support. Such a rotor is said to have three planes of freedom. It is free to rotate in any plane in relation to the base and is so balanced, that with the gyro wheel at rest, it will remain in any position in which it is placed. Restricted or semi-

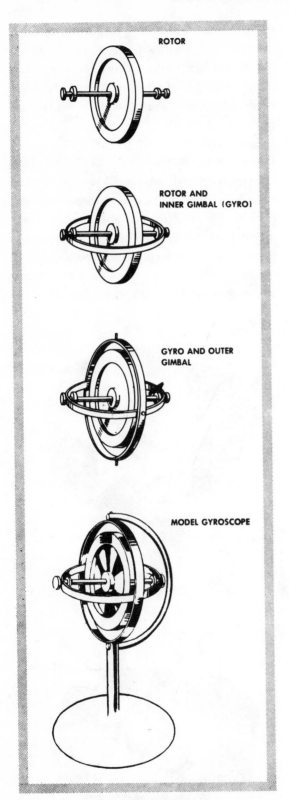

Fig. 214. Primary elements of a standard gyroscope.

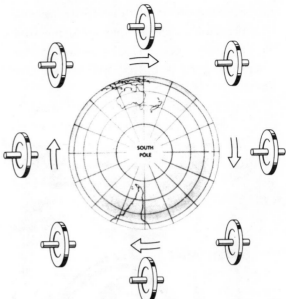

Fig. 215. Action of a freely mounted gyroscope.

Of course, the gyroscope illustrated in Fig. 214 is only a model. Two important design characteristics of a regular instrument gyro are great weight, or high density, for its size and rotation at high speeds with low-friction bearings.

*Properties of Gyroscopic Action*

All practical applications of the gyro are based on two fundamental properties of gyroscopic action—rigidity in space, and precession.

RIGIDITY IN SPACE. When the rotor of a gyro is spinning, it has the ability to remain in its original plane of rotation regardless of how the base is moved. However, since it is impossible to have bearings without some friction, there is some deflective force upon the wheel.

PRECESSION. An operating gyro resists a force which attempts to change the direction of its spin axis, but it moves in response to such a force or pressure. The movement is not a direct one in response to the force; it is a resultant movement. The gyro axis is displaced, not in the direction of the applied force, but at right angles to the applied force, and in such a way as to tend to cause the direc-

rigidly mounted gyros are those so mounted that one of the planes of freedom is held fixed in relation to the base.

tion of the rotation of the rotor to assume the direction of the torque resulting from the applied force. This property of an operating gyro is called gyroscopic precession.

For example, when a force is applied upward on the inner gimbal, as shown in Fig. 216, it is as if the same force were applied to the rim of the rotor at F. (See Fig. 217.) The force at F is opposed by

the resistance of the gyroscopic inertia, preventing the rotor from being displaced about the axis y-y. However, with the rotor spinning clockwise, the precession takes place 90° ahead in the direction of rotation at P. (See Fig. 218.) The rotor turns about axis z-z in the direction of the arrow at P. (See Fig. 219). The rate at which the wheel precesses is proportional to the deflective force applied (minus the friction in the gimbal ring, pivots and bearings.) If too great a deflective force is applied for the amount of rigidity in the wheel, the wheel precesses and topples over at the same time.

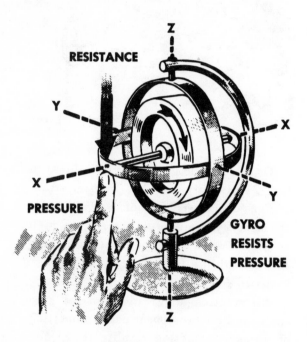

Fig. 216. Force applied to a gyro.

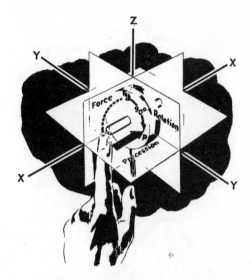

Fig. 218. Direction of precession.

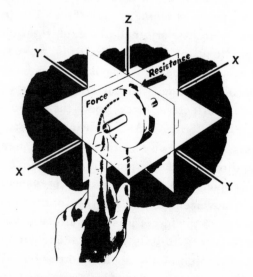

Fig. 217. Transmission of force.

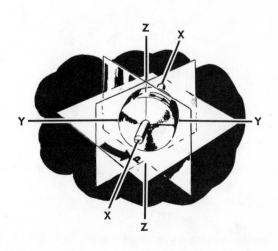

Fig. 219. Precessional movement.

It is this property of gyroscopic precession as well as the property of rigidity, or gyroscopic inertia, that are utilized in gyroscopic instruments. Gyroscopic inertia establishes a reference in space unaffected by any movement of the supporting body. Precession is utilized to control the effects of drift, whether it is apparent drift or mechanical drift; it maintains the reference in the required position.

DRIFT. A free gyro (one not provided with an erection system) maintains its axis fixed in relation to space, and not in relation to the surface of the earth. For example, imagine such a gyro at the equator, starting with the spin axis horizontal and pointed in an east-west direction. The earth turns in a west-to-east direction with an angular velocity of one revolution every 24 hours. To an observer out in space, the spin axis of the gyro would appear to maintain its direction pointing east.

However to an observer on the earth, stationed where the gyro is, the spin axis would appear gradually to tilt or drift. At the end of three hours the spin axis would have tilted 45°; at the end of six hours, the spin axis would have tilted 90° and would be in a vertical position. At the end of 12 hours the spin axis would be horizontal again but pointing west; at the end of 24 hours it would be back where it started. (See Fig. 220.) This action of a free gyro is known as apparent drift. To overcome apparent drift as well as mechanical drift caused by bearing friction or slight unbalance, a gyroscopic instrument must be provided with an erecting device which maintains the spin axis in the required position. This erecting device applies a force to the gyro whenever drift occurs. Precession returns the spin axis to its normal position, maintaining an accurate reference. (See Fig. 221)

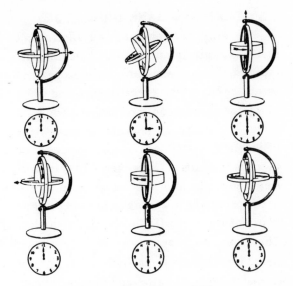

Fig. 220. Apparent drift.

Fig. 221. Precession controlling drift.

*Gyro Instruments*

The three basic gyro instruments are the turn-and-bank indicator, the heading indicator, and the horizon indicator. The turn-and-bank indicator utilizes the gyroscopic property of precession and is a semi-rigidly mounted instrument. The heading indicator is freely mounted; it utilizes the gyroscopic property of rigidity in space to establish a reference plane and the gyroscopic property of precession to maintain the vertical axis of the rotor perpendicular to the earth's surface.

## TURN-AND-BANK INDICATOR

The only suction-operated instrument still maintained on most new naval aircraft is the turn-and-bank indicator. This is not because the electric turn-and-bank indicator is no good but, rather, because it is necessary to provide a means for emergency instrument flight in case of electrical failure. However, this instrument now plays a secondary role. It is used primarily for cross-checking other instruments or for flight on partial panel. Therefore, many new aircraft have a two-inch instead of three-inch dial on the turn-and-bank indicator, and the instrument is placed in a less central position on the panel.

The turn-and-bank indicator was one of the first modern instruments to be used for controlling an aircraft without visual reference to the ground or horizon. It is a combination of two instruments, a ball and a turn needle. The ball part of the instrument is directly actuated, while the turn indicator depends on the gyroscopic property of precession for its indications.

*The Ball*

The ball part of the turn-and-bank indicator consists of a sealed, curved glass tube containing water-white kerosene and a black agate or common steel ball-bearing which is free to move inside the tube. The fluid provides a dampening action and insures smooth and easy movement of the ball. The tube is curved so that when it is held in a horizontal position the ball has a natural tendency to seek the lowest point, which is the center. A small projection on the left end of the tube contains a bubble of air which compensates for expansion of the fluid during changes in temperature. Two strands of safety wire are wound around the glass tube as reference markers to indicate the correct position of the ball in the tube. The plate to which the tube is fastened and the

reference wires are usually painted with a luminous paint.

Fig. 222. Turn-and-bank indicator.

The natural forces acting on the ball in straight-and-level flight are: (1) gravity, which acts toward the center of the earth, and (2) the force exerted by the bottom of the tube which is always perpendicular to the tangent at the point of contact. It acts from the point where the ball makes contact with the tube through the center of the ball.

In a coordinated turn, the natural forces acting on the ball are: (1) gravity which pulls toward the center of the earth, (2) the force exerted by the bottom of the tube, and (3) centrifugal force which acts in the horizontal plane and outward from the center of turn.

The ball assumes a position between the reference markers when the resultant of centrifugal force and gravity acts midway between the reference markers. When the forces acting on the ball become unbalanced, the ball moves away from the center of the tube.

In a skid, the rate of turn is too great for the angle of bank. The centrifugal force is excessive, and the resultant of centrifugal force and gravity is not opposite the mid-point between the reference markers, but toward the outside of the turn. Consequently, the ball moves in that direction. Correcting to coordinated flight calls for increasing the bank or decreasing the rate of turn, or a combination of both.

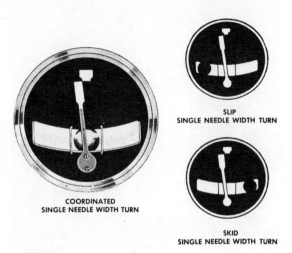

Fig. 223. Indications of the turn-and-bank indicator.

In a slip, the rate of turn is too slow for the angle of bank. There is not enough centrifugal force, and the resultant of centrifugal force and gravity causes the ball to move toward the inside of the turn. Correcting to coordinated flight requires decreasing the bank or increasing the rate of turn, or a combination of both.

The ball instrument serves to check your coordination. It is actually a "balance" indicator, because it indicates the relationship between the angle of bank and the rate of turn. It tells you the "quality" of the turn; whether the aircraft has the correct angle of bank for its rate of turn.

### The Turn Needle

The turn needle is actuated by a gyro. A restrictor valve to control the suction on the turn needle gyro is installed between the main suction line and the instrument. On the older systems, the restrictor valve control is behind the instrument panel and is not accessible to the pilot. Newer-model aircraft have a valve control on the instrument panel, which enables you to adjust the suction on the turn needle while in flight. On some models, the suction gage may also be switched to the turn needle, enabling you to know the actual suction on the instrument.

The desired vacuum on the turn-and-bank indicator is 1.9 to 2.0 inches of mercury (Hg); it should be set between the limits of 1.8 in. Hg and 2.1 in. Hg.

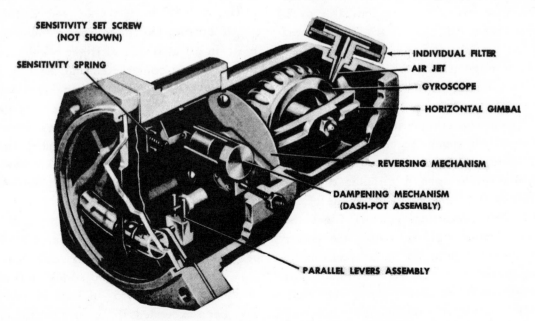

Fig. 224. Cutaway view of turn-and-bank indicator.

Low vacuum causes a lower rotor rpm and reduces the indication from what it would be if the rotor rpm were within limits. High vacuum causes the deflection to be greater than normal.

The turn needle indicates the rate (number of degrees per second) at which the aircraft is turning about its vertical axis. By using the turn-and-bank indicator, you can check for coordination and balance in straight flight and in turns. If you cross-check this instrument against the airspeed indicator, you can determine the relation between the lateral axis of the aircraft and the horizon (angle of bank). For any given airspeed there is a definite angle of bank necessary to maintain a coordinated turn at a given rate.

## GYRO HEADING INDICATOR

The gyro heading indicator is a suction-operated directional gyro. It is fundamentally an instrument designed to facilitate the use of the magnetic compass. Any pilot can imagine the difficulties he would have to contend with in instrument flying if he had to depend for directional information solely on the magnetic compass. The gyro-driven heading indicator overcomes these difficulties. It is not affected by the centrifugal force of turns, by rough air, by magnetic disturbances, or, within certain limits, by the orientation of the aircraft.

The instrument operates on the principle of rigidity in space of a universally mounted gyroscope. The rotor turns in the vertical plane, and a circular compass fixed at right angles to the plane of the rotor (to the vertical gimbal). Since the rotor remains rigid in space, the points on the card hold the same position in space relative to the vertical plane. The case simply revolves about the card. During turns, of course, the rotor may deviate from the vertical plane of rota-

tion, but the erecting mechanism quickly returns the rotor to its normal plane of rotation.

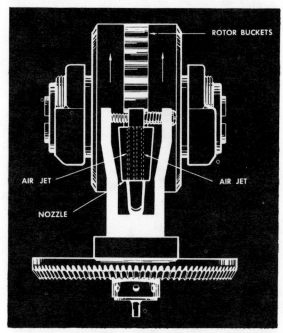

Fig. 225. Heading indicator gyro rotor and nozzle assembly.

The heading indicator can operate properly with a suction gage reading as low as 3.5 in. Hg or as high as 5.0 in. Hg, but the limits used for adjustment should be between 3.75 in. Hg and 4.25 in Hg, with 4.0 in Hg the desired reading.

Of course, the instrument cannot operate in all attitudes of flight because of the way it is constructed and the way it operates. The stop or limiting factor in the instrument is the caging arm. In the uncaged position, the caging arm rests on the bottom of the vertical gimbal ring and in that position restricts the movement of the vertical gimbal ring about the rotor or the horizontal gimbal.

The limits of operation of the instrument, for all practical purposes, are 55° of pitch and 55° of bank. *On some headings*, though, the gyro does not spill or tumble even though 55° of bank or pitch have been exceeded. If the rotor is aligned with the longitudinal axis of the aircraft, it will not tumble even though the pitch attitude of the aircraft exceeds 55°.

When the horizontal gimbal touches the stop, the precessional force causes the card to spin rapidly. You can correct this by caging and uncaging the instrument.

No gyroscope yet designed has eliminated precession from the original plane of rotation. In the gyro heading indicator, this precession causes the card to drift, or creep, away from the true reading. The chief cause of creep or drift is friction. An unbalanced condition of the gimbal ring also causes errors. If the gyro unit is out of balance, there is a force applied to the rotor which causes precession.

Another cause of error is the effect of the rotation of the earth, which causes a universally mounted gyroscope to precess, the amount depending on the position of the aircraft. At the equator there is no effect. Above and below the equator, the precession increases according to the distance from the equator in opposite directions in the Northern and Southern Hemispheres. The effect of the earth's rotation is counteracted by balancing the gimbal rings. Then, so long as the plane flies somewhere near the same latitude, there is no problem. However, in a flight entailing great changes of latitude the error would become apparent, particularly if the equator were crossed. If the instrument were corrected for error in the Northern Hemisphere and flown in the Southern Hemisphere, the error and correction would act in the same direction, and cause a noticeable amount of creep.

When considering the errors in this instrument, it is well to remember that error in the heading indicator is frequently the result of an improper setting from the magnetic compass. Incidentally, you adjust the card of the heading indicator by means of the caging mechanism. This rotates the vertical gimbal by gears or a clutch, depending on the design of the particular model.

Before take-off, ground check the heading indicator to determine whether it is operating properly. To do this, first see that there is sufficient vacuum. While the engine is warming up, check whether the rotor is turning by first caging and then uncaging the instrument with a gentle twisting motion. If the rotor is turning, the card will stop as soon as the instrument is uncaged. To assure the proper speed of operation, allow the gyroscope to run up for five minutes before take-off. During taxiing, you can check the gyro headings if the limits are exceeded and the gyro is indicating large amounts of creep. The gyro heading indicator is extremely useful during take-off under instrument conditions since it is not affected by the acceleration of the aircraft.

During flight, the gyro heading indicator is used to maintain straight flight and make turns to headings. Whether you set the card with the compass or use the heading of zero, you use the magnetic compass as the reference. Be careful in reading the compass. Unless you check the compass deviation card, the indicator may appear to drift several degrees during a turn. *Check the gyro heading indicator at least every 15 minutes against the magnetic compass.* After setting the instrument, uncage it by pulling the caging knob straight out. If there is an error of more than 3° in a period of 15 minutes, turn in a "squawk."

During maneuvers which exceed the limits of the instrument, it should be caged. At all other times the instrument may be left uncaged. It is obvious that frequent aerobatic flight with the instrument uncaged shortens the life of the gyro unit. A great deal of force is applied to the bearings if the limits are exceeded and the gyro is "spilled."

## SUCTION-OPERATED HORIZON INDICATOR

The suction-operated horizon indicator is virtually obsolete. It is generally found only in aircraft manufactured before 1950. This manual will therefore not discuss the theory and construction of this instrument in any detail. Like all horizon indicators, it has a horizon bar which moves in such a way that the position of the miniature airplane in relation to the horizon bar corresponds to the position of the aircraft in relation to the actual horizon.

which is held level by the gyro. The bank of the aircraft is thus accurately reflected by the bank of the miniature airplane in relation to the horizon bar. The pitch of the airplane is indicated by the vertical position of the minature airplane in relation to the horizontal bar.

The basic mechanism of the instrument is a freely mounted gyroscope which always remains in a constant plane relative to the earth when the instrument is operating. This gyro is driven by suction which should be within 0.25 in Hg. of the desired vacuum of 4.0 in. Hg.

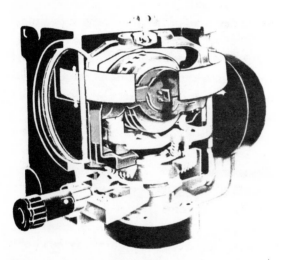

Fig. 226. Cutaway view of suction-driven heading indicator.

Fig. 227. Suction-operated horizon indicator.

The miniature airplane is supported from the base on the front of the case and is approximately in the center of the instrument face. The horizon bar is supported by an arm which extends back on the right side of the instrument to a pivot at the back of the horizontal frame. The pivot allows the horizon bar to move up and down but allows it no lateral motion.

The horizon bar is held constantly horizontal since the frame on which it is mounted is held horizontal laterally by the gyro. In other words, the miniature airplane moves with the case and with the actual airplane around the horizon bar

The gyro rotor and gyro housing can be held rigidly in a horizontal plane with respect to the instrument case by use of the caging mechanism. To cage the gyro, pull the caging knob on the face of the instrument and turn it clockwise as far as it will go; then push in. To uncage, pull the knob and then turn it counterclockwise as far as it will go; then push the knob in.

The limits of the horizon indicator are determined by its construction—100° of bank, and 70° of pitch. Maneuvers in excess of these limitations cause the gyro to precess violently, upset, and become useless. It remains useless until it erects itself or is caged and then uncaged in level flight.

*Errors*

The horizon indicator is subject to slight errors in both bank and pitch due to the effect of the erecting mechanism in a turn. The bank and pitch errors are greatest in a slow turn and after 180° of turn. The indications should return to normal after 360° turn.

The bank error causes the instrument to indicate slightly less than the actual amount of bank during a turn, or a slight bank in the opposite direction after level flight has been resumed. The pitch error causes the horizon bar to dip slightly below its correct position for level flight. This error is small; however, if you follow the indications of the horizon indicator in slow turns without reference to other instruments, you may enter a gradual descent and, in time, lose considerable altitude. The action of the erecting mechanism corrects these bank and pitch errors in a short time after level flight has been resumed.

Acceleration can also give wrong indications by causing the erection mechanism to react in such a way as to make the horizon bar move downward. This results in a tendency to dive the aircraft while accelerating. Deceleration has the opposite effect—causing the horizon bar to move upward. Both these errors are proportional to the amount of acceleration or deceleration and to the elapsed time involved.

Other errors in the indications of the instrument may be caused by precession of the gyro as a result of worn or dirty gimbal bearings or an out-of-balance condition in any of the moving parts. A loss of vacuum due to dirty filters or other causes will also keep the instrument from operating properly.

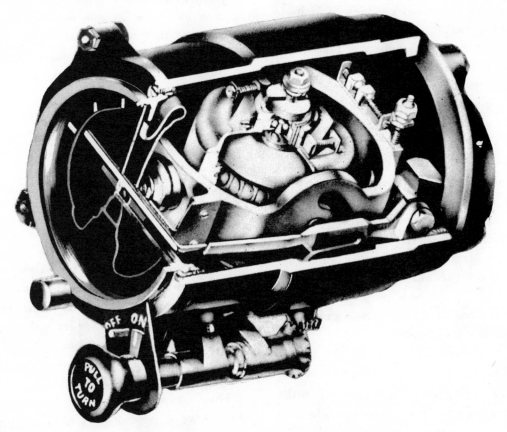

Fig. 228. Cutaway view of horizon indicator.

*Using the Horizon Indicator*

Because of frequent errors of indication, it is necessary to coordinate the suction-driven horizon indicator with the other flight instruments. In straight-and-level flight, the pilot who relies too much on the suction-driven horizon indicator will most likely find his flight erratic. You must therefore cross-check it with the turn-and-bank indicator, heading indicator, and altimeter. In turns, the pitch error causes an improper attitude to be shown by the instrument. Constant cross-checking with the other instruments is again necessary. In climbs and descents, the acceleration and deceleration of the aircraft causes pitch error. You must take this into consideration in order to have a proper attitude for the maneuver.

In addition, remember that the indications of the horizon indicator are only approximations of the exact pitch attitude, because of the small changes of attitude caused by variation in the airspeed, load, and air density. To help you take these changes into account, the instrument has an adjustment knob with which the miniature aircraft may be moved upward or downward inside the case.

*Caging the Instrument*

When the limits of the instrument are exceeded, it will spill or tumble. You must avoid this because it brings a force to bear against the rotor which produces very violent precession until the opposite limit is reached and there is an abrupt stop in the precession. This may result in cracked, flattened, or loosened bearings, any one of which causes excessive friction and precession.

If you expect to exceed the limits, therefore, you should cage the instrument, although flying with the instrument in the caged position does cause considerably more than normal wear. Exceeding the limits of the horizon indicator may be compared to driving an automobile into a stone wall; flying with the instrument caged can be compared to stopping the same automobile by slamming on the brakes before hitting the stone wall. You avoid immediate damage but you do cause excessive wear.

The suction-driven horizon indicator should be uncaged only in level flight. The indications of the instrument depend on the position of its universally mounted gyro, and if you uncage it in an unlevel attitude, it tends to remain in an unlevel plane, except for the action of the erecting mechanism. When uncaging the instrument, be sure that it is fully uncaged. If you're not careful to see that this is done, the clamps in the caging mechanism will decrease the maneuvering limits, and the instrument will spill even in a normally safe maneuver.

Be particularly careful in caging the horizon indicator. Rough, forceful caging causes the instrument to be spilled many times. The damaging results similar to those caused by exceeding the limits of the instrument caged wears it excessively; therefore, it should be caged only when the limits are to be exceeded.

In summary, remember that the horizon indicator is the most realistic attitude instrument on the panel and its indications are close approximations of the actual attitude of the aircraft itself. Don't be too concerned with its errors. Just remember what they are and take them into account in interpreting its indications. Finally, remember that the instrument should always be left uncaged unless its limits are to be exceeded.

## MAGNETIC INSTRUMENTS

This chapter discusses instruments which have a more-or-less auxiliary role in instrument flight, but which are nevertheless important.

Fig. 229. Magnetic compass.

*Magnetism and Magnetic Fields*

A simple bar magnet has two centers of magnetism which are called poles. Lines of force flow out from each pole in all directions, eventually bending around and returning to the other pole. The area through which these lines of force flow is called the field of the magnet. The poles usually are designated *north* and *south*. If you place two bar magnets near each other, the north pole of one will attract the south pole of the other.

There is a magnetic field surrounding the earth, too. It acts very much as though there were a huge bar magnet running along the axis of the earth with its ends several hundred miles below the surface. However, the magnetic and geographic poles of the earth do not coincide. The north magnetic pole is located in Baffinland at 73° N., 96° W., and the south magnetic pole at 72° S., 155° E.

The lines of force in the earth's magnetic field are parallel to the earth's surface at the magnetic equator but point increasingly downward when moving toward the magnetic poles themselves. Speaking technically, the lines of force have a vertical component which is zero at the equator but builds up to 100 percent of the total force at the poles. If a magnetic needle is held along these lines of force, this vertical component causes a dip of the needle, a deflection downward. It is this deflection which causes some of the larger compass errors.

## PANEL-TYPE MAGNETIC COMPASS

The panel-type magnetic compass is simple in construction. It contains two steel magnetized needles mounted on a float around which is mounted the compass card. The needles are parallel, with their north-seeking ends pointed in the same direction. The compass card has letters for cardinal headings, and number every

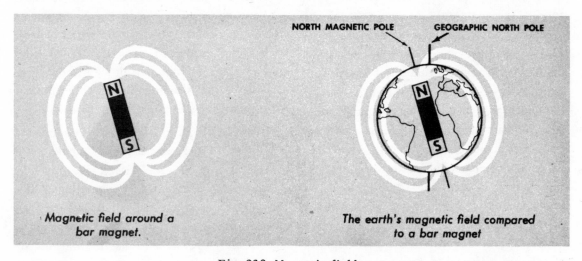

Magnetic field around a bar magnet.

The earth's magnetic field compared to a bar magnet

Fig. 230. Magnetic fields.

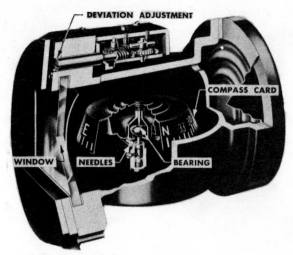

Fig. 231. Cutaway and front view of panel-type
magnetic compass.

30° in between. The last zero of the degree indication is omitted. Between these numbers the card is graduated for each 5°.

The float assembly, which consists of the magnetized needles, compass card, and float is housed in a bowl filled with acid-free white kerosene. This liquid dampens out excessive oscillations of the compass card, and its buoyancy relieves part of the weight of the float from the bearings. The liquid also provides lubrication and prevents rust within the instrument case.

On the bottom of the bowl is a pedestal on which the float rests. Jewel bearings are used to mount the float assembly on top of the pedestal. At the rear of the compass bowl there is a diaphragm to allow for any expansion or contraction of the liquid and prevent the formation of bubbles or possible bursting of the case.

The glass face of the compass is an integral part of the bowl and has mounted behind it a lubber line, or reference line, by which compass indicators are read. If the face is broken, the fluid is lost and the compass becomes inoperative. On top of the compass is a compensating device consisting of several small bar magnets which are adjustable by two set-screws

labeled N-S for north-south and E-W for east west.

*Compass Errors*

VARIATION. In navigation, course computations on aeronautical charts are based on the relation of the course to the true geographic North Pole. The magnetic compass, however, points to magnetic north—not to the true North Pole. The angular difference between true and magnetic north is known as variation. It is different for different spots on the earth. Lines of equal magnetic variation are called isogonic lines and are plotted on aeronautical charts with the amounts shown in degrees of variation east or west. A line connecting the 0° points of variation is termed the agonic line. These lines are replotted periodically to take care of any change which may occur as a result of the shifting of the poles or any changes in local magnetic deposits.

DEVIATION. Electrical equipment mounted in the aircraft and accessories made of iron or steel, such as guns and armor plate, may affect the reading of the magnetic compass. The difference between the indications of a compass on a particular aircraft and the indications of an unaffected compass at the same point

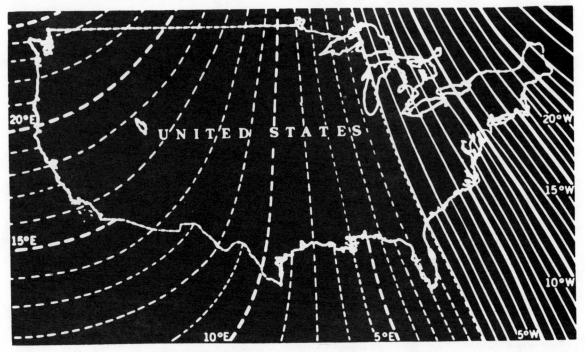

Fig. 232. Magnetic variation in the United
States.

on the earth's surface is called deviation. To counteract the magnetic effect of the aircraft equipment and reduce this deviation, compensating magnets on the compass are adjusted as follows:

On a surveyed compass rose, the aircraft is pointed toward magnetic north and compensated with the N-S screw until the compass reads correctly. This is repeated on a heading of east, and the error is adjusted by use of the E-W screw. On headings of south and west, half the error is taken out by adjusting the compensating screws. Then the compass is swung through 360°, and the errors at each 30° mark are noted. These remaining errors are entered on the compass deviation card in the cockpit.

Deviation may change for each piece of electrical equipment turned on. In addition, the magnetism of the aircraft itself may change as a result of severe jolts. Therefore, it is necessary to swing the compass periodically and prepare a new correction card. Deviation also changes with latitude, so the compass should be swung on arrival at a new base of materially different latitude from the old base.

MAGNETIC DIP. The tendency of the magnetic compass to point down as well as north in certain latitudes is known as magnetic dip. This is responsible for the northerly and southerly turning error as well as the acceleration and deceleration error on headings of east and west.

At the magnetic equator, the vertical component of the earth's magnetic field is zero and the magnetic compass is not disturbed by this factor. As you fly from the magnetic equator to the higher latitudes, the effect of the vertical component of the earth's magnetic field becomes pronounced.

This tendency is not noticed in straight-and-level unaccelerated flight because the compass card is mounted in such a way that its center of gravity is below the pivot point and the card is well balanced in the fluid.

When the aircraft is banked, however, the compass card banks, too, as a result of the centrifugal force acting on it. While the compass card is in this banked attitude in northern latitudes, the vertical component of the earth's magnetic field causes the north-seeking ends of the compass to dip to the low side of the turn, giving the pilot an erroneous turn indication. This error called northerly turning error, is most apparent on headings of north and south. In a turn from a heading of north, the compass briefly gives an indication of a turn in the opposite direction; in a turn from a heading of south, it gives an indication of a turn in the proper direction but at a more rapid rate than is actually the case. In southern latitudes, all these errors are reversed. They are called southerly turning error.

ACCELERATION ERROR. Acceleration error is also due to the action of the vertical component of the earth's magnetic field. Because of its pendulous-type mounting, the compass card is tilted during changes of speed. This deflection of the card from the horizontal results in an error which is most apparent on headings of east and west. When the aircraft is accelerating or climbing on either of these headings, the error is in the form of an indication of a turn to the north; when the aircraft is decelerating or descending the error is in the form of an indication of a turn to the south. Acceleration error is constantly present during climb and descent.

OSCILLATION ERROR. Oscillation error is due to the erratic swinging of the compass card, probably the result of rough air or rough pilot technique. The fluid serves to reduce this oscillation.

The magnetic compass, if you understand its errors and characteristics thoroughly, offers you a reliable means of determining the direction in which your aircraft is headed. When reading the compass to determine direction, be sure that the aircraft is as steady as possible, is not in a turn, and is flying at a constant airspeed.

## Uses of the Panel Compass

In modern aircraft, the panel compass is principally a standby instrument. It is used for training or cross-check purposes and when an electrical or other failure renders the remote-indicating compass or salved gyro heading indicator useless.

One of the principal reasons for its reduced importance is the large and variable amount of deviation present, especially near the panel. Electrical and electronic gear, armament, and nose landing gear create deviation errors which vary as that equipment is used, and the compass correction card cannot allow for all possible variations in the amount of deviation. The other compasses, discussed in Chapter 4, largely eliminate this problem.

The panel-type compass is so mounted that when the aircraft is in straight-and-level, unaccelerated flight, the vertical component of the earth's magnetic field has no effect on the compass indication. When the aircraft is banked, however, on or near a heading of north or south, or when it is accelerated or decelerated on or near east or west headings, the compass indications are erroneous. Because of this dip error, precision flying without the use of a suction-driven or electrically driven heading indicator is difficult, especially in rough air. Another disadvantage is that the fluid in which the panel compass is immersed to dampen oscillation is subject to swirl which may create noticeable error. Additionally, the comparatively small size of the compass bowl restricts the use of efficient dampening vanes.

In the extreme latitudes (near the North and South Poles) the panel-type magnetic compass is practically useless. The horizontal component of the earth's magnetic field is very weak, and the lines of flux cannot make the needles line up with them. Therefore compasses may spin erratically or indicate incorrectly in the Artic and Antarctic regions.

# ATTITUDE INSTRUMENT FLYING
## FOR PROPELLER AIRCRAFT
### CHAPTER 15

This chapter deals with the basic procedures and considerations of instrument flying for prop aircraft. It does not give you the specific procedures for each type. It assumes a typical assortment of instruments and presents and explains the typical procedures to be followed. To apply this information in practice, be sure to consult the operating handbook for the particular aircraft you fly and follow the specific procedures given there.

Instrument flight, like visual flight, depends on complete and accurate control of the aircraft. This, in turn, is based on the principles of aerodynamics and the way they affect the attitude of the aircraft under various conditions. A full under-standing of these factors will help you do a better job of controlling the attitude of your airplane in both visual and instrument flight.

## ATTITUDE INSTRUMENT FLYING

The attitude of an aircraft is the relationship of its longitudinal axis (or fuselage), its lateral axis (or wings), and the earth's surface or any plane parallel to the earth's surface. Attitude instrument flying is controlling the attitude of an aircraft through reference to flight instruments.

Attitude instrument flying is like visual flying in that both use reference points to determine the attitude of the aircraft.

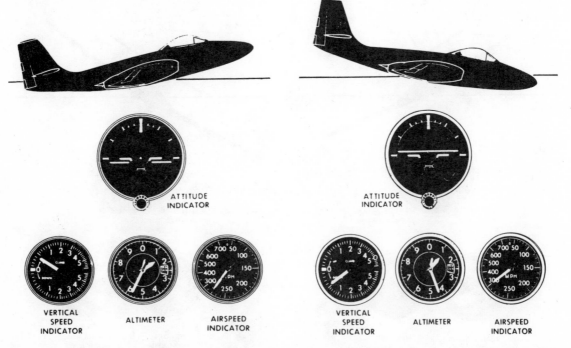

Fig. 233. Attitude instruments as they might appear in a climb.

Fig. 234. Attitude instruments as they might appear in a descent.

While flying by visual reference to flight instrument, you determine the attitude of the aircraft by observing indications on the instruments which give you essentially the same information as you get by visual reference to the earth's surface.

Another similarity between attitude instrument flying and visual flying is the way in which the aircraft is controlled. You use exactly the same control techniques while flying by reference to instruments as you do in visual flying. The largest single learning factor in attitude instrument flying is that of interpreting the flight instruments to determine the attitude of the aircraft.

*Attitude Instrument Flying Skills*

Attitude instrument flying consists of three major types of skills—instrument coverage (scanning); instrument interpretation; and aircraft control.

INSTRUMENT COVERAGE. Instrument coverage is commonly termed *scanning*. Experiments in scanning have shown that

a pilot whose instrument flying proficiency is at a high level cross-checks his instruments much more often than a pilot whose proficiency is at a lower level. In fact, the lack of precision in instrument flying can often be traced back to slow and inaccurate cross-checking. The best way to improve proficiency is through practice.

The most common faults in instrument scanning are:

1. Omitting an instrument entirely from the scan.

2. Placing too much emphasis on a single instrument.

3. Gazing too long at the wrong instrument.

As an example of how improper scanning occurs, consider the case of a pilot attempting to reduce the airspeed and hold straight-and-level flight. As the power is reduced, he observes the manifold pressure gauge so closely in order to make the proper adjustments that he neglects to observe the instruments which would indicate a deviation from straight-and-level

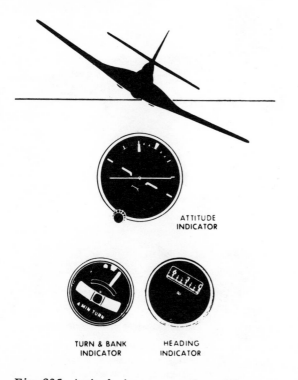

Fig. 235. Attitude instruments in a right turn.

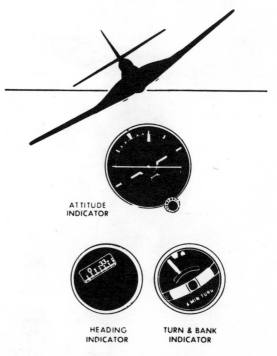

Fig. 236. Attitude instruments in a left turn.

flight. This failure to observe the proper instruments sufficiently could very well be the underlying cause for poorly executed maneuver.

There is no one set order to follow while scanning the instruments; it depends on the type of maneuver to be executed. During certain maneuvers, one instrument or group of instruments may be of prime importance; during other maneuvers, other instruments may be of prime importance.

INSTRUMENT INTERPRETATION. The second major type of attitude instrument flying skill is instrument interpretation; experience has shown that this is difficult to learn. However, since proper instrument interpretation is essential to precision instrument flying, you must apply yourself fully in order to attain the desired precision. The first step, of course, is learning the construction and principle of operation of each flight instrument. This reduces the difficulty of learning to use the instruments and usually results in higher standards of proficiency.

The final step is being able to interpret each instrument indication automatically in terms of the attitude of the aircraft. If the position of the nose is to be determined, the airspeed indicator, the altimeter, the vertical-speed indicator, and the horizon indicator must be interpreted. (See Fig's 233 and 234.) If the position of the wings is to be determined, the indications of the horizon indicator, and the turn-and-bank indicator must be interpreted. (See Fig's 235 and 236.) The indications on the flight instruments should be interpreted in terms of the attitude of the aircraft at all times. Each pilot should use primary and secondary instruments for proper instrument interpretation.

AIRCRAFT CONTROL. The third attitude instrument flying skill is aircraft control. In visual flight, you know the relationship between your movements of the controls and the attitude of the aircraft. You know what control pressures to use, for you see the results, and you coordinate the controls to place the aircraft in the desired attitude.

Instrument flying is essentially the same with the instruments substituted for the visual reference points. Your control movements necessary to produce a given attitude by reference to instruments are the same as those in visual flight and so are your thought processes.

Aircraft control is composed of four coordinated steps: (1) pitch control, (2) bank control, (3) power control, and (4) trim.

Pitch control is controlling the movement of the fuselage about the lateral axis; it is accomplished by movement of the elevators. After interpreting the pitch attitude of the aircraft from the proper flight instruments, you exert control pressures on the elevators to effect the desired pitch attitude with reference to the earth's surface.

Bank control is controlling the angle made by the wing and the earth's surface; in other words, the movement of the wings about the longitudinal axis. After interpreting the bank attitude from the proper instruments, you exert the necessary control pressures to attain the desired bank attitude.

Power control, which is control of the power-plant, is used to achieve the desired airspeed and flight path.

Trim control is achieved by relieving all possible control pressures after the desired attitude has been attained. Precision instrument flying is difficult when pressures must be held manually; therefore, trim control must be exercised to relieve as many control pressures as possible.

Remember, of course, that pitch, bank

power, and trim control are performed in a coordinated manner, and the breakdown given here is only an analytical treatment of the subject. Remember, too, that good instrument flying techniques are difficult when you are tense. Tenseness results in erratic and abrupt control movements and in holding pressures on the controls in opposition to the trim. One way of overcoming tenseness is to hold the controls lightly and trim the aircraft to maintain the desired attitude.

## INSTRUMENT COCKPIT CHECK

One basic requirement for a successful instrument mission is the proper operation of all the instrument flying equipment in the aircraft. The only way to be sure of this is to make a thorough instrument check before take-off, following the procedures specified in the handbook provided with the airplane. In general, however, here are some of the main points involved in the instrument check.

*Suction Gauge (or Inverters).*

Check the source of motivating power for the gyro instruments to make sure the output is proper. If the gyros are driven by a vacuum system, check the suction gauge for the proper indications of 3.75" to 4.25". If the gyros are electrically driven, check the generators and inverters for proper operation.

*Airspeed Indicators.*

The airspeed indicator needle should indicate zero. Check the airspeed calibration card for any deviations at the speed range that you intend to fly.

*Heading Indicator.*

Uncage the suction-driven heading indicator before starting the engine(s). Allow 5 minutes after starting engine(s) for the gyro rotor to attain its proper speed. Then cage the gyro, and while uncaging it, simultaneously pull out and turn the knob. If the card continues to turn after the knob is pulled out, the gyro is not operating properly and should be

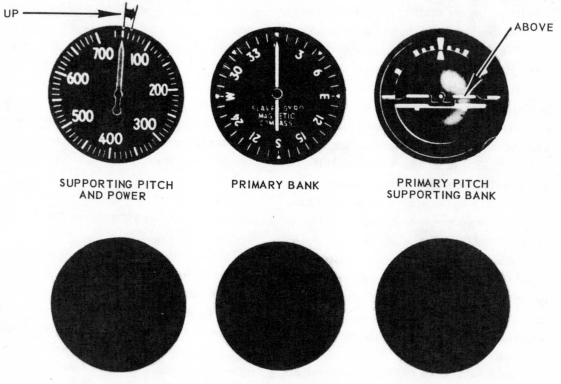

SUPPORTING PITCH AND POWER     PRIMARY BANK     PRIMARY PITCH SUPPORTING BANK

Fig. 237. Instruments used before leaving ground on instrument takeoff.

replaced. If it is operating properly, set the gyro to a known heading while taxiing straight. Recheck the accuracy of this heading just before take-off. If the error is large, the instrument is unreliable.

*Horizon Indicator.*

Uncage the suction-driven horizon indicator before starting the engine(s). After starting engine(s) allow the instrument five minutes to attain rotor speed. Then adjust the miniature aircraft so that the hairline is barely visible on the staff below (unless a different position is required for the particular aircraft). If the horizon bar erects quickly to the horizontal position and remains at the correct position for the attitude of the aircraft, or if it begins to vibrate after this attitude is reached and then slowly stops vibrating altogether, the instrument is operating properly. If the horizon bar fails to remain in the horizontal position while you are taxiing straight, the instrument is unreliable. If the horizon bar tips in excess of 5° during a taxiing turn, an unbalanced condition is indicated, probably caused by a low rotor speed or clogged erection mechanism.

If you have allowed sufficient time for gyro warm-up, the horizon indicator should have erected to a wings level attitude, and should indicate the nose attitude of the aircraft on the ground. Set the miniature aircraft level with the 90° marks on the side of the case. This should give approximately the level flight attitude at normal cruising airspeed.

*Altimeter*

Set the altimeter to the station altimeter setting as reported by the tower and check to determine if the altimeter indicates the altitude of the field. If there is a difference between the actual field elevation and the indication on the altimeter, either the altimeter setting is incorrect or there is a scale error in the instrument. If the error is more than 75 feet, the instrument should be replaced. If the deviation is less than 75 feet, set the altimeter at field elevation and note the difference between the tower altimeter setting and the reading in the Kollsman window. Apply this figure to all subsequent altimeter settings received.

*Turn-and-Bank Indicator.*

Turn the aircraft to the right and left while taxiing and note the reaction of the turn needle. If its indications are not positive, or if the needle is sluggish and does not return to the center promptly when the turn is stopped, the instrument is not operating properly. If the instrument is mounted in a shock-mounted panel, you can make this same check when the aircraft is not moving by pressing in one side of the panel and then releasing it. Check the ball to be sure it moves freely in the race, and that the tube is filled with liquid.

*Vertical-Speed Indicator.*

With the aircraft on the ground, the needle should indicate zero. If it does not, gently tap the panel. If it does not return to zero, adjust it by using a small screw driver to turn the screw in the lower left corner of the instrument. While making this adjustment, gently tap the panel to check the accuracy of the new setting. If you cannot adjust the needle to zero, you must use its ground indications as the zero position in flight.

*Panel Magnetic Compass.*

Check to see whether the magnetic compass has sufficient fluid. Determine its accuracy by comparing its indications with a known heading while the aircraft is taxiing straight. If a Remote Indicating Compass is installed, check its indications in the same way.

## THE INSTRUMENT TAKE-OFF

Instrument take-off techniques vary

slightly with different types of aircraft, but the techniques discussed here are successful for any type of aircraft if you consider the original attitude on the ground.

Before attempting an instrument take-off, complete an instrument cockpit check as specified in the aircraft handbook. After being cleared for take-off, align the aircraft with the center of the runway and allow it to roll straight for a short distance before stopping, making sure that the nose wheel or tail wheel is straight. Lock the tail wheel if the aircraft is so equipped, and hold the brakes firmly to prevent creeping. Set the suction-driven heading indicator on the 5° mark nearest the published runway heading, and recheck to be sure that it is uncaged. If you use the electric heading indicator rotate it so that the heading needle is under the index at the top of the instrument.

Advance the power to an rpm that will provide partial rudder control. Release the brakes, and advance the throttle(s) smoothly to take-off power. During the take-off roll, hold the heading constant on the heading indicator by use of rudder. If necessary, in multi-engine propeller-driven aircraft, use the throttles to assist in maintaining directional control. Use the brakes only as a last resort because braking usually results in over-controlling and lengthening the take-off roll. You must counteract any deviation in heading immediately to return to the desired heading.

As flying speed is approached adjust the nose attitude to make the desired take-off attitude show on the horizon indicator. Establish this attitude by raising the nose of the aircraft (with tricycle landing gear) or by allowing the tail of the aircraft to rise slightly if it is equipped with conventional landing gear. As the aircraft approaches flying speed, and immediately after leaving the ground, control the nose and bank attitudes by reference

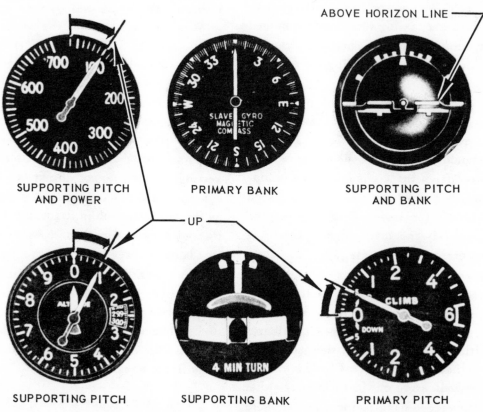

Fig. 238. Instruments used right after leaving ground on instrument takeoff.

to the heading indicator. Continue to maintain the heading by reference to the heading indicator. Maintain the nose attitude by reference to the horizon indicator until the altimeter and vertical speed show a positive rate of climb. When a predetermined safe altitude (generally, about 100 feet) is attained or when the aircraft cannot make a safe wheels-down landing, raise the landing gear. Once you raise the gear, the horizon indicator is the primary pitch instrument until the climbing airspeed is attained. However, the altimeter, vertical-speed indicator, and airspeed indicator are the secondary instruments and you must scan them closely at this critical time.

Maintain a nose attitude on the horizon indicator that will result in a continuous climb and a smooth increase in airspeed. As soon as you attain a safe altitude and airspeed, raise the flaps if they are down. Cross-check the indications of the altimeter and verify the altitude by the limit switch of the radar altimeter. After you attain single-engine airspeed and reach an altitude of 200 to 400 feet above the terrain as shown on the altimeter, reduce power to climbing settings and accomplish the climb-out as a constant airspeed climb. When you raise the gear and flaps, the nose attitude may change unless you counteract it by control pressures.

Adjust the trim tabs for take-off before starting the take-off roll. Don't change this setting until after the aircraft becomes airborne. After the aircraft is airborne, use the trim tabs to relieve control pressures as described before.

*Common Faults in Instrument Take-Off*

1. Failure to make an adequate cockpit check of all instruments before take-off.

2. Swerving and failure to maintain accurate directional control on the ground. Remedy this by making adequate small movements of the rudder pedals the instant the heading indicator shows a change. Neutralize the rudders after the correction has been made.

3. Failure to maintain take-off attitude after becoming airborne. This is just an invitation to a stall.

4. Nosing down after take-off, thereby flying back into the ground.

5. Failure to scan instruments after take-off.

6. Reducing power too soon after take-off.

## PITCH CONTROL FOR LEVEL FLIGHT

The pitch (or nose) attitude of an aircraft is the angular relation of the longitudinal axis of the aircraft to the true horizon (Fig. 239). In level flight, the pitch attitude varies with airspeed. The aircraft flies nose-high at low speeds and nose-low at high speeds. The pitch attitude of the aircraft for level flight at a constant airspeed also changes with differences in load.

The instruments that are used for pitch control are the horizon indicator, altimeter, vertical-speed indicator, and airspeed indicator.

*Horizon Indicator*

The aircraft you fly may have an electric horizon indicator or it may have a suction-driven horizon indicator. One or the other of these instruments is installed in an aircraft, sometimes both. For instructional purposes and for better reading in this chapter, the phrase *horizon indicator* will be used for both electric and suction-driven indicators.

In visual flight, you attain the proper pitch attitude by raising or lowering the nose in relation to the horizon. In instrument flight, the horizon indicator supplants the real horizon. You follow exactly the same procedure in raising or lowering the nose of the miniature aircraft on the

Fig. 239. The pitch attitude of an aircraft is the angular relation of the longitudinal axis of the aircraft to the true horizon.

artificial horizon. With the horizon indicator, you can quickly place the aircraft in approximately the correct pitch attitude for any condition of flight. However, you cannot know the exact attitude in advance. You must determine this by the movement or lack of movement of the other pitch instruments.

For reliable indications and maximum upset limits, you must uncage the horizon indicator only in straight-and-level attitude, as indicated by the other attitude instruments. Of course, the electric horizon indicator has no tumble limits; however, you should not rely on the suction-driven horizon indicator after exceeding 70° of pitch, up or down.

When you make pitch corrections, your control pressures should be extremely light and you should observe the horizon indicator to attain the correct pitch attitude. The normal movement of the horizon bar should not exceed one to one and a half times the width of the bar. Use the vertical-speed indicator in conjunction with the horizon bar to determine over-controlling in pitch attitude.

*Altimeter*

The altimeter gives you an indirect reading of the pitch attitude of the aircraft in straight-and-level flight. Since the altitude should remain constant in level flight, any deviation from the desired altitude shows a need for a change

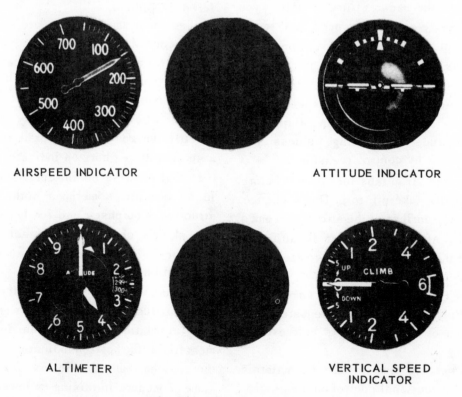

AIRSPEED INDICATOR

ATTITUDE INDICATOR

ALTIMETER

VERTICAL SPEED INDICATOR

Fig. 240. Pitch instruments.

LEVEL FLIGHT
(CONSTANT POWER)

NOSE HIGH ATTITUDE
(CONSTANT POWER)

NOSE LOW ATTITUDE
(CONSTANT POWER)

Fig. 241. Indications of attitude by altimeter

in pitch. If you are losing altitude, raise the nose; if you are gaining altitude, lower the nose. (Fig. 241.)

The rate at which the altimeter is moving aids you in determining the pitch attitude. A slow movement of the altimeter indicates a small deviation from the desired pitch attitude; a fast movement indicates a large deviation. Take corrective action promptly, with light control pressures. Remember, too, that movement of the altimeter should always be corrected by two distinct changes of attitude. The first in a change of attitude to stop the altimeter; the second, a change of attitude to return smoothly to the desired altitude.

At low altitudes, however, for example in carrier landings, the barometric altimeter has too much lag to be safe. The radar altimeter is much better.

*Vertical-Speed Indicator*

The *initial* movement of the vertical-speed needle is usually almost instantaneous. It indicates the trend of the vertical movement of the aircraft. You must realize, however, that it takes a little while for the vertical-speed indicator to reach its maximum point of deflection after a correction has been made. This time element is commonly referred to as *lag*. The lag is directly proportional to the speed and magnitude of the pitch change. Train yourself to use smooth control techniques by using light pressures to make any adjustment in pitch attitude; then, the vertical-speed indicator will be easy to interpret. You can stop over-controlling by relaxing pressure on the controls, allowing the pitch attitude to stabilize, and then re-adjusting the

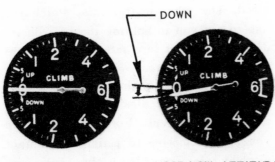
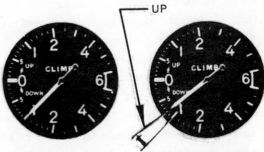

CONSTANT PITCH ATTITUDE
DURING LEVEL FLIGHT
(CONSTANT POWER)

NOSE-LOW ATTITUDE
(CONSTANT POWER)

CONSTANT ATTITUDE
DESCENT
(CONSTANT POWER)

NOSE-HIGH ATTITUDE
1,000 FPM DESCENT
(CONSTANT POWER)

Fig. 242. Vertical-speed indicator.

pitch attitude by utilizing the indications of the other pitch instruments.

Occasionally, the vertical-speed indicator may be slightly out of calibration and indicate a slight climb or descent when the aircraft is really in level flight. If you are unable to readjust the vertical-speed indicator properly, take this error into consideration when you use the vertical-speed indicator for pitch control.

### Airspeed Indicator

The airspeed indicator gives you an indirect reading of the pitch attitude. With a given power setting and pitch attitude, the airspeed remains constant. If the airspeed increases, the nose is too low and should be raised; if the airspeed decreases, the nose is too high and should be lowered. A rapid change in airspeed indicates a large change in pitch, and a slow change in airspeed indicates a small change in pitch. There is very little lag in the indications of the airspeed indicator, so when you make pitch changes, they are reflected immediately by a change of airspeed. Altitude, however, is a function of power. Remember—nose attitude controls airspeed, power controls vertical speed, (in other words, altitude).

### Scanning

The interpretation of the individual pitch instruments has been discussed in the preceding paragraphs. Observing and interpreting two or more of these instruments to determine and maintain the attitude of the aircraft is known as scanning. The importance of scanning cannot be over-emphasized. Even in visual flight, you must scan the flight instruments to see whether you are holding the proper attitude. As an example, though you can maintain a level attitude by visual reference, you must also check the altimeter to see whether this attitude is maintaining level flight. During instrument flight the instruments serve a dual purpose. They permit you to visualize the attitude of the aircraft, and also to determine whether that attitude will maintain the desired condition of flight. The control technique is identical with that of visual flight. Accurate control during instrument flight depends on your ability to scan and properly interpret the instruments most important for the maneuver you are executing.

Individual pilots may differ in the exact method of scanning, but they all use the same basic system. They use the instruments which give the best information for controlling the aircraft in any given maneuver. They also scan the other instruments to aid in maintaining the important, or primary, instruments at the desired indications.

The primary instrument is always the instrument that gives the most pertinent information for any particular maneuver; it is usually the one that you should hold at a constant indication. The horizon indicator, for example, is always the primary instrument for pitch attitude in level flight, especially in conditions such as thunderstorms where there are exceptionally strong vertical currents. As already explained, you can use any of the pitch instruments to hold a level attitude (or with the proper power setting, reasonably level flight), but none of these instruments except the horizon indicator will give you the exact information desired. The other instruments, which you use to aid you in holding the horizon indicator constant, are referred to as supporting instruments.

There are times when you use a supporting instrument almost as much as the primary instrument. For example, when you are attempting to maintain constant pitch by reference to the horizon indicator, the altimeter and the vertical-speed indicator will show you whether you are succeeding and will show you the direction (up and down) of any variation from the desired pitch. Scanning can thus be a real help because the sooner you determine the need for a correction, the smaller the corrective action you need.

*Trim*

Proper trim techniques are essential to smooth and accurate instrument flying. Use trim to relieve control pressures and not to initiate attitude changes. Sometimes, when the control pressures have apparently been relieved by trimming, there may be very small pressures which you can't feel. Therefore, release the controls slowly and observe the instruments to determine if the aircraft will maintain the desired attitude. If it will not, apply pressures to the controls again to attain the desired attitude, and retrim the aircraft. Repeat this procedure until the aircraft will maintain the desired attude without pressure on the controls.

## BANK CONTROL TO PRODUCE COORDINATED STRAIGHT FLIGHT

The bank attitude of an aircraft is the angular relation of the lateral axis of the aircraft to the true horizon. To maintain a straight course in visual flight, you must keep the wings of the aircraft level with the true horizon. Assuming that the aircraft is trimmed properly and is in coordinated flight, any deviation from a wings-level attitude produces a turn.

The instruments used for bank control are the horizon indicator, the heading indicator, and the turn-and-bank indicator. (Fig. 243).

### Horizon Indicator

In instrument flight, the miniature airplane and the horizon bar of the horizon indicator are substituted for the real aircraft and the true horizon (Fig. 244). The horizon indicator is a direct-reading instrument. The attitude of the aircraft is indicated on its face instantly through the relative position of the miniature aircraft with respect to the horizon bar. For easy interpretation of this instrument, the pilot imagines himself "flying" the miniature aircraft.

The angle of bank is indicated by the

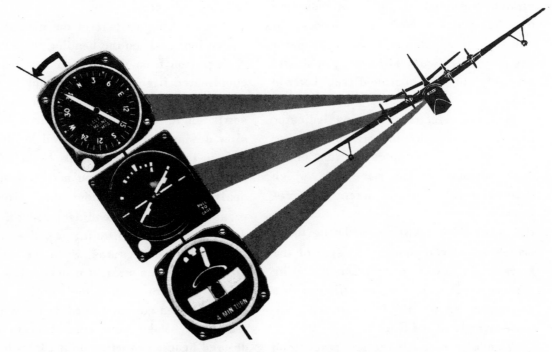

Fig. 243. Instruments used for bank control.

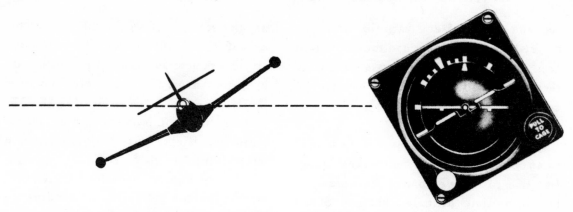

Fig. 244. Banking attitude as shown on the horizon indicator.

pointer on the banking scale at the top of the instrument. On some horizon indicators, you can readily determine small angles of bank (which you may not see while observing the miniature aircraft) by referring to the banking scale pointer.

You can determine pitch and bank attitude simultaneously on the horizon indicator. Even though the wings of the miniature aircraft are not level with the horizon bar, you can determine pitch attitude by observing the relative position of the nose of the miniature aircraft with respect to the horizon bar.

Uncage the horizon indicator only in straight-and-level attitude, as indicated by the other attitude instruments. Of course, the electrical horizon indicator has no tumble limits; however, you should not rely on the suction-driven horizon indicator after exceeding 100° of bank.

Both the electrical horizon indicator and the suction-driven horizon indicator may show small misrepresentations of the bank attitude during maneuvers which involve turns. You can detect this precession immediately by closely scanning the other bank instruments during these maneuvers. Even though the gyro of the horizon indicator may precess during certain maneuvers, you can still use this instrument as an aid in controlling the bank attitude of the aircraft.

You will normally notice precession when you roll out of a turn. If, on the completion of the turn, the wings of the miniature aircraft are level and the aircraft is still turning, make a small change in the bank attitude to center the turn needle and stop movement of the heading indicator.

### Heading Indicator

Some aircraft you fly will have an electric heading indicator, and some will have a suction-driven heading indicator. One or the other of these instruments will be installed, but not both. To cover both, the term "heading indicator" is used here for both electric and suction-driven gyro heading indicators.

The banking attitude of the aircraft is shown indirectly on the heading indicator. A deviation from the desired heading in coordinated flight suggests a bank in the direction that the aircraft is turning. A small angle of bank is indicated by a slow deviation from the desired heading, and a large angle of bank by a rapid change in heading. If you notice a turn, apply coordinated rudder and aileron pressures until the heading indicator indicates a constant heading. When an aircraft is banked, it turns. When the wings are level, it flies straight if in coordinated flight. Therefore, when the heading indicator shows a constant heading the wings are level. Make your correction to the desired heading by using an angle of bank no larger than the number of degrees to be turned. In this correction, do not exceed the angle of bank required for a standard rate turn.

The suction-driven heading indicator has no direction-seeking qualities and should be adjusted while the aircraft is in straight-and-level flight so that its indication coincides with the magnetic heading. Check it frequently against the magnetic indicator for precessional error. The limits of operation of the suction-driven heading indicator are approximately 55° of pitch and/or bank.

*Turn-and-Bank Indicator*

When the turn needle is exactly centered, the aircraft is in straight flight. When the turn needle is displaced from center, the aircraft is turning in the direction of the displacement. Thus, in coordinated flight, if the turn needle is to the left of center, the left wing is low; re-centering the turn needle will produce straight flight.

Close observation of the turn needle is necessary to interpret accurately small deviations from the desired position. In turbulent air, the turn needle oscillates from one side to the other, and you must average the fluctuations to determine the banking attitude. When the deflection is greater on one side of center than the other, the aircraft is banking in that direction. To determine whether the turn needle is out of adjustment, place the aircraft in straight flight, as indicated by observing the other banking instruments. If the turn needle indicates a deflection, you should interpret this position as the center position.

Use the ball of the turn-and-bank indicator to determine whether the ailerons and rudder are coordinated. If the wings are level and you have the aircraft properly trimmed, the ball will remain in the center, and the aircraft will maintain straight flight. If the ball is not centered, the aircraft is improperly trimmed.

To trim the aircraft properly, use the aileron pressure required to maintain a wings-level attitude (by reference to all available instruments); then center the ball with rudder pressure. To relieve these individual pressures, adjust the appropriate trim control. Release the controls slowly and observe the instruments to determine whether the aircraft will maintain straight flight. If it does not, again apply pressures to attain the desired attitude and retrim the aircraft. Repeat this procedure until the aircraft will maintain straight flight without pressures on the controls.

*Scanning*

You should practice the combined use of all available bank-control instruments to produce straight flight. Both the heading indicator and the turn needle indicate when the aircraft is turning. Either the horizon indicator or the ball of the turn-and-bank indicator can show you the cause of the turn. In straight flight, the horizon indicator is the primary instrument for bank control. If it is not available (inoperative, unreliable, etc.), maintain straight flight by reference to the turn needle and the heading indicator.

Throughout your practice of the techniques described in this chapter, remember that control of pitch and bank attitude is of equal importance. Therefore, as you learn the use of each of the bank instruments, you must include it in the sequence of scanning previously used. As the number of instruments you must observe increases, the speed of scanning also must increase.

## POWER CONTROL IN STRAIGHT-AND-LEVEL FLIGHT

At any given airspeed, the power setting determines whether the aircraft is in level flight, in a climb, or in a descent.

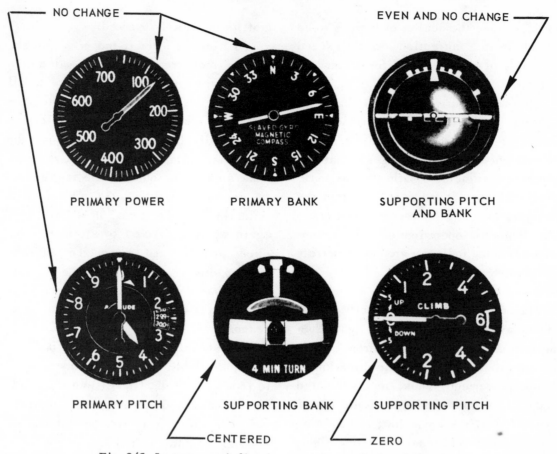

Fig. 245. Instruments indicating straight - and - level flight.

In other words, power controls altitude. For example, cruising airspeed maintained with cruising power will result in level flight. If you increase the power setting and hold the airspeed constant, the aircraft will climb. Conversely, if you decrease the power and hold the airspeed constant, the aircraft will descend.

If you hold the altitude constant, the power determines the airspeed. For example, at a constant altitude, cruising power results in cruising airspeed. Any deviation from the cruising power setting results in a change in airspeed.

To maintain level flight when you change power and airspeed, you will need considerable elevator pressures in all types of aircraft. You will also need various rudder pressures in propeller-driven aircraft, because of torque changes. When you add power to increase the air-speed, the aircraft tends to assume a nose high attitude and climb without any movement of the elevators or the elevator trim. The opposite effect occurs when you reduce power: the aircraft tends to assume a nose-low attitude and descend. These changes in attitude are caused by the changes in vertical lift, which, in turn, are caused by changes in power. Also, when you increase power, the nose of the aircraft tends to yaw to the left. This yawing effect, which is most pronounced in single-engine, propeller-driven aircraft, and to lesser extent in multi-engine, propeller-driven aircraft, is absent in aircraft with counter-rotating propellers and in jet aircraft. To counteract the tendency of the aircraft to change attitude, retrim the aircraft.

During a change in power, you should make an accurate interpretation of the altimeter. Then counteract any deviation from the desired altitude by appropriate pressure on the elevator control. If the altitude is low and the airspeed is high, or vice versa, a change in pitch alone may return the aircraft to the proper altitude and airspeed. If both airspeed and altitude are low, or if both are high, then a change in both power and pitch is necessary.

To make power control easy when changing airspeed, you should know the approximate power settings for the various airspeeds which will be flown. When you wish to change the airspeed any appreciable amount, adjust the power so that the manifold-pressure gauge shows approximately 3 to 5 inches more change than you anticipate will be required to maintain the new airspeed. This is sometimes called the power differential. As the airspeed changes, you must control the pitch and bank attitudes to maintain a constant altitude and heading. As you approach the desired airspeed, adjust the power to the new cruising power setting. Overpowering and underpowering 3 to 5 inches of manifold-pressure is the normal procedure. This results in a change of airspeed at a moderate rate, which allows ample time to trim the aircraft. In certain types of aircraft these figures will not apply.

In changing airspeed any appreciable amount, use the manifold-pressure gauge to give you the power required for the airspeed you want. When making the change, the manifold-pressure gauge is momentarily the primary power-control instrument. However, as the airspeed approaches the desired speed, the airspeed indicator becomes the primary instrument for power control.

Since power changes effect aircraft attitude, scanning the attitude-indicating instruments is continued during all power transitions.

As you can see, the necessity for power control thus adds the power-control instruments to the pitch and the bank instruments which you must scan to produce straight-and-level flight. With a constant power setting, a normal scan should be satisfactory. When you change the power, however, you must increase the speed of the scan to cover the pitch and bank instruments adequately as well as the power-control instruments. This is necessary to counteract any deviations immediately.

## CONSTANT AIRSPEED CLIMBS, DESCENTS AND LEVEL-OFFS

For any power setting and load condition there is only one attitude which will give the most efficient rate of climb. Climb data for the type of aircraft you are flying gives you the best climbing airspeed and power settings for different altitudes. In a climb or a descent at a constant airspeed and power setting, you must accept whatever vertical speed results. The manifold-pressure gauge is the primary instrument for power control.

To enter a climb from cruising airspeed, raise the nose to the approximate climbing attitude; after the airspeed drops to about 5 knots above the desired climbing airspeed, apply climbing power. It takes only a very small amount of back pressure to complete the change from level to climbing attitude. Follow the horizon indicator in accomplishing the change in attitude. It is the primary instrument for pitch. Hold this established rate of climb constant. This causes the airspeed to decrease smoothly. As the desired airspeed is approached, lower the nose slightly to stop and maintain the airspeed on the desired indication.

Although the horizon indicator is the primary instrument for pitch, it is important that you use the vertical-speed indicator

PRIMARY POWER     PRIMARY BANK     SUPPORTING PITCH
                                   AND BANK

PRIMARY PITCH     SUPPORTING BANK     SUPPORTING PITCH

Fig. 246. Level off from either climb or descent.

as an aid to maintain a constant airspeed. For example, if the vertical speed is 800 fpm (feet per minute) after the entry, you should hold this rate of climb until the airspeed shows a change. If the airspeed decreases 2 knots below that desired, you should adjust the attitude on the horizon indicator to establish a rate of climb of 700 fpm. This should regain the desired airspeed, but if it does not, make another correction. If the initial change were as much as 5 knots, it would be advisable to make a 200 fpm correction on the vertical-speed indicator. Maintain directional control as in straight flight. Be sure to use the proper trim technique throughout the climb.

Entering a climb without the horizon indicator is the same except that you must use the airspeed indicator and the trend of the vertical speed indicator for pitch control. Applying power, will normally bring the nose up and you will not have to apply back pressure to attain the desired vertical speed. Hold this vertical speed until the airspeed approaches the climbing airspeed. From this point the procedure is the same as when all the instruments are available.

Start the level-off from a climb before reaching the desired altitude. Although the necessary amount of lead varies with the aircraft and pilot technique, the most important factor is the vertical speed. Normally, the lead for each 500 fpm rate of climb will be 20 to 30 feet. When you reach the proper altitude for starting the level-off, the altimeter becomes primary for pitch. (Fig. 246). Adjust the nose attitude to the level-flight attitude for that airspeed. Cross-check the altimeter and vertical speed indicator to determine whether you have attained level flight at the proper altitude. Follow changes in nose attitude with appropriate trim adjustments when necessary.

To enter a climb when already at climbing airspeed (Fig. 247), advance the

Fig. 247. Entry into a climb at climbing airspeed.

throttle to the climbing power setting and adjust the nose attitude on the horizon indicator to maintain a constant airspeed. As you apply power, the airspeed indicator becomes primary for control of the nose attitude. Then use the relationship between the vertical speed and the airspeed for control of the nose attitude as previously described.

If you want to cruise at climbing airspeed, accomplish the level-off with a coordinated change of power and pitch. When the aircraft reaches the point of level-off, reduce the power smoothly to maintain airspeed and adjust the nose attitude to level off on the desired altitude.

A constant airspeed descent may be performed at any airspeed, but you must determine the airspeed before entry. Regardless of the airspeed, the technique is basically the same.

To descend at an airspeed lower than cruising, reduce power to the descending setting and maintain a constant altitude. When you approach the descending airspeed, adjust the nose attitude to establish a descent at the desired airspeed. Use the horizon indicator as the primary instrument. Then, when the descent is started, cross-check the airspeed indicator. Use the vertical-speed indicator as previously described in a climb.

To enter a descent from descending airspeed, reduce the power and adjust the pitch simultaneously to maintain a constant airspeed. The horizon indicator is the primary pitch instrument throughout the descent. Use the airspeed indicator and the vertical-speed indicator exactly as in a climb to aid in controlling the nose attitude.

To level off at descending airspeed, simultaneously advance the power to the setting necessary to maintain this airspeed in level flight and adjust the nose to level-flight attitude. As in a climb, a lead is necessary to level-off at a desired altitude. This lead is approximately 40 to 60 feet for each fpm rate of descent. When you reach the proper altitude for starting the level off, the horizon indicator becomes the primary instrument for pitch and the airspeed is primary for power.

To level off at an airspeed lower than descending airspeed, use the same lead and primary instruments as just discussed for levelling off at descending airspeed. Here's what you do. When you reach the level-off point, adjust the pitch as necessary to maintain level flight as the airspeed is reduced. As the airspeed approaches the speed desired, adjust the power to maintain that airspeed in level flight. The power used in some descents may be too high to allow the airspeed to change at a normal rate. This may require a reduction in power as you adjust the nose attitude in the level-off.

To level off at an airspeed higher than that used for the descent, you must advance the power before reaching the level-off point. The new power setting should be the one necessary to maintain the desired airspeed in level flight. Add the power at the point that will allow you to attain the desired airspeed at the time you reach the level-flight attitude. This point varies with different types of aircraft, with the amount of change in airspeed, and with the rate of descent. The horizon indicator becomes the primary instrument for pitch as you add the power (Fig. 248). Hold this rate of descent constant until you reach the lead point for changing the pitch to the level-flight attitude. At this time the altimeter becomes primary for pitch and the airspeed indicator primary for power.

During straight climbs and descents, the heading indicator is primary for bank control. You must relieve control pressures by use of trim, as in all instrument maneuvers.

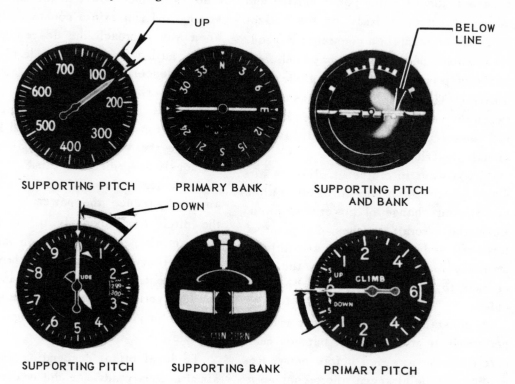

Fig. 248. Leveling off from a descent at cruising airspeed.

## RATE CLIMBS AND DESCENTS

Rate climbs and descents are excellent maneuvers for developing and improving precision aircraft control.

The procedures, scan, and aircraft control for constant-rate climbs and descents are very similar to those just described for climbs and descents at a constant airspeed. The key principle, as stated before, is that the nose attitude controls airspeed and power controls vertical speed, which means altitude. The horizon indicator is primary for pitch control. The heading indicator remains the primary turn control instrument, because the assumption is that, at this point, you are making climbs and descents on a constant heading.

For training purposes, rate climbs or descents are often entered from climbing or descending airspeed. This may not always be possible or desirable in actual instrument conditions. The rate utilized in these maneuvers is one that is practical for the type of aircraft. Normally, in prop aircraft, you make the climbs and descents at 500 fpm.

To enter a climb at a definite rate, increase the power to the approximate setting for the desired rate. At the same time, raise the nose of the aircraft to the climbing attitude for the desired airspeed and rate of climb. As you add the power, the airspeed indicator is primary for pitch control until the vertical speed approaches the desired rate (Fig. 249). At this time, the vertical-speed indicator becomes the primary instrument for pitch control. Change the nose attitude of the aircraft as required to maintain the desired indication (Fig. 250). However, the vertical-speed indicator may be inaccurate to some extent. Check the change in altitude against the time interval while performing a rate climb or descent. This will determine whether the vertical-speed indicator is properly calibrated. Start by establishing a rate of climb or descent. Then check the altimeter every 15 seconds for the proper change in altitude. For example, if you

PRIMARY PITCH     PRIMARY BANK     SUPPORTING PITCH AND BANK

SUPPORTING PITCH     SUPPORTING BANK     SUPPORTING PITCH

Fig. 249. Entering into rate climbs and descents.

PRIMARY POWER     PRIMARY BANK     SUPPORTING PITCH
                                        AND BANK

SUPPORTING PITCH     SUPPORTING BANK     PRIMARY PITCH

Fig. 250. Instruments used during rate climbs and descents.

use a 500 fpm rate, the altitude should change 125 feet every 15 seconds. If the change in altitude is more or less, adjust the vertical speed accordingly. Repeat the procedure until you determine what indication will produce the desired rate. If you find any error, take it into account in later rate climbs and descents.

When the vertical-speed indicator becomes primary for pitch control, the airspeed indicator becomes primary for power control. Adjust the power to maintain the desired airspeed. Pitch and power corrections must be closely coordinated. Thus, for example, if the vertical speed is correct but the airspeed is low, add power. As you increase the power you must lower the nose slightly to avoid increasing the vertical speed. Adjust the nose attitude smoothly to avoid over-controlling. Small power corrections are usually sufficient to bring the airspeed

back to the desired indications.

To enter a descent at a definite rate, decrease the power to the approximate setting for the desired rate and aircraft configuration. At the same time, lower the nose to maintain the airspeed. The airspeed indicator is the primary instrument for pitch control until the vertical speed approaches the desired rate. The vertical-speed indicator is then the primary instrument for pitch control. Maintain it at the desired indication. Coordinate power and pitch control as described for climbs, and use an identical scan.

Proper trim technique is essential in climbs and descents at a definite rate, and helps prevent over-controlling the pitch attitude.

Level-offs from climbs and descents at a definite rate are accomplished in the same manner as level-offs from climbs and descents at a constant airspeed.

## TURNS: ENTRY, TURNING, AND RECOVERY

A turn made by reference to instruments should be made at a definite rate. Turns described in this section are those which do not exceed a standard rate (3° per second) as indicated in the turn-and-bank indicator. The true airspeed determines the angle of bank necessary to maintain a standard rate turn (single needle width for 3° per second with the two-minute turn needle, or two needle widths with the four-minute turn needle). At high speeds (above 220 knots true airspeed) a ½ standard rate turn (1½° per second) is desirable to avoid steep banks.

To enter a turn, apply steady, coordinated pressure on the ailerons and rudder in the direction of the desired turn. The horizon indicator is the primary bank instrument, and the turn needle is the secondary instrument. Use the turn needle as an aid in maintaining a constant rate of turn.

In level turns, as in straight-and-level flight, the horizon indicator is the primary pitch instrument and the altimeter is secondary (Fig. 251). During the entry into a turn, you must change the nose attitude to compensate for the loss of vertical lift caused by the banking of the aircraft. Therefore, you must observe the pitch instruments while rolling into a turn. Remember, however, that you should not apply corrective action until the flight instruments indicate a deviation from the desired condition of flight. As you raise the nose of the aircraft to hold altitude, add power necessary to maintain the desired airspeed. Proper trim technique is especially valuable at this time since you must vary the control pressures during the turn entry.

When you attain the desired angle of bank, you may have to apply a slight opposite pressure to the ailerons to prevent the bank from increasing beyond the desired amount. It is very important that

PRIMARY POWER        SUPPORTING BANK        SUPPORTING PITCH AND BANK

PRIMARY PITCH        PRIMARY BANK        SUPPORTING PITCH

Fig. 251. Instruments for level turns.

you maintain the desired angle of bank accurately, since any change in bank changes the vertical component of lift, thus necessitating a change in pitch to maintain level flight.

To return to straight-and-level flight, apply coordinated pressure to the ailerons and rudder in the direction opposite to the turn. The rate of roll-in and roll-out should be the same. To accomplish this, use the rate of roll-in as a guide during the roll-out. As the angle of bank decreases, the vertical lift increases and you must lower the nose of the aircraft to maintain the desired altitude. At the same time, you must make the proper power adjustment to maintain the desired airspeed.

You can enter a turn with rudder alone, but this results in a skid instead of a coordinated entry (Fig. 252). You can also enter a turn by use of ailerons alone, but the resulting aileron drag causes a mo-

mentary slip (Fig. 252). Simultaneous use of the ailerons and rudder will produce a coordinated entry. The ball of the turn-and-bank indicator shows whether the aircraft is in coordinated flight. Observe the ball during your scan throughout the turn, so that you may apply pressures to keep it centered.

To make sure of the calibration of the turn needle in case the horizon indicator fails, calibrate your turn needle on the first turn after take-off. Set your airspeed and, using the horizon indicator, bank the aircraft at the proper angle for a standard rate turn at that airspeed. Time your turn through at least 30° (10 seconds), checking your turn needle to see how far it deflects. You then know how much your turn needle deflects for a standard rate turn—whether it is actually a single needle width or is off somewhat. Then, if you lose your horizon indicator, you know accurately the significance of the turn needle deflection.

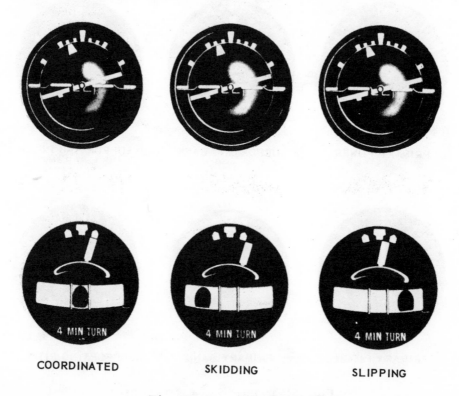

COORDINATED                SKIDDING                SLIPPING

Fig. 252. Turn indications.

*Steps in executing turn.*

Remember that three distinct steps are utilized in executing a turn:

1. START the turn at a normal rate, coordinating aileron and rudder.

2. STOP the rotational movement of the wing when the desired angle of bank is achieved with necessary aileron force.

3. HOLD the desired angle of bank with the necessary aileron force. Remember that the three steps should be coordinated into one continuous movement.

Coordinating ailerons and rudder means that you apply pressures simultaneously to rudder and aileron. Good coordination requires that you don't skid or slip the aircraft in executing a turn. By referring to the altimeter and vertical-speed indicator frequently, you can apply immediate corrective action if you observe any tendency for the aircraft to climb or descend. Check the heading indicator frequently during the turn, and start the recovery in sufficient time to stop on the desired heading.

## HEADING INDICATOR TURNS

In the section "Bank Control to Produce Coordinated Straight Flight," you learned that turning and banking in coordinated flight are the same. An aircraft will continue to turn as long as the wings are banked; therefore, you must start the recovery from a turn to a heading on the heading indicator before the desired heading has been reached. The amount of this lead varies with the relationship between the rate of turn and the angle of bank and with the individual pilot's rate of recovery. If you analyze the following examples, you will see the reasons for varying the amount of lead necessary to roll out on a given heading.

As a guide, when you recover from a 3° per second rate of turn, use a lead of

PRIMARY POWER          PRIMARY BANK          SUPPORTING PITCH
                                              AND BANK

PRIMARY PITCH          SUPPORTING BANK        SUPPORTING PITCH

Fig. 253. Rolling out on a heading.

one-half the angle of bank; when you re-cover from a 1½° per second rate of turn, use one-third the angle of bank as a lead. As an example, suppose you are turning at a rate of 3° per second, using a 24° bank. Lead your roll-out point by 12°. If you are turning at a rate of 1½° per second, using a 24° bank, lead your roll-out point by 8°. Use these amounts of lead until you are able to determine the exact amount required for your particular aircraft and technique.

To roll out on a given heading (Fig. 253), use the same technique as you would during a normal roll-out from any turn, except that you should start the recovery the instant you reach the predetermined lead on the heading indicator. Check the heading indicator after you have the turn needle centered to determine whether or not you used the proper lead. Any devia-tion from the desired heading on the head-ing indicator will then indicate a need for a change in the number of degrees of lead used. For example, if you used 13° of lead to roll out of a 26° angle of bank, and the roll-out was 2° beyond the desired heading, the proper lead would be 15°. The rate of entry and recovery should be the same. During the turn, use the normal scan technique and the primary instru-ments you use in any turn. To determine when you start the recovery, however, add the heading indicator to the scan as the aircraft approaches the desired heading.

## USE OF THE MAGNETIC COMPASS

The direct-reading panel magnetic compass (Fig. 254) is the only heading indicator that does not become inoperative with the loss of suction and/or electrical current. Therefore, it is important that you be able to turn your aircraft to a magnetic compass heading and maintain it. To do this, you should understand and remember the following:

Fig. 254. Magnetic compass.

*Characteristics of the magnetic compass:*

1. If the aircraft is on a northerly heading and you start a turn toward the east or west, the indication of the compass lags, or indicates a turn in the opposite direction.

2. If the aircraft is on a southerly heading and you start a turn toward the the east or west, the indications of the compass precede the turn and indicate a greater amount of turn than has actually been made.

3. When the aircraft is on an east or west heading, no error is apparent while turning toward north or south.

4. If the aircraft is on an east or a west heading, an increase in airspeed causes the compass to indicate a turn toward the north.

5. If the aircraft is on an east or a west heading, a decrease in airspeed causes the compass to indicate a turn toward the south.

6. If the aircraft is on a north or south heading, no error is apparent while climbing, diving, or changing airspeed.

Obviously, then, it is best to read the compass only when the aircraft is flying straight and level at a constant speed. If you do that, you will reduce errors to the minimum.

When you make turns on the magnetic compass, use an angle of bank that gives a standard-rate turn, but this angle should not exceed 18°. You must hold this angle of bank accurately to be successful in turning to magnetic compass headings. In a turn to north or south, the amount of lead or lag in the indications of the magnetic compass depends on the latitude at which the turn is being made. In fact, it is approximately equal to the latitude. This lead or lag is at the minimum over the equator and increases as the latitude increases, reaching its maximum in the polar regions. Besides this lead or lag, you must consider also the normal lead necessary for the roll-out of a turn. To understand this, consider turns to cardinal headings.

When you turn to a heading of north, the number of degrees of lead necessary is equal to the latitude plus the number of degrees required for the roll-out. For example, during a left turn to a heading of north, using a 15° angle of bank at a TAS of less than 220 kts in a locality where the latitude is 30° N, you should start the roll-out when the magnetic compass reads 37½° (30° plus one-half of 15).

To turn to a heading of south, turn past south the number of degrees equal to the latitude, minus the number of degrees required for the roll-out. For example, when you turn to the right to a heading of south, at a TAS of less than 220 kts, start the roll-out when the magnetic compass reads 202½° (180° plus 30° minus 7½°).

In a turn from north to east or west, the magnetic compass initially shows a lag. As the heading approaches the east or west heading, the magnetic compass starts to turn faster than the aircraft is turning. For this reason, you must start the roll-out when the magnetic compass indicates approximately 10° ahead of 90°

or 270°. For example, start the roll-out at approximately 80° when turning to east; start at 280° when turning to west.

In a turn from south to east or west, the magnetic compass initially shows a lead. As the heading approaches east or west, the rate of turn of the compass card decreases and you must start the roll-out only 5° ahead of 90° at 270°.

## STEEP TURNS

Any turn with an angle of bank greater than 30° is considered a steep turn (Fig. 255). This type of turn is seldom necessary or advisable in routine instrument flight. However, all-weather jet interceptors employ precise steep turns on instruments as a matter of routine. Therefore, the ability on the part of prop-aircraft pilots to perform these maneuvers on instruments as evasive action against all-weather jets is very desirable. A steep turn is also a good maneuver to increase your ability to react quickly and smoothly to rapid changes in attitude.

Regardless of the angle of bank, the techniques of entry, control during the turn, and recovery are the same in steep turns as in normal turns. You will find it more difficult to control the pitch attitude, however, because of the greatly reduced vertical lift when you increase the angle of bank. This produces a tendency to lose altitude in steep turns. In addition, with some horizon indicators, precession during the turn makes it more difficult to maintain the desired attitude. Therefore, to maintain a constant altitude, you must take immediate corrective action as soon as the necessity is indicated on the flight instruments. It is important, however, that you do not initiate a correction before the necessity arises. Since this correction involves an increase in the angle of attack, the drag increases and the airspeed decreases. Apply the necessary power to

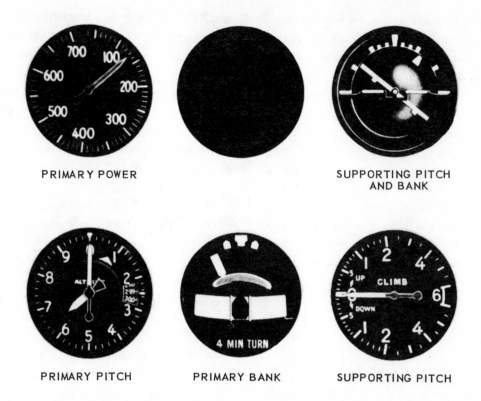

PRIMARY POWER                    SUPPORTING PITCH
                                   AND BANK

PRIMARY PITCH      PRIMARY BANK      SUPPORTING PITCH

Fig. 255. Steep turn.

maintain a constant airspeed if this is desired.

When making any corrections, refer to the horizon indicator even though the precession of the instrument is apparent. To accomplish this, note the need for a correction on the vertical-speed indicator or the altimeter; check the attitude indicated on the horizon indicator; and effect the change on the horizon indicator for this indication. After you make this change, again check the altimeter and vertical-speed indicator to determine whether or not the correction was adequate.

If the horizon indicator is not available, note the need for correction on the vertical-speed indicator and altimeter. Initiate the correction action immediately and observe the altimeter and vertical-speed indicator closely to determine whether or not the correction was adequate. Use the turn needle in your scan to maintain a constant rate of turn.

Your recovery should be smooth and with a normal rate of rollout. As you roll the aircraft out of the turn, the vertical lift will increase and the aircraft will tend to climb if you do not effect the necessary corrections as soon as you note the need on the instruments. Remember to adjust the power to maintain the desired airspeed.

## RECOVERIES FROM UNUSUAL ATTITUDES

An unusual attitude is any attitude of the aircraft not required for normal instrument flight. It may result from any one factor or a combination of several factors, such as turbulence, vertigo, instrument failure, confusion of the pilot, or carelessness in scanning the instruments.

If you are flying a conventional aircraft with suction-driven gyro instruments or electric gyros which are not non-tum-

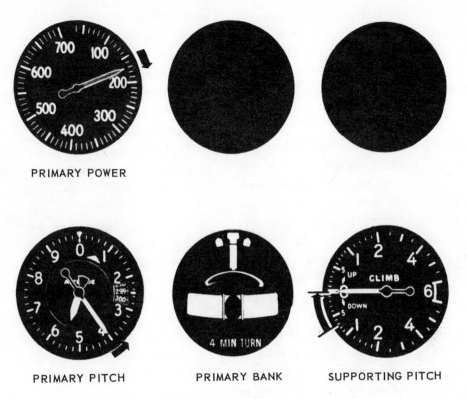

Fig. 256. Recovery from unusual attitude.

bling, you make the recovery from any unusual attitude by utilizing the airspeed indicator, the altimeter. the turn needle, and the vertical-speed indicator (Fig. 256).

In any event, recovery must be effected so as to resume straight and level flight with a minimum loss of altitude, yet, at the same time, without exceeding the stress limits of the aircraft.

There are two general procedures for recoveries from unusual attitudes. One of these procedures is used for recoveries from nose-high unusual attitudes; the other is used to recover from nose-low unusual attitudes.

As soon as you detect an unusual attitude, check the airspeed indicator and the altimeter to determine whether the nose of the aircraft is above or below the horizon. Because of the lag in the vertical-speed indicator, disregard it during the initial part of the recovery. If the nose is below the horizon, and the airspeed is

high, reduce the power and level the wings by centering the turn needle; then correct the pitch attitude to level flight. Level flight will be indicated when the altimeter is constant on an altitude. If the nose is above the horizon and the airspeed is low, correct the bank to a wings-level attitude; then, as you lower the nose, add power. At the time the airspeed indicator and the altimeter reverse their indications, the nose of the aircraft has passed through the level-flight attitude for the airspeed indicated at that time. Again, level-flight attitude will be indicated when the altimeter is constant on an altitude and the turn needle is centered.

Change all components of control almost simultaneously, with only a slight lead of one over the other; however, this lead should be in the sequence just mentioned. To establish and maintain a level flight attitude, observe the altimeter and turn needle closely as the aircraft approaches level flight. Also, since the control pressures you usually use in recoveries from unusual attitudes are greater than those necessary for normal flight, you should use care to neutralize these pressures as you approach straight-and-level flight.

If the aircraft is equipped with electrical horizon and heading indicators, you may use them as the aircraft approaches level-flight attitude to assist you in the full recovery. Remember, however, that the flight attitude indicated on the horizon indicator may not be the exact aircraft attitude because of gyro precession.

A spin is indicated by a low airspeed, extreme displacement of the needle in the direction of the spin and a rapid loss of altitude. The ball may be displaced in either direction depending on the spin characteristics of the aircraft. To recover from a spin, use the same mechanical procedures as you use in visual flight to stop the spin. Once you have the spin stopped, make the remainder of the recovery the same as for a nose-low unusual attitude.

*Rules to recover from unusual attitudes:*

1. Check the airspeed indicator and altimeter as soon as you detect any unusual attitude in flight.

2. If the aircraft is in a nose-low attitude, simultaneously reduce power and correct the bank, then correct the pitch attitude.

3. If the aircraft is in a nose-high attitude, correct the bank to a wings-level attitude, then simultaneously lower the nose and add power.

Because of the very nature of the occurrence of an unusual attitude, corrective action must be prompt. Speed is essential in the recovery. Excessive loss of altitude is undesirable and may be dangerous. Start a climb or descent back to the original altitude and heading as soon as you attain full control of the aircraft and a safe airspeed.

# Glossary of Aeronautical Terms

AILERON. A hinged control surface on the wing to aid in producing a bank, or rolling about the longitudinal axis.

AIRFOIL. Any member, or surface, on an airplane whose major function is to deflect the airflow.

AIRPLANE. A mechanically driven flying machine which derives its lift from the reaction of the mass of air which is deflected downward by fixed wings.

AIRPORT. A tract of land, or water, which has been established as a landing area for the regular use of aircraft.

AIRSPEED. The speed of an airplane in relation to the air through which it is passing.

AIRWORTHY. The status of being in condition suitable for safe flight.

ALTIMETER. An instrument for indicating the relative altitude of an airplane by measuring atmospheric pressure.

ALTITUDE. The elevation of an airplane. This may be specified as above sea level, or above the ground over which it flies.

ANEMOMETER. A device for measuring the velocity of the wind, in common use at airports.

ATTITUDE. The position of an airplane considering the inclination of its axes in relation to the horizon.

AUTOMATIC PILOT. A gyroscopic device for operating the flight controls without attention from the pilot. Commonly installed in large airplanes used for flights of considerable duration.

AXIS. The theoretical line extending through the center of gravity of an airplane in each major plane: fore and aft, crosswise, and up and down. These are the longitudinal, lateral, and vertical axes.

BAIL OUT. To jump from an airplane in flight.

BALANCED CONTROL SURFACE. A surface with some area ahead of the hinge line to aid in reducing the force necessary to displace it.

BANK. To tip, or roll about the longitudinal axis of the airplane. Banks are incident to all properly-executed turns.

BIPLANE. An airplane having two main supporting surfaces, one above the other.

BOOST. Used to denote air increase in manifold pressure or throttle setting.

BOOSTER. (1) An electrical device, either induction coil or auxiliary magneto to aid in starting an airplane engine, or (2) a device for aiding, with power, in the movement of the flight controls in heavy airplanes.

BUFFETING. The beating effect of the disturbed airstream on an airplane's structure during flight.

BUNT. An acrobatic maneuver involving a dive to inverted position from level flight. A bunt amounts to the first half of an outside loop.

CANOPY. (parachute) The main supporting cloth surface of the parachute.

CEILING. (meteorology) The height of the base of the clouds above the ground.

CEILING. (aircraft) The maximum altitude the airplane is capable of obtaining under standard conditions.

CENTER OF GRAVITY. The point within an airplane through which, for balance purposes, the total force of gravity is considered to act.

CENTER SECTION. The central panel of a continuous wing.

CHECK LIST. A list, usually carried in the pilot's compartment, of items requiring the airman's attention for various flight operations.

CHECK POINT. In air navigation, a prominent landmark on the ground, either visual or radio, which is used to establish the position of an airplane in flight.

CIRCUIT BREAKER. A device which takes the place of a fuse in breaking an electrical circuit in case of an overload. Most aircraft circuit breakers can be reset by pushing a button, in case the overload was temporary.

COCKPIT. An open space in the fuselage with seats for the pilot and passengers; also used to denote the pilot's compartment in a large airplane.

COMPASS, MAGNETIC. A device for determining the direction of the earth's magnetic field. Subject to local disturbances, the compass will indicate the direction to the north magnetic pole.

COMPRESSIBILITY. The effect encountered at extremely high speeds, near the speed of sound, when air ceases to flow smoothly over the wings, and "piles up" against the leading edge, causing extreme buffeting and other similar effects.

CONTROLS. The devices used by a pilot in operating an airplane.

CONTROL SURFACES. Hinged airfoils exposed to the air flow which control the attitude of the airplane and which are actuated by use of the controls in the airplane.

COORDINATION. The movement or use of two or more controls in their proper relationship to obtain the results desired.

CROSS FEED. A system in a large airplane by which fuel, or oil, may be transferred from engine to engine, or from tank to tank.

CRUISE CONTROL. The procedure for the operation of an airplane, and its power plants, to obtain the maximum efficiency on extended flights.

CUSHIONING EFFECT. The temporary gain in lift during a landing due to the compression of the air between the wings of an airplane and the ground.

DEVIATION. The error induced in a magnetic compass by steel structure, electrical equipment and similar disturbing factors in the airplane.

DIVE. A steep descent with or without power at a greater air speed than that normal to level flight.

DOWNWASH. The downward thrust imparted on the air to provide lift for the airplane.

DRAG. Force opposing the motion of the airplane through the air.

DRIFT. Deflection of an airplane from its intended course by action of the wind.

DRIFT METER. A navigation instrument for determining visually the amount of drift, in degrees.

ELEVATOR. A hinged, horizontal control surface used to raise or lower the tail in flight.

EMPENNAGE. Term used to designate the entire tail group of an airplane, including the fixed and movable tail surfaces.

ENERGIZER. A flywheel device incorporated in large engine electric starters which is turned up to a high speed before engaging the starter to aid in overcoming the static friction of the engine.

FAIRING. A member or structure the primary function of which is to produce a smooth outline and to reduce drag.

FIN. A fixed airfoil to increase the stability of an airplane. Usually applied to the vertical surface to which the rudder is hinged.

FLAP. An appendage to an airfoil, usually the wing, for changing its lift characteristics to permit slower landings.

FLARE OUT. To round out a landing by decreasing the rate of descent and air speed by slowly raising the nose.

FLARES. Magnesium lights of high intensity, usually electrically-operated, which can be dropped suspended from small parachutes for night emergency landings.

FLIGHT PLAN. A detailed outline of a proposed flight usually filed with an Airways Communication Station before a cross-country flight.

FLIPPER. Any movable control surface.

FLOAT. A buoyant water-tight structure which is a part of the "landing gear" of a seaplane.

FRONT. The line of demarcation between two different types of air mass.

FUSELAGE. The body to which the wings, landing gear, and tail are attached.

GASCOLATOR. A type of fuel strainer incorporating a sediment bulb.

GLIDE. Sustained forward flight in which speed is maintained only by the loss of altitude.

GOSPORT. A speaking-tube system, attached to the student's helmet, or to earphones, to aid in conversation in the air.

GROUND LOOP. An uncontrollable violent turn on the ground.

HOMING. To fly with the airplane's heading directly toward a radio station at the destination by use of a loop-equipped radio.

HORN. (control horn) A projection from a hinged control surface for the attachment of the actuating cable or push-pull tube.

HORSEPOWER. A unit for measurement of power output of an engine. It is the power required to raise 550 pounds one foot in one second.

INCIDENCE, ANGLE OF. The angle between the mean chord of the wing and the longitudinal axis of the airplane.

INDUCED DRAG. The drag produced indirectly by the effect of the induced lift.

INDUCED LIFT. That lift caused by the low pressure of the rapidly-flowing air over the top of a wing.

INTERPHONE. (intercommunication) An electrically-operated inter-communication system between various members of the crew of an airplane.

JURY STRUT. A secondary structural member, often used to brace a main strut near its center.

KINESTHESIA. The sense which detects and estimates motion without reference to vision or hearing.

KNOT. A unit speed equalling one nautical mile per hour.

LANDING. The act of terminating flight and bringing the airplane to rest, used both for land and seaplanes.

LANDING AREA. Any area suitable for the landing of an airplane.

LANDING GEAR. The under structure which supports the weight of the airplane while at rest.

LAND PLANE. An airplane designed to rise from and alight on the ground.

LEADING EDGE. The forward edge of any ailfoil.

LIFT. The supporting force induced by the dynamic reaction of air against the wing.

LIFT COMPONENT. The sum of the forces acting on a wing perpendicular to the direction of its motion through the air.

LIGHT GUN. An intense, narrowly-focused spotlight with which a green, red, or white signal may be directed at any selected airplane in the traffic on or about an airport. Usually used in control towers.

LOAD. The forces acting on a structure. These may be static (as with gravity) or dynamic (as with centrifugal force) or a combination of static and dynamic.

LOAD FACTOR. The sum of the loads on a structure, including the static and dynamic loads, expressed in units of G, or one gravity.

LOG. To make a flight-by-flight record of all operations of an airplane, engine, or pilot, listing flight time, area of operation, and other pertinent information.

LONGERON. The principal longitudinal structural member in a fuselage.

LUBBER LINE. The small reference line used in reading the figures from the card of an aeronautical compass.

MANEUVER. Any planned motion of an airplane in the air or on the ground.

MONOCOQUE. A type of aircraft construction in which the external skin constitutes the primary structure. (An egg is of monocoque construction.)

MONOPLANE. An airplane having one supporting surface.

NACELLE. Inclosed shelter for a power plant or personnel. Usually secondary to the fuselage or cabin.

NOSEHEAVY. A condition of rigging in which the nose tends to sink.

NOSE-OVER. The turning of an airplane on its back on the ground by rolling over the nose.

NOSE-WHEEL. A swivelling or steerable wheel mounted forward in tricycle-geared airplanes.

OLEO. A shock-absorbing strut in which the spring action is dampened by oil.

ORIENTATION. The act of fixing position or attitude by visual or other reference.

OVERSHOOT. To fly beyond a designated area or mark.

PERIODIC INSPECTION. The airframe and engine inspection of an airplane by a certificated mechanic, required at specified intervals by regulations.

PILOT. One who operates the controls of an airplane in flight.

PITCH. (airplane) Angular displacement in reference to any line.

PITCH. (propeller) The angle of its blades measured from its plane of rotation.

PITOT TUBE. A tube exposed to the air stream for measuring impact pressure or for measuring outside undisturbed static pressure.

PLANE. An airfoil section for deflection of air; surface or field of action in any two dimensions only; to move over the water (seaplanes) so the weight is supported by dynamic reaction of the water, rather than by displacement.

PORPOISING. In seaplanes, pitching while planing.

PROPELLER. Any device for producing thrust in any fluid; generally, a device for measuring angles. Usually used in navigation to determine compass courses on a chart.

PROTRACTOR. A device for measuring angles. Usually used in navigation to determine compass courses on a chart.

PUSHER. An airplane in which the propeller is mounted aft of the engine, and pushes the air away from it.

PYLON. A prominent mark, or point, on the ground used as a fix in precision maneuvers.

RATE-OF-CLIMB INDICATOR. An instrument which indicates the rate of ascent or descent of an airplane.

RHUMB LINE. The line drawn on a Lambert chart between points for navigational purposes. In practice it is the line on the map which the pilot attempts to follow.

RIG. Adjustment of the airfoils of an airplane to produce desired flight characteristics.

ROLL. Displacement around the longitudinal axis of an airplane.

RUDDER. A hinged, vertical, control surface used to induce or overcome yawing moments about the vertical axis.

RUDDER PEDALS. (or bar) Controls within the airplane by means of which the rudder is actuated.

RUNWAY. A strip, either paved or improved, on which take-offs and landings are effected.

SEAPLANE. An airplane equipped to rise from and alight on the water. Usually used to denote an airplane with detachable floats, as contrasted with a flying boat.

SAILING. In seaplanes, the use of wind and current conditions to produce the desired track while taxiing on the water.

SEQUENCE REPORT. The weather report transmitted hourly to all teletype stations, and available at all C.A.A. Communication Stations.

SKID. Sideward motion of an airplane in flight produced by centrifugal force.

SLIP. (or sideslip) The controlled flight of an airplane in a direction not in line with its longitudinal axis.

SLIPSTREAM. The current of air driven astern by the propeller.

SOLO. A flight during which a pilot is the only occupant of the airplane.

SPAR. The principal longitudinal structural member in an airfoil.

SPIN. A prolonged stall in which an airplane rotates about its center of gravity while it descends, usually with its nose well down.

SPIRAL. A prolonged gliding or climbing turn during which at least 360° change of direction is effected.

STABILITY. The tendency of an airplane in flight to remain in straight, level, upright flight, or to return to this attitude if displaced, without attention of the pilot.

STABILIZER. The fixed airfoil of an airplane used to increase stability; usually, the aft fixed horizontal surface to which the elevators are hinged.

STALL. The abrupt loss of lift when the air speed decreases to the minimum which will support an airfoil at the existing loading.

STEP. A "break" in the bottom of a float of a seaplane's float to improve planing characteristics on the water.

STRUT. A compression or tension member in a truss structure. In airplanes, usually applied to an external major structural member.

SWINGING THE COMPASS. Checking the indications of an installed compass by comparing them with an accurate compass rose laid out on the ground.

TAB. A small auxiliary airfoil, usually attached to a movable control surface to aid in its movement, or to effect a slight displacement of it for the purpose of trimming the airplane for varying conditions of power, load or airspeed.

TACHOMETER. An instrument which registers in revolutions per minute (RPM) the speed of the engine.

TAIL GROUP. The airfoil members of the assembly located at the rear of an airplane.

TAILHEAVY. A condition of trim in an airplane in which the tail tends to sink.

TAILSKID. A skid, or runner, which supports the aft end of the airframe while on the ground.

TAIL SLIDE. Rearward motion of an airplane in the air; commonly occurs only in a whip stall.

TAIL WHEEL. A wheel which serves the same purpose as the tailskid.

TAXI. To operate an airplane under its own power on the ground, except that movement incident to actual take-off and landing.

TERMINAL FORECASTS. Weather forecasts available each six hours at all C. A. A. Communications Stations, covering the airways weather eight hours in advance.

TERMINAL VELOCITY. The hypothetical maximum speed which could be obtained in a prolonged vertical dive.

THRUST. The forward force on an airplane in the air, provided by the engine acting through a propeller in conventional airplanes.

TORQUE. Any turning, or twisting force. Applied to the rolling force imposed on an airplane by the engine in turning the propeller.

TURN INDICATOR. A gyroscopic instrument for indicating the rate of turning. Often combined with a ball bank indicator.

TURTLEBACK. The top of the fuselage aft of the cabin; originally detachable in older airplanes.

ULTIMATE LOAD. The load which will, or is computed to, cause failure in any structural member.

USEFUL LOAD. In airplanes, the difference, in pounds, between the empty weight and the maximum authorized gross weight.

$V_1$. (transport category airplanes) The indicated airspeed at which it has been determined that a specific multi-engine airplane can continue controlled flight after one engine has become suddenly inoperative, or can be brought to a stop within the runway available.

$V_2$. The indicated airspeed which has been determined to give a rate of climb which meets minimum requirements in a specified multi-engine airplane with one engine inoperative.

VECTOR. The resultant of two quantities (forces, speeds, or deflections); used in aviation to compute load factors, headings, or drift.

VENTURI. (or Venturi Tube) A tube with a restriction used to provide suction to operate flight instruments by allowing the slip stream to pass through it.

VISCOSITY. The measure of body, or "thickness" in a fluid. Important in determining the correct lubricating oil for any engine.

VISIBILITY. The greatest horizontal distance which prominent objects on the ground can be seen. (Used to denote weather conditions.)

WASH. The disturbed air in the wake of an airplane, particularly behind its propeller.

WASHIN. A greater angle of incidence (and attack) in one wing, or part of a wing, to provide more lift; usually used to overcome torque.

WASHOUT. A lesser angle of incidence to decrease lift. (See above.)

WEATHER-VANE. The tendency of an airplane on the ground or water to face into the wind, due to its effect on the vertical surfaces of the tail group.

WIND SHIFT. (or wind shift line) An abrupt change in the direction or velocity, or both, of the wind. Usually associated with a front.

WIND SOCK. A cloth sleeve, mounted aloft at an airport to use for estimating wind direction and velocity.

WIND TEE. An indicator for wind or traffic direction at an airport.

WING. An airfoil whose major function is to provide lift by the dynamic reaction of the mass of air swept downward.

WING BOW. The former at the wing tip used to provide a rounded conformation. Sometimes used to denote the wing tip.

WING HEAVY. A condition of rigging in an airplane in which one wing tends to sink.

WING-OVER. A flight maneuver in which the airplane is alternately climbed and dived during a 180° turn.

WING ROOT. The end of a wing which joints the fuselage, or the opposite wing.

WING TIP. The end of the wing farthest from the fuselage, or cabin.

YAW. To turn about the vertical axis. (An airplane is said to yaw as the nose turns without the accompanying appropriate bank.)

ZOOM. To zoom is to climb for a short time at an angle greater than the normal climbing angle, the airplane being carried upward by momentum.